Arch

Archaeopoetics

WORD, IMAGE, HISTORY

MANDY BLOOMFIELD

The University of Alabama Press
Tuscaloosa

For Megan

The University of Alabama Press
Tuscaloosa, Alabama 35487-0380
uapress.ua.edu

Inquiries about reproducing material from this work should be addressed to the
University of Alabama Press.

Typeface: Minion

Manufactured in the United States of America
Cover photograph: Frontispiece from *Veil* by Charles Bernstein, 1987; courtesy of
Charles Bernstein
Cover design: Michele Myatt Quinn

∞

The paper on which this book is printed meets the minimum requirements of American National Standard for Information Sciences—Permanence of Paper for Printed
Library Materials, ANSI Z39.48-1984.

Library of Congress Cataloging-in-Publication Data

Bloomfield, Mandy, 1971–
Archaeopoetics : word, image, history / Mandy Bloomfield.
pages cm. — (Modern and contemporary poetics)
Includes bibliographical references and index.
ISBN 978-0-8173-5853-2 (pbk. : alk. paper) — ISBN 978-0-8173-8965-9 (e book)
1. Poetry, Modern—History and criticism. 2. Imagery (Psychology) in literature. 3.
Visual perception in literature. 4. Poetics. I. Title.
PN1271.B57 2016
809.1'04—dc23
                                                              2015033019

Contents

Illustrations

Acknowledgments

This book probably would not have existed without the encouragement, intellectual inspiration and generosity of Peter Middleton, who has been this project's guiding light from its inception. I am also grateful to Nicky Marsh for invaluable guidance in the early days as well as continuing friendship and dialogue. Thanks to Robert Hampson and Gail McDonald for their careful reading and expert advice. Thanks as well to the anonymous peer reviewers at the University of Alabama Press whose insightful comments, helpful recommendations, and excellent suggestions have helped improve this book significantly. Thanks also to the series editors Charles Bernstein and Hank Lazer for supporting and guiding the publication of this work. I am especially grateful to Dan Waterman for his patience and professionalism during the process of seeing this book into print, and to Kevin Fitzgerald for his scrupulous editing work.

The project that led to *Archaeopoetics* was funded by the Arts and Humanities Research Council in the United Kingdom. I am grateful to them and to the University of Southampton for the financial assistance and institutional support that enabled me to complete the initial research and write an early draft. Archival research at University of California, San Diego, was facilitated by Lynda Claassen. The assistance of Stephanie Cannizzo at the Berkeley Art Museum and Pacific Film Archive helped make my visit there productive. Special thanks are due to Michael Davidson for his intellectual encouragement, wonderful hospitality, and friendship during my time in California and ever since. I also owe debts of thanks to Maggie O'Sullivan and Susan Howe not only for their work but also for productive dialogue and encouragement.

Many of the ideas and materials in this book have benefited from presentations at conferences, symposia, and research seminars. In particular, I am grateful to the organizers of seminar series at the University of Southampton and Birkbeck, University of London and conferences at Sussex, Durham,

Aberystwyth, and Lancaster to name but a few. Thanks also to the editors of scholarly journals and essay collections for opportunities to publish earlier versions of some of the chapters, and to the anonymous peer reviewers for these publications. A previous version of chapter 2 appeared in *Textual Practice*, edited at the time by Peter Nicholls and then Peter Boxall. Earlier incarnations of chapter 4 appeared in the *Journal of British and Irish Innovative Poetry* edited by Robert Sheppard and Scott Thurston and in the *Salt Companion to Maggie O'Sullivan* from Salt Publishing.

The long process of writing this book has been enriched by the support and stimulus of numerous colleagues and friends whose presence has provided the community, provocation, collegiality, and often the solace without which I may have ground to a halt long ago. Special thanks to Alice Barnaby and Gareth Farmer for friendship and solidarity during some particularly challenging days, to Jesse Ransley and Christer Petley for camaraderie and conversations about archaeology and history, and to Lucy Watson, Helen Cross, Liam Connell, Kerry Myler, Julia Banister, Catherine Edgecombe, and Victoria Sheppard for being wonderful friends and colleagues. And finally thanks to my family for enduring support, patience, love, and good times, most especially to Adam and Megan Bloomfield and also Ruben Moon.

Permissions

Permission to reprint copyrighted material has been obtained wherever possible. The author gratefully acknowledges permission to reprint from the following sources:

From *The Nonconformist's Memorial* by Susan Howe, copyright © 1993 by Susan Howe. Reprinted by permission of New Directions Publishing Corp.

From *Singularities* by Susan Howe © 1990 Susan Howe. Reprinted by permission of Wesleyan University Press.

From Theresa Hak Kyung Cha's *DICTEE* © 2001 The Regents of the University of California and the video work *Mouth to Mouth* (1987). Reproduced by permission of University of California, Berkeley Art Museum.

From *that bread should be* by Maggie O'Sullivan published by Etruscan Books © 1997 Maggie O'Sullivan and *red shifts* by Maggie O'Sullivan published by Etruscan Books © Maggie O'Sullivan. Reprinted by permission of the author and Etruscan books.

From *murmur: tasks of mourning* by Maggie O'Sullivan, published by Veer Press © 2011 Maggie O'Sullivan. Reproduced by permission of Maggie O'Sullivan.

From *Middle Passages* by Kamau Brathwaite, published by Bloodaxe Books

Archaeopoetics

1
Archaeopoetics

When the attentions change / the jungle
leaps in
      even the stones are split
            they rive
[. . .]
But the E
cut so rudely on that oldest stone
sounded otherwise,
was differently heard

                   Charles Olson, "The Kingfishers"

History weighs like a nightmare on the lives of modern poetry. Charles Olson's famous 1949 poem "The Kingfishers" marks a pivotal moment in poetry's long and obsessive engagement with the cultural past. Mindful of the elongated shadow cast by Auschwitz and the atom bomb and alert to the dawning of a new era of cold war, Olson's poem casts a skeptical eye toward hegemonic Western history and turns away to "hunt among stones" of the marginal and archaic. Ranging through the remains of multiple histories and traditions, from the ruins of Angkor Wat to the "E on the stone" (*Collected Poems* 87) at Delphi to Mayan ritual, the poem's attention decisively moves beyond the post-Homeric "Western Box" privileged by Eliot and Pound (Olson, *Selected Writings* 129). In so doing, it anticipates a proliferation of revisionist histories in the 1960s and '70s and a concurrent reshaping of the "poem including history" (Pound). It also raises a question that has come to haunt these endeavors: how do we recover histories hitherto rendered silent, marginal, or irrecuperable? This question begins to surface with heightened urgency in "The Kingfishers." This is also a poem that suggests an especially archaeological way of proceeding, a poetics of excavating material remains. Olson's trip to work on a dig of Mayan ruins in Yucatan in the early '50s provided a practical grounding for a poetics that took fieldwork as a methodological model. An archaeological sensibility is already apparent in "The Kingfishers," though in 1949 this, in itself, was nothing new. As Brian McHale points out, archaeology has been a persistent master trope of modernism (*Obligation* 102–3). By taking up archaeology as a poetic model, Olson drew from the tradition apparent in Eliot's *The Waste Land* and especially Pound's *Cantos*, though Olson's approach is distinct from these precursors. Olson constitutes the poem as an archaeological site not for the deposit of cultural treasures, as it was for Pound and Eliot, but as a space for reflecting on *how* the past is encountered.

"The Kingfishers" marks a transformation of the "poem including history" into something else—something that might be described as the poem contemplating historiography. As Michael Davidson so astutely remarks, a poem like Olson's "mak[es] historical speculation its subject" ("Hunting" 197). *Archaeopoetics* is a book about recent poetry that continues and intensifies this activity. The contemporary writers whose work I discuss in the following chapters—American poet Susan Howe, Korean American artist Theresa Hak Kyung Cha, British poet Maggie O'Sullivan, and diasporic Caribbean writers Kamau Brathwaite and M. NourbeSe Philip—engage with an array of elided, effaced, and unacknowledged histories. Such a pursuit of histories not readily available for contemporary scrutiny engenders investigations into those forms of knowledge, representation, and power that mediate our cultural pasts and the contemporaneity they continue to shape. These poetries do not recover marginalized histories but present a series of inquiries into how existing *modes* of historical knowledge might be reshaped. In other words this poetry's concern is not so much with *what* we might know of our cultural past as with *how* it might be encountered differently.

Similarly, what is unearthed and brought into the light in "The Kingfishers" is not so much some deeply significant cultural find but the problem of engaging with histories that are at best only partially recoverable, a problem that becomes most apparent in the poem's contemplation of the inscrutable Delphic "E / cut so rudely on that oldest stone" (88). This reference to Plutarch's essay "The E at Delphi," which charts a frustrated attempt to uncover the meaning of the inscription, highlights the dilemma of interpreting remains whose cultural traditions are lost and whose meanings are thus unknowable. While Olson's poem may advocate a practice of "hunting among stones," it finds only indecipherable and fragmented traces of lost pasts. What becomes evident is a version, or an intimation at least, of the "corrosive epistemological uncertainty" (*Obligation* 115) that McHale associates with postmodern writing in general and postmodern archaeological poetry in particular (although McHale himself associates Olson with a much more self-assured modernist tradition). However, this uncertainty does not amount to an abandonment of epistemology altogether in Olson's poem, nor in the poetries I examine in later chapters. Rather it feeds into speculation about alternative ways of understanding dimensions of historical experience that are palpable though not necessarily intelligible.

Olson's poem looks to the practices of archaeological fieldwork for direction. Sasha Colby convincingly argues that "what appeals to Olson about archaeological modes of knowing is tangibility, object-knowledge, and direct particularity" (95). Indeed, for Olson, the notion of direct physical engagement with concrete specificities not only offers ways of countering the generalizing and totalizing aspirations of Eliot's and Pound's historicist poetics, but also forms the basis for the alternative epistemology toward which "The Kingfishers" strains. The poem's meditation on the E of the Delphic stone is not an attempt at interpretation so much as an encounter with its (imagined) physical qualities—the raw materiality of the inscription, the direct physicality of the stone's age—that promise to yield a kind of palpable knowledge.

Furthermore, this attention to concrete particulars extends to the poem's own material forms, most notably its appearance on the page. While Olson's use of the page as a very literal spatial field may not be as dramatic here as in some of his later *Maximus* poems, "The Kingfishers" contains numerous visual techniques, including degrees of indentation (including a three-stepped line akin to William Carlos Williams's contemporaneous variable foot); widely differing line lengths; the isolation of single words, phrases, or lines; the insertion of extra spaces into the middle of lines; and unconventional uses of diacritical marks, especially quotation marks and the forward slash. Such manipulations of typography and layout make a significant contribution to the poem's enactment of the archaeological method it proposes. In the first of the lines in the epigraph above, for example, the caesura performed by the forward slash—a recurrent Olsonian technique—plays a key role in the advancement of the poem's particular archaeological mode. In "Projective Verse," Olson celebrated the capacities of the typewriter to convey the poet's intended sounding of the poem. He states that he uses the slash in place of a comma to indicate "a pause so light it hardly separates the words" (*Selected* 23). But as Eleanor Berry rightly points out, the effects of the slash are more complicated; she suggests that it "visually and immediately conveys a sort of equivalence in weight, as between two items on a balance scale" (61). Indeed, in the poem's first line "what does not change / is the will to change" and in its penultimate line "shall you uncover honey / where maggots are?" the slash certainly does appear to work this way, as a simultaneously visual and conceptual pivot around which contrasting images are balanced. The slash in the epigraph above introduces a further complexity by virtue of the line break that severs the subject and predicate in the second clause, which introduces a distinct sense of *im*balance. And this imbalance puts something in motion: first, in progressing from one half of the second clause to its severed and deferred predicate, the reading eye makes a movement that echoes the "leap" of the "jungle." This spatial movement leads to a sequence of stepped lines whose visual arrangement embodies a series of kinetic shifts, and these shifts in turn add force to the verbal image of stones in motion, actively splitting. In other words, these lines enact, by means of typographic marks and layout, a dynamic, even revolutionary (groundbreaking), process that develops out of a moment "[w]hen the attentions change." By creating a dialogue between the linguistic meanings of these lines and their spatial arrangement on the page, the poem induces a parallel change of attentions: one that takes into account the physical dimensions of the poetic page that normally go unnoticed. A practice of attending to concrete particulars, the poem suggests, creates the possibility of an opening into which "the jungle / leaps," where "the jungle" may be taken to encompass all that has been excluded, Othered, and thereby positioned as textual and historical wilderness. In this way "The Kingfishers" proposes that a poetics attentive to material specificities offers ways of imagining how history might be "sounded otherwise" and "differently heard" (88).

The poetry examined in the later chapters of this book shares this conviction. The work of Howe, Cha, O'Sullivan, Brathwaite, and Philip constitutes a material turn in contemporary historicist poetry in which shifts of attention become vital. Joan Retallack has remarked that "[n]oticing becomes art when, as contextualizing project, it reconfigures the geometry of attention, drawing one into conversation with what would otherwise remain silent in the figure-ground patterns of history" (10). The work I explore in this book is noticing-as-art, and indeed art-as-noticing, which reorients attention in the ways that Retallack so wonderfully describes and Olson's poetry performs. It is not the case that all of the poets I examine explicitly draw on Olson as a predecessor or overtly invoke archaeology as a model for their practice. Nevertheless, their work develops and extends an archaeological poetics akin to "The Kingfishers." Like Olson's poem, the work of these five poets reflects on the potentials of palpable knowledge and material meaningfulness conveyed through the physical dimensions of the poetic page.

My discussions of this work will predominantly focus on the visual manifestations of this physicality. The visual aspects of the written word, when foregrounded, are one of the most emphatic ways of shifting "the geometry of attention" precisely because they are so often the dimensions of writing least attended to. As the artist Robert Smithson puts it, "[l]ook at any *word* long enough and you will see it open up into a series of faults, into a terrain of particles each containing its own void" (*Collected* 107). When we notice the visual surfaces of the written page, we perceive its physicality, and this noticing leads beyond the customary routes of linguistic semantics to tensions, presences, and absences not reducible to normative parameters of discursive cognition.

Insofar as such textual properties have been theorized at all, critics have generally associated emphasis on the word as matter with an inevitable breakdown of signification. Walter Benn Michaels scathingly equates a "commitment to the material object" (7) and most particularly the "transformation of text into material object" (8) with a "commitment to meaninglessness" (7) or else a valorization of proliferating meanings so multiplicitous as to amount to meaninglessness.[1] He argues that to focus on what he calls the "shape of the signifier" is to make a fundamental mistake about what a text is and what reading is. The poets I examine provoke a reconsideration of what a text is, what it means to read, and of what meaningfulness might comprise. My engagement with their work seeks to challenge entrenched oppositions between meaning and (meaningless) materiality, signification and "mere mark" (Fried 198), and interpretation and phenomenological experience upon which critics like Michaels rely. While the work examined in this book does not smooth over the discursive power of these ingrained dualisms, it proposes a notion of *material meaningfulness*, and in so doing explores the possibilities for articulating emergent forms of knowledge. In other words, I want to suggest that the work of the five poets I examine demonstrates not only how visual materiality contributes to poetic meaning but also offers forms of meaningfulness that have implications for the ethics and politics of historical encounter, especially Retallack's "geometries of attention." By tracing the relationship between the visual aesthetics and historicist impulses of this poetry, my investigations seek to widen the compass of poetic meaning by offering openings for reflecting upon and enlarging prevailing epistemic frontiers.

The work of the poets I examine in this book has to be read in the context of a wider impulse in the humanities to seek the gaps and silences of history. Yet this work refuses assimilation into discursive theoretical projects; instead, it proposes specifically aesthetic modes of engaging questions about historical encounter. In his book *The Obligation toward the Difficult Whole*, McHale identifies a genre of "archaeo-poetry," which he describes as "poetry of stratification and excavation, of fragments and ruins" (102). Extending this generic classification, I want to propose a notion of archaeo*poetics* implicit in McHale's illuminating discussion. By embodying a poetic mode of inquiry that foregrounds the material dimensions of experience and knowledge, archaeopoetry suggests an archaeo*poetics*. If poetics theorizes about aesthetic forms, then archaeopoetics both performs and reflects upon the capacities of aesthetic forms to perform the work of archaeological investigation. I coined the term *archaeo*poetics rather than using a term like "historicopoetics" because (very broadly speaking) history as a disciplinary field implies a focus on texts, records, and narratives, while archaeology draws clues about the past from material culture and offers, as Olson knew, inherently spatial and embodied modes of dialogue with the past. The lines between history and archaeology are, of course, highly permeable, and I do often use the terms somewhat interchangeably. But my privileged metaphor of archaeology is meant to suggest an emphasis on material encounter and forms of tangible knowledge even when the apparatus of investigation and the sources excavated are textual, as they very often are. Drawing on archaeology's engagement with physical artifacts, archaeopoetics foregrounds the palpable but not necessarily intelligible traces of the past not just as subject matter but also in terms of *formal* strategies. It explores the possibilities and limitations of historical encounter by pushing at the edges of existing epistemic frameworks. Archaeopoetics is the poem's own formally and materially enacted exploration of what a poem can be and do as a form of historical inquiry.

Archaeopoetics also gives rise to a reflective activity that extends beyond poetic or aesthetic questions. I refer to this as archaeo*critique*. By this I mean a mode of critical inquiry that, broadly following a Kantian sense of critique, investigates the conditions of possibility for historical knowledge. Archaeocritique raises questions about the grounds for prevailing forms of historical consciousness. It is the philosophical dimension of archaeopoetics; where archaeopoetics explores the capacities of aesthetic modes of inquiry, archaeocritique makes wider theoretical points about the power relationships underpinning certain historiographical paradigms or the implications of particular theories of history. There is, of course, a large overlap between these activities, and it is often difficult—and indeed artificial—to separate out these "levels" or moments of poetic inquiry. I place emphasis on this critical dimension because, quite simply, poetry participates in philosophical and theoretical activities and not just aesthetic ones. The aesthetic is a mode of theorizing. In parallel with Lynn Keller, I argue for "thinking poetry" (the title of her recent book), poetry that "like philosophy or political theory enacts a significant intellectual engagement with . . . important and challenging issues" (2).

In its development of these new critical concepts and in its broader emphasis on experimental poetry's historiographic focus, *Archaeopoetics* addresses a somewhat neglected aspect of modern and contemporary poetics. The dominant critical discourse in this field has tended to discuss poetic practices in terms of an "innovation" that is implicitly rooted in a future-oriented present. One need only consult a small selection of recent book titles to discern the pervasiveness of this approach: Jed Rasula's *Syncopations:*

The Stress of Innovation in Contemporary American Poetry (2004), Aldon Lynn Nielsen's *Integral Music: Languages of African American Innovation* (2004), Evie Shockley's *Renegade Poetics: Black Aesthetics and Formal Innovation in African American Poetry* (2010), and Craig Dworkin's edited collection *The Consequence of Innovation* (2008). Key anthologies of experimental poetry have also embraced this prevailing narrative as a way of framing what is important about contemporary poetries. Once again this is evident just from a glance at some titles: *Out of Everywhere: Linguistically Innovative Poetry by Women in North America and the UK* (1996) edited by Maggie O'Sullivan, *Every Goodbye Ain't Gone: An Anthology of Innovative Poetry by African Americans* (2006) edited by Aldon Lynn Nielsen and Lauri Ramey, and *Lyric Postmodernisms: An Anthology of Contemporary Innovative Poetries* (2008) edited by Reginald Shepherd. The practice of emphasizing the innovative is perhaps even more pronounced in the United Kingdom, where the only academic journal entirely devoted to experimental poetry is entitled *The Journal of British and Irish Innovative Poetry*. Perpetuating the residual logics of "making it new," the rhetorics of the "innovative" and the "avant-garde" are so ubiquitous as to be increasingly naturalized in the world of poetics.[2]

In part, the tenacity of this critical narrative owes much not only to the commonplace notion that modernism's defining trait is its attempt to break with the past but also to the legacy of certain aspects of Language-centered poetics that have been thoroughly assimilated into current critical frameworks. "To make the word the basis of *extensions*. Instead of a derivative (sublimate) of previously established connections, the word as 'the dwelling place,' where meaning will insist on spinning out of the closed circuit of the sign, or to reach or act on the world (not only as it is, as it could be)" (Andrews, "Writing" 136), for example, is to see the poem—and the active reading of the poem—as an event occurring in the present and as generative of future potentials. Furthermore, as Peter Middleton and Tim Woods indicate, such articulations of "diminished reference" tend "to put almost any recognizable representation of the past into question" (*Literatures* 2). In Peter Nicholls's formulation, Language writing saw itself as "distinctively new" because its various critiques of language's referential function "repudiate a whole tradition of writing about remembered experiences of the lyric self, turning attention instead to the 'tense-less' condition of language as medium" ("From Gertrude Stein" 116). I do not wish to reject the valuable legacies of Language poetics but merely to indicate how some of its most portable tenets have shaped the temporal alignments of contemporary discussions of poetry. Nor do I wish to take an oppositional stance by, for example, critiquing the logics of formal innovation as problematically replicating the processes of late capitalism, as did Frederic Jameson, J. H. Prynne (qtd. in Perril par. 48), and Alan Shapiro in various ways in the 1980s and '90s. Rather, I want to suggest that contemporary poetry has been just as preoccupied with investigating history and historical consciousness as it has been in future-orientated innovation. After all, the contemporary is, as Retallack states, "made out of the residue of the past. What, after all, is there materially but all that is after?" (10). A focus on how poetry explores the pasts of the contemporary can offer valuable perspectives on its present moment.

The chapters that follow explore the ways in which a range of archaeological poetries offer theoretical reflections on contemporary paradigms of historical knowledge. It is the task of this introductory chapter to sketch out key theoretical and aesthetic reference points for the archaeopoetic activities of Howe, Cha, O'Sullivan, Brathwaite, and Philip. The work of these five writers draws on, extends, and rethinks the historicist, poetic, and visual strategies of a range of philosophical and aesthetic modernisms. Paradigmatic for their activities and a guiding figure for my analysis of these poets' historiographic modes is Walter Benjamin, whose infamous notion of "brush[ing] history against the grain" I now want to excavate in some detail.

History Brushed Against the Grain

The five writers upon which *Archaeopoetics* focuses all came of age as poets amid the rise of revisionist histories that emerged out of the social movements of the 1960s and '70s and in the context of a proliferation of debates about the possibilities and limitations of historical recuperation. Theories of the postmodern announced the decline of totalizing frameworks of knowledge or "grand narratives," and promoted an understanding of history as heterogeneous and multiple, a "profusion of entangled events" (Foucault, "Nietzsche, Genealogy, History" 155). New Historicists and Cultural Materialists emphasized "the textuality of history and the historicity of texts" (Montrose 20), proclaiming that history could only be known through its textual and cultural practices, which are themselves thoroughly embedded in the power relations of both their moment of production and interpretation. Various feminisms attempted to read between the lines of official histories for traces of the feminine while debating the implications of psychoanalysis and poststructuralism for their praxis; if both the writing and the rewriting of history take place within a patriarchal symbolic and social order that positions women as Other, how can their voices be recovered? Postcolonial critics faced a related set of problems. In 1985 Gayatri Spivak notoriously declared "the subaltern has no history and cannot speak" ("Subaltern" 83); the voices and histories of colonized and subjugated peoples cannot be simply recovered, nor should the contemporary critic attempt to help them speak through ventriloquism. Rather they must be heard as a kind of "speaking silence" in the gaps and fractures of colonial and neo-colonial discourse. Meanwhile, trauma theorists working from a Freudian model of repression argued that the unassimilability of some events, such as the Holocaust, problematizes access to the "truth" of such histories even while the effects of such events continue to return, belatedly, to haunt the present. In one way or another these critical and theoretical endeavors have aimed, as Walter Benjamin puts it, "to brush history against the grain" (*Illuminations* 248) to reveal its unacknowledged dimensions. With the rise of revisionist historicizing in Anglo-American academia in the 1970s and '80s, Benjamin's philosophy experienced a critical resurrection of its own, providing a model of history repeatedly invoked, whether explicitly or implicitly, in these debates.

This complex of overlapping and often conflicting discourses forms the intellectual context for the poetic archaeologies of Howe, Cha, O'Sullivan, Brathwaite, and Philip, and these critical currents have, to different degrees and with varying emphases, informed their historical investigations. The work of these writers confronts more acutely than Olson's "Kingfishers" the power structures that elide some histories while endorsing others; as Howe puts it, "a dark wall of rule supports the structure of every letter, record, transcript: every proof of authority and power" (*Birth-mark* 4). For these poets, the work of challenging this "dark wall of rule" involves projects that engage both the operations of hegemonic power and the fissures and contradictions that offer glimpses of other, multiple, alternatives. In common with the various discourses about questions of historical recovery, the work of each of these five poets also implicitly takes up and rethinks a Benjaminian philosophy of history that not only "brushes history against the grain" but also seeks to *redeem* the unfulfilled potentials of its fragmented remains. The Benjamin who declared "[t]here is no document of civilization which is not at the same time a document of barbarism" (248) and that history must be read "against the grain" in an attempt to recover the traces of multiple untold histories has been widely embraced by various revisionist historicisms, and has also been frequently invoked in relation to the particular kinds of poetic historical endeavor performed by the poets discussed in this book (see, for example, Back, Naylor, Wong). But critics who draw on Benjamin's model of historicism have tended to sidestep the theologically inflected interplay of catastrophe and redemption that structures his thought. The mystical associations of redemption sit uncomfortably with the Marxist, poststructuralist, and psychoanalytical dimensions of historical revisionism in an age in which the very notion of redemption seems suspect and untenable. Like the well-known allegorical image of the puppet controlled by a hidden dwarf that opens Benjamin's "Theses on the Philosophy of History," the academic embrace of his thought, especially in literary and cultural studies, has for the most part kept the "wizened" theological puppet master of a very particular brand of historical materialism out of sight. These dimensions of Benjamin's thinking are worth attending to and can cast this rather overfamiliar model of historicizing in an altered light.

At the heart of Benjamin's philosophy of history is the fragment and its dual character both as an index of the catastrophe of modernity and as the embodiment of a redemptive possibility. In the celebrated "angel of history" passage of "Thesis IX," Benjamin depicts history as an ongoing "catastrophe" that results in an ever-expanding accumulation of the shattered fragments of a broken world:

> This is how one pictures the angel of history. His face is turned toward the past. Where we perceive a chain of events, he sees one single catastrophe which keeps piling wreckage upon wreckage and hurls it in front of his feet. The angel would like to stay, awaken the dead, and make whole what has been smashed. But a storm is blowing from Paradise; it has got caught in his wings with such violence that the angel can no longer close them. This storm irresistibly propels him into the future to which his back is turned, while the pile of debris before him grows skyward. This storm is what we call progress. (*Illuminations* 249)

Apocalyptic as this scene might seem, in the rubble of history that piles up at the angel's feet Benjamin detects something worth rescuing: the remains of "spark[s] of hope in the past" (*Illuminations* 247). Underlying this frequently cited passage is a co-presence of cataclysm and redemption that runs through Benjamin's entire philosophy of history. The "sparks" that the angel seems incapable of recovering, but which Benjamin urges his historical materialist to heed, derive from the Lurianic Kabbalistic account of the "breaking of the vessels" (see Scholem, 262–5). According to Luria's interpretation of the *Zohar*, God's divine light was supposed to be contained in ten *sefirot* or special vessels, but the light was too powerful for them and they broke apart. Falling to earth, their shattered remains became the *kelipot* or "husks" of all that is malevolent in the world. However, sparks of divine light or *shekhinah* remain mixed among the *kelipot*, and the recovery and restoration of these sparks to their place in the "ideal order," as Gershom Scholem puts it, is "the secret purpose of existence" (264). In Benjamin's "Theses," the malign "husks" are analogous to the disastrous history of bourgeois culture that heaps "wreckage" at the angel's feet. It is the task of his historical materialist to sift through the debris of this history for *shekhinah*-like "spark[s] of hope in the past." Brought to bear on the present, grasped as part of the "constellation which [the historian's] era has formed with a definite earlier one," these luminous shards have a transformative capacity to constitute the present as "the 'time of the now' . . . shot through with chips of Messianic time" (*Illuminations* 255). In other words it is only in the moment of their recuperation into the present historical moment that the revolutionary promise of the fragments of the past can be glimpsed, and this transformative capacity inheres not in some essence of the fragments themselves but in the fleeting light that they can cast on the calamity of contemporary modernity and the prospects for imagining it "otherwise."

Through their archaeopoetic engagement with the fragmented remains of the past, the poetries I examine in the later chapters of this book perform and reflect on a parallel activity. Furthermore, in so doing they archaeocritically rethink and reshape this model of historiography in relation to the particularities and pluralities of the histories with which they are concerned. Brathwaite, for example, describes his poetic project in terms of an aspiration "to find the rhythm, the metaphor, the image that would unite 'whole' and 'hole,' that would create a sweep and an ancestry out of the broken cordilleras" ("Caliban's Guarden" 4). Drawing on the geography and history of his native island of Barbados, Brathwaite's vision of history as structured by "catastrophe" (4) and possible regeneration echoes, but also recasts, Benjamin's messianism. O'Sullivan, meanwhile, describes the poetic page as a "place of damage, savagery, pain, silence: also a place of salvage, retrieval and recovery" ("Writing / Conversation"). In this manner she conceives the very place of writing in terms of a dialectic of trauma and tentative recuperation of dormant potentials. Such articulations seek to "salvage" hitherto suppressed, and potentially revolutionary, dimensions of poetic and cultural experience; in so doing they also reflect on the implications of this mode of historical inquiry in a number of different contexts.

To "brush history against the grain" in a Benjaminian sense is not simply to consider history's "barbarism" as inseparable from its claims to "civilization" nor is it to simply recover "the anonymous toil" of peoples unacknowledged in dominant versions of history; it is to embark on a quest to recover unfulfilled cultural potentials, moments whose possibilities and significance have gone unrecognized, and to rejuvenate present political endeavors with the vigor of their latent promise. Benjamin's attempt to incorporate theology into a Marxist historical materialism has proved highly contentious among his commentators. As his "Theses" amply demonstrate, Benjamin broadly agrees with the Marxist maxim that "[t]he history of all hitherto existing society is the history of class struggles" (Marx and Engels 219) insofar as his concept of history aims to rescue "[t]he tradition of the oppressed" and to bring to attention the "anonymous toil" of those whose unacknowledged labor is secreted in the "cultural treasures" presided over by history's "victorious." Furthermore, he sees unequal economic and power relations between classes as producing a "'state of emergency' in which we live" and which is "not the exception but the rule" of modernity (*Illuminations* 248). However, Benjamin departs from orthodox Marxism in his abandonment of the notion of history as a developmental process. The idea of class struggle as a productive driving force behind a progressive history seemed untenable in the light of the political context in which he was writing; for him, the increasingly oppressive regime created in the name of Marxism under Stalin, the rise of Fascism in Germany, and the Hitler-Stalin alliance in 1939 signaled the failure of a progressive Marxist materialist project. According to Rolf Tiedemann, Benjamin's messianism responds to this political situation by attempting to inject a "revolutionary stimulus" that "had long since disappeared from the calcified theory of official materialism" ("Historical Materialism" 204). This move is part of Benjamin's own archaeocritical process. For him, "progress" is the apocalyptic storm by which the angel of history is blown backwards, stripped of agency, into a future he cannot glimpse. For Benjamin, neither history nor politics can be understood as teleological. Rather, his philosophy of history aspires to reinvigorate historical materialism by proposing that the very notion of history as a "continuum" must be "blast[ed] open" (*Illuminations* 254) and that political thought and action occur not by a gradual process of class struggle but by practices that radically juxtapose past and present moments in a "constellation"(255) capable of delivering a revolutionary "shock" (254) to the social and cultural configurations of the contemporary moment.

Some critics, such as Susan Buck-Morss, see the relationship of the theological and materialist axes of Benjamin's thought as complementary or even dialectical. As Buck-Morss states, "[w]ithout theology (the axis of transcendence) Marxism falls into positivism; without Marxism (the axis of empirical history) theology falls into magic" (249). Each acts as a corrective to the other's critical dangers. For Tiedemann, however, this combining of historical materialism and theology is an "attempt to unite the irreconcilable" ("Historical Materialism" 199). Jürgen Habermas essentially agrees, remarking that this endeavor

> must fail, because the materialist theory of social development cannot simply be fitted into the anarchical conception of the *Jeztzeiten* that intermittently break through fate as if from above. Historical materialism, which reckons on progressive steps not only in the dimen-

sion of productive forces but in that of domination as well, cannot be covered over with an antievolutionary conception of history as with a monk's cowl. (113–4)

Furthermore, this failure means that as far as Habermas is concerned, Benjamin's "semantic materialism" (123) cannot amount to a mode of political action: "[t]he liberation from cultural tradition of semantic potentials that must not be lost to the messianic condition is not the same as the liberation of political domination from structural violence" (120). Benjamin's "semantic materialism" may philosophically rescue a "tradition of the oppressed" (Benjamin, *Illuminations* 248), but his recovery of the latent "semantic potentials" of historical vestiges does not necessarily translate into a political liberation of the oppressed. For Habermas, Benjamin's "rescuing critique" is valuable not so much in its implications for political action but rather in its capacity to emphasize "a *further* moment in the concepts of exploitation and progress: besides hunger and oppression, failure; besides prosperity and liberty, happiness" (121). What Benjamin's theologically informed stance suggests, argues Habermas, is that emancipation, without taking account of this "*further* moment," risks becoming meaningless: "Without the influx of those semantic energies with which Benjamin's rescuing critique was concerned, the structures of practical discourse—finally well established—would necessarily become desolate" (123). In spite of—or perhaps even because of—the uncomfortable fit between these differing aspects of Benjamin's thought, his "semantic materialism," in its messianic rescue of as yet unrealized potentials, proposes ways of infusing the "practical discourse" of historical materialism with new kinds of meaning.

Habermas's notion of "semantic potentials"—and the possibilities and problems it engenders—becomes especially relevant when discussing an archaeological poetics whose concern is to explore *language's* capacities to harbor hitherto suppressed dimensions of historical experience. To "critique radical radical visible subsurface" (*Nonconformist's* 98), as Howe's poem "Melville's Marginalia" has it, is to critically excavate language in search of the (emphatically repeated) "radical" forces that inhere as its "subsurface." Importantly, Howe's line, surrounded by lines printed vertically, diagonally, and overlapping each other, foregrounds the "visible" as a textual dimension with particularly rich potentials. The work of Howe and the four other poets explored in this book deploys visual materiality, in particular, as a way of putting into play *further* dimensions of signification by which hitherto unapprehended meanings might be detected. Again the question of political efficacy arises, reverberating with long-running debates among practitioners and critics of experimental poetry. The mobilization of extra-linguistic semantic possibilities in a poetic work does not and cannot amount to a full-scale recovery of a lost past nor result in any kind of social emancipation in the present for those whose pasts have been covered over: "semantic potentials" do not simply "translate" smoothly into political change. Indeed, the poetry I examine in this book refuses such models of efficacy by contesting the notion that their various fragments can be resolved into a totality or co-opted to a coherent political project. Because this work archaeocritically engages the forms of representation and knowledge that mediate any understanding of cultural pasts and the contemporaneity those pasts continue to shape, it can inform an attentiveness to dimensions of language and culture that might otherwise go unacknowledged. It performs, in other words, an orientational function, pointing the way to alternative dimensions of meaningfulness and modes of historical knowledge. Failure is also always a possibility.

In light of this, while Habermas's account of Benjamin does in the end manage to reconcile the theological and materialist aspects of this thinking, perhaps it is also worth keeping hold of his initial insistence that Benjamin's project, too, "must fail" if its philosophical accomplishment is measured according to the extent to which the tensions between its constituent dimensions can be resolved. Given Benjamin's own insistence on the juxtaposition of different historical moments and the value he places on the "shock" produced, the very incompatibility of the theological and materialist dimensions of his thinking might be viewed in a parallel light: as a forcing-together of diverse impulses with contradictory implications that may overlap and inform each other but refuse to entirely settle their differences. It is precisely these contradictory multifarious vectors that contemporary poet Charles Bernstein values in a recent recasting of Benjamin's thought. In an interview in *The Argotist* Bernstein describes Benjamin's thinking as "multipolar, rather than linear . . . . I mean this as a way of rethinking what is often called fragmentation or disjunction. Think of fragments not as discontinuous but as overlays, pleats, folds" ("Interview"). For him, Benjamin transforms the notion of fragmentation into something else, something more resembling a midden of overlapping deposits, profoundly palimpsestual, composed of layers that create moments of adhesion capable of generating connections or "sparks" of apperception. In his libretto *Shadowtime*, written for an opera by Brian Ferneyhough on Benjamin's life and thought, Bernstein conducts an archeological mining of the strata of these "overlays." He brushes Benjamin's own writing "against the grain" in order to salvage its transformative implications for his own contemporary moment: "In the libretto, I have the angel of history say the opposite of what Benjamin writes in 'The Concept of

History.' Benjamin writes that 'the angel would like to stay, awaken the dead, and make whole what has been smashed.' Our angels, in contrast, ask that we 'imagine no wholes from all that has been smashed.' Because for me . . . it's very important *not* to imagine a totality, but rather a multiplicity, the shards, and the sparks around the edges. We don't live in a Messianic moment, the scales have not fallen from our eyes, our seeing is double and triple, not unitary. The Benjaminian 'now time' (*jetzeit*) lets us hear the cathected material moment amidst the multiplicity of omnivalent vectors" ("Interview"). Benjamin's own angel may not have been able to let go of the impulse to create a totality, but his writing offers glimpses of the possibility of that multiple, fragmented version of history as an alternative—or an infinity of alternatives. And although "we don't live in a Messianic moment," Bernstein's version of the angel of history scene retains the messianic potential of "shards" and "sparks" that are tangible precisely in the disjunctive "edges" of a multiplicity of fragments and in the irreconcilability of these fragments. This is precisely what keeps the "sparks" alive.

Imag(in)ing History

Benjamin's historicism has more to offer when considering archaeological poetics. Most especially, the notion of the "dialectical image" (475, N10a, 3) that his unfinished *Arcades Project* both proposes and embodies anticipates some of the formal strategies traced in the later chapters of *Archaeopoetics*. The messianic possibility of a historical vision that is double, triple, and multiple is most apparent in Benjamin's visually oriented rethinking of dialectics. While he rejects the developmental notion embedded in the Marxist dialectic, he does not want to do away with dialectics altogether, maintaining that "dialectical thinking is the organ of historical awakening" (*Arcades* 13). The "awakening" he envisages is a sudden emergence from a collective dream state by which modern bourgeois societies keep their subjects in thrall into a state of political awareness. What Benjamin values about the dialectical model is the revolutionary energy produced by bringing conflicting forces together. He deeply distrusts the developmental process posited by Hegelian and Marxian dialectics in which tensions get resolved in the movement toward synthesis or sublation. As Paul Naylor points out, in the moment of sublation, "something gets covered over" (22). Oppositional tensions and alternative potentials become contained and subsumed "[a]s if all history were a progress . . . [a] single thread of narrative" (Howe, *Nonconformist's* 7). For Benjamin, such a process not only closes down possibilities; it also too easily echoes the form of the soothing "once upon a time" (*Arcades* 473, N3, 4) story that sustains modernity's slumbers. In the search for a non-developmental, non-narrative mode of historical understanding, Benjamin's philosophy of history turns to visual paradigms as offering alternative models:

> It's not that what is past casts its light on what is present, or what is present its light on what is past; rather, image is that wherein what has been comes together in a flash with the now to form a constellation. In other words, image is dialectics at a standstill. For while the relation of the present to the past is a purely temporal, continuous one, the relation of what-has-been to the now is dialectical: is not progression but image, suddenly emergent. (*Arcades* 462, N2a, 3)

As the vocabulary of "light" and the "flash" might suggest, this image-based notion of dialectics borrows from Benjamin's long-running fascination with film and photography. Indeed, the photograph constitutes a concrete model for his "dialectical image." In his 1931 essay "A Small History of Photography," Benjamin describes the seductive power of old photographs that compel the beholder to seek out "the tiny spark of contingency, of the Here and Now, with which reality has so to speak seared the subject, to find the inconspicuous spot where in the immediacy of that long-forgotten moment the future subsists so eloquently that we, looking back, may rediscover it" (243). The photograph, in Benjamin's hands, performs an odd and uncanny temporal conflation. As a concretization of an arrested moment of some forgotten past, it has the potential to tell us something of our own moment, the "Here and Now" that "subsists" as a hitherto submerged stratum or unfulfilled possibility of that earlier reality. But it is "not that what is past casts its light on what is present": the fleeting "spark" of the present can only be apprehended by "looking back" from the vantage point of a very particular "Here and Now" to a very particular and fleeting "immediacy" in the past that the photograph makes present (243). Furthermore, the photograph discloses what might otherwise remain hidden: "photography reveals . . . the physiognomic aspects of visual worlds which dwell in the smallest things, meaningful yet covert enough to find a hiding place in waking dreams" (243). It compels us to see again, to attend more carefully to details we might otherwise miss, and to rethink what we find "meaningful." So, too, the dialectical image is an arrested instant of intersection between the "what-has-been" and "the now," which Benjamin differentiates from a more generalized sense of "past" and "present." Like the photographic image, this dialectical image figures history not as a temporal unfolding but as a concretized site of contact between different but very specific historical realities. The instantaneous "flash" of this convergence produces a "now of particular recognizability"

(*Arcades* 463, N3, 2), a "suddenly emergent" moment of historical recognition that is both an "awakening" to and a "re-cognition" of one's historical conditions. The dialectical image is not a window on the world but an aperture of political possibility.

This transformative potential depends on the opening up rather than the closing down or resolution of dialectical tensions. Whereas in Hegelian and Marxist dialectics the progressive moment of synthesis resolves conflicting forces (even if only temporarily), the Benjaminian image is arrested at the moment "where the tension between dialectical opposites is greatest." It is "a constellation saturated with tensions" (475, N10a, 3). As Susan Buck-Morss puts it, the dialectical image's "principle of construction is that of montage, whereby the image's ideational elements remain unreconciled, rather than fusing into one 'harmonizing perspective'" (67). While this formulation emphasizes "ideational elements," Benjamin draws just as much upon the physical juxtapositions carried out by the practices of montage, for these concretize and keep in play dialectical tensions as unresolved nodes of the "constellation." Buck-Morss relates Benjamin's notion of the dialectical image to the avant-garde practices of Berlin Dada artist John Heartfield, but one might just as legitimately cite Cubist collage and the techniques of Russian experimental filmmakers such as Sergei Eisenstein and Vsevolod Pudovkin (whom Benjamin mentions approvingly in his "Photography" essay) as equally likely models. The techniques of Cubist and Dada collages exemplify a practice of severing fragments from their original contexts and redeploying them in new contexts in ways that produce new kinds of meaning, while the radical juxtapositions of an Eisenstein montage typify the capacity of such arrangements to produce sudden and illuminating "shocks." Indeed it is at least partly the physical tangibility of productive frictions in such practices that Benjamin seeks to capture in his own historical method. In other words, in his archaeocritique of prevailing modes of historical thinking, he turns to recent developments in the arts and aesthetic experiences of his time to propose alternative kinds of historical consciousness rooted in new cultural foundations. He asks, "In what way is it possible to conjoin a heightened graphicness <*Anschaulichkeit*> to the realization of the Marxist method? The first stage in this undertaking will be to carry over the principle of montage into history" (461, N2, 6). The translation here of *Anschaulichkeit* as "graphicness" is an attempt to convey the striking intensity and immediacy of pictorial knowledge, a quality that Benjamin's dialectical images seek to encapsulate by emulating the principles of montage.

The principles of Benjamin's dialectical image are embedded not only in the structures of his historical thinking but also in the very compositional process of *The Arcades Project*, his unfinished book in which the dialectical image is the core theoretical proposal. We might say, then, that Benjamin's archaeocritique is enacted through a kind of archaeopoetics even though this work was not strictly a work of poetry or art. At his death in 1940, the manuscript comprised a huge unwieldy collection of fragmented notes and quotations that are arranged in themed sections or "Convolutes" whose central subject was to be the nineteenth-century shopping arcades of Paris and the forms of bourgeois consumerism they concretized. What Benjamin had intended for this mass of materials can never fully be known, but at one point in the notes he proclaims, "Method of this project: literary montage. I needn't say anything. Merely show. I shall purloin no valuables, appropriate no ingenious formulations. But the rags, the refuse—these I will not inventory but allow, in the only way possible, to come into their own: by making use of them" (460, N1a, 8). This is a mode of writing history that eschews narration and explanation in favor of a "making use." To make use in the Benjamin sense somewhat contrasts with the instrumentalist connotations of the phrase in that it aims simply to present a constellation of undigested materials whose very juxtapositions allow them "to come into their own." The spatial logic of montage takes over from narrative, and the historian remains silent, merely selecting artifacts and arranging them, more a curator than an originator of "ingenious formulations." Henceforth, "[t]o write history . . . means to *cite* history" (476, N11, 3).

Benjamin's philosophy of history draws on the image and on the visual cultural practices of his time for the ways in which they seemed to embody a spatialized, concrete form of thinking that suggests alternatives to discursive modes of knowledge. Thus to "brush history against the grain" is not just to read it for its omissions but to *physically* brush it, to lay palpable hold upon histories understood as material. Like Olson's "Kingfishers," Benjamin proposes a method of historical encounter that attempts to imagine history "otherwise" by engaging with its remains in all their physicality, in an archaeopoetic mode.

Indeed, Benjamin was himself no stranger to the archaeological trope of modernism. In a short essay fragment of the early 1930s, he writes:

> He who seeks to approach his own buried past must conduct himself like a man digging. Above all, he must not be afraid to return again and again to the same matter; to scatter it as one scatters earth, to turn it over as one turns over soil. For the "matter itself" is no more than the strata which yield their long-sought secrets only to the most meticulous investigation. That is to say, they yield those images that, severed from all earlier associations, reside as treasures in the sober rooms of our later insights. ("Excavation and Memory" 576)

By regarding the past as "matter" to be physically sifted and revisited time and again, Benjamin's archaeologist of modernity transforms "the rags, the refuse" of an earlier age into the illuminating images, the "treasures" that, wrested from their prior contexts, take on new meaning and value in the "sober" light of contemporaneity. His archaeological, image-led model of historicism hopes to recover concrete relations with the world of things that in his thinking, according to Rolf Tiedemann, were lost to an "abstracting cognition" related to the "achievements of language and writing" ("Dialectics" 934). Benjamin, Tiedemann continues, "was concerned about 'palpable knowledge,' which 'not only feeds on the sensory data taking shape before his eyes, but can very well possess itself of abstract knowledge—indeed, of dead facts—as something experienced and lived through.' Images take the place of concepts" (934). As Adorno puts it, "Benjamin does not weave a relation to the absolute out of concepts, but rather seeks it through corporeal contact with the material" ("Benjamin's Schriften" 4). Benjamin makes a claim for the palpable, physical encounter embodied in the qualities of the visual image as an alternative to a mode of historical knowledge dominated by the conceptual abstractions of a discursive logic.

By proposing a spatialized logic, a practice of citation and collage, and a foregrounding of the physicality of historical traces, especially in the process of their decontextualization and recontextualization, the dialectical image finds its successors in the practices and poetics of Cha, Howe, O'Sullivan, Brathwaite, and Philip. If to write history is to cite history, then "to transplant words onto paper with soil sticking to their roots" (Howe, *Souls* 16) is also to carry forward a Benjaminian sense of historical particulars as concrete "matter" with transformative potential nurtured through its physical transplantation into other contexts. Or, alternatively, in Cha's formulation:

> Words cast each by each to weather
> avowed indisputably, to time.
> If it should impress, make fossil trace of word,
> residue of word, stand as a ruin stands,
> simply, as mark
> having relinquished itself to time to distance
> (*DICTEE* 177)

The material word wrenched from the continuum of historical narrative has the capacity to "stand as a ruin stands," as a "fossil trace" in all its tangibility and physical particularity. It also has the ability to serve as a "mark" of concretized relations with other materials that offer alternatives to established pathways of meaning and discursive logic.

From Ideogram to Open Field

The visual and historicist impulses discernible in the work of the five poets I examine have antecedents not only in Benjamin's thinking but also in the aesthetic practices of modernism. Indeed, Benjamin's attempt to formulate a mode of thinking that combines the unresolvedness of montage with the concreteness of a visual "graphicness" had contemporary aesthetic counterparts not only in the visual arts and filmmaking but also in the poetic avant-gardes of the early twentieth century. The image has long been considered a central and defining feature of poetry. However, in the early decades of the twentieth century, poets were attending in new ways to the literal kinds of visuality and physicality implied by the very notion of the poetic image. For example, in a move that resonates strikingly with Benjamin's notion of the dialectical image as constellation, Mallarmé's seminal *Un Coup de dés* pursued a highly abstract and dynamic poetic language, perhaps rather paradoxically, via a poetic "CONSTELLATION" realized through the spatial and material resources of the poetic page. Likewise, Apollinaire reinvented the pattern poem in his shaped *Calligrammes*, which Gabriel Arbouin, a contemporary commentator, described as displaying "an ideographic logic leading to a spatial order of distribution completely at odds with that of normal discursive order" (qtd. in Drucker, *Visible Word* 165). Marinetti performed a "Typographic Revolution," as his 1913 manifesto has it, in poems that energetically exploded the visual conventions of the poetic page and insisted on the mimetic immediacy of visual and sonic physicality. Russian Futurists such as Velimir Khlebnikov and Aleksei Kruchenykh emphasized the graphic and phonic materiality of "The Word as Such" and even "The Letter as Such," which became the titles of two of their manifestos. Meanwhile, American poets such as e. e. cummings and William Carlos Williams were experimenting with typographic manipulation in their poetry, and Pound was developing his "ideogrammic" method. These are only some of the ways that modernist poets explored the possibilities for visual languages of typography and spatial organization to revolutionize poetry's semantic capacities. By bestowing upon words the physical qualities of visual images, these modernist poets aimed to deliver a variety of visually informed jolts to historical consciousness in ways that form noteworthy parallels to Benjamin's notion of dialectical images. But it is Pound, most of all, who brought an intensified form of visual sensibility to bear on the writing of the "poem including history." His legacy is most pertinent for contemporary poets writing in this vein.

In his early Imagist phase, Pound's endorsement of "direct treatment of the 'thing'" (Flint 94) involves a highly visual conception of the poetic image.

When recounting the process of composing his celebrated poetic response to the experience of stepping off the Paris metro, he remarks that he "found, suddenly, the expression . . . not in speech but in little splotches of color" (Ruthven 153). "I realized," he goes on, "that if I were a painter . . . I might found a new school of . . . painting that would speak only by arrangements in colour." What Pound seeks is a poetic equivalent of painting's ability to "speak" via the physical relations embodied in its "arrangements." In its first 1913 printing, "In a Station of the Metro" retains this visual sensibility in the layout of the components of its verbal image:

The apparition   of these faces   in the crowd
Petals   on a wet, black   bough
(Ruthven 152)

The large white spaces in this printing, as K. K. Ruthven remarks, function as a means of "making the lines look as though they are composed of six detachable fragments; and as a means of getting the reader to regard the words on the page as 'things'" (153). Such a sensitivity to the capacity of visual arrangements of the printed word to emphasize the thingness of words, and thereby inflect the poem's meaning, was surely shaped by Pound's awareness of European avant-garde movements such as Cubism and Dada, and in particular his contact with Marinetti's radical typographical experimentation. But it was his engagement with the work of Orientalist scholar Ernest Fenollosa on Chinese written characters that most influenced Pound's development of a visually inflected poetics. The Chinese ideogram seemed to answer Pound's desire for a language that, like painting, functions concretely as a physical relational field. Fenollosa argued that by combining signs so that "two things added together do not produce a third thing but suggest some fundamental relation between them," Chinese writing operates not arbitrarily but pictorially, and not just on a simple, mimetic level (46). Drawing on Fenollosa, Pound believed (albeit somewhat erroneously) that the ideogram compressed together simple but vivid images superimposed on one another to form a complex of condensed meaning. For Pound, the ideogram was a model of "language charged with meaning to the utmost possible degree" (*ABC* 28), a densely layered intersection of concepts concretized in a set of physical relations.

Chinese ideograms increasingly make their way into Pound's *Cantos* from Canto 52 onwards where, in the words of Jerome McGann, they function as "an index of the kind of attention all scripted forms demand" (*Textual Condition* 146). But for all his emphasis on the visual, concrete properties of Chinese writing, and his early use of visual and painterly metaphors in his pronouncements about the poetic image, Pound primarily valued the ideogram not so much for its own material qualities as for the poetic method it suggests. In its physical compounding of two or more images, the ideogram represents a process of "heaping together the necessary components of thought" (*Selected Prose* 209). It is this process that underpins Pound's "ideogrammic method" and that, in *The Cantos*, becomes a way of "including history." The ideogrammic method advocates the incorporation of historical and cultural fragments into the poem without providing syntactical or explicit conceptual links between them: "[t]he artist seeks out the luminous detail and presents it. He does not comment" (Pound, *Selected* 23). Rather, these fragments' physical juxtaposition with other elements should "suggest some fundamental relation between them" (Fenollosa 46). The ideogram thus gives rise to an archaeopoetics that presents research materials according to a spatial logic, and this enables the *Cantos* to suggest, but not explicate, historical patterns.

In *The Cantos* this spatial mode of negotiating history is often manifested in the layout of the poem, particularly in the later *Rock Drill* and *Thrones* Cantos. At one point in Canto 96, for example, Pound's exploration of the Canto's central theme of commerce and right governance takes the form of a grid of words and word clusters that utilizes the space of the page to set up relations between its different elements (679) (see figure 1). The right-hand column of the word grid consists of the Chinese ideograms for "purple," "to go to," "surpass," and "vermilion," which can be translated as "purple goes far in surpassing red" (Terrell 604). This sequence resonates with a reference on the previous page to "Hyacinthinis," which is Latin for "vermilion" and is taken from Jules Nicole's nineteenth-century translation into modern Greek and Latin of *Eparch's Book of Leo the Wise*, a commercial manual of the Byzantine era. Pound translates this Latin term as "fake purple" (678), which according to Carroll F. Terrell's *Companion* is a reference to the early days of cloth dyeing when purple "was an exclusively royal color sold legally only to royalty" (603). This meditation on purple also invokes Confucius's words "I hate the way purple spoils Vermilion . . . I hate sharp mouths (the clever yawp, mouths set on profits) that overturn states and families" (Terrell 603). In Pound's word grid, the sequence of Chinese ideograms should be read not only vertically but horizontally across the page in spatial relation to terms such as the Greek words for "retail dealers," "hucksters," and "babbler" and the English "that is 'mouthy.'" These apparently arbitrary references drawn from culturally and historically disparate sources coalesce around ideas of counterfeiting (vermilion is a kind of counterfeit purple) and the "babbling" mouths of hectoring "hucksters," who would contravene the laws of commerce and "just price" to make a profit (*Cantos* 679). The poem suggests that a wider set of economic and social relations might be

verberator et bonis mulcator

παιδευέσθω καὶ εἰσκομιζέσθω

register all silk purchases over ten aurei

δέκα νομισμάτων (Nicole: purpureas vestes) τὰ βλαττία

but the ἀναιδῶς is rather nice, Dr. Nicole,

before the μὴ αὐξάνοντες ἢ ἐλαττοῦντες τὴν τιμήν

and the idea of just price is somewhere,

       the haggling, somewhere,

also

    ἀλογίστους quite beautifully used

        tho' utopian

tzu³

χαπηλεύων   or

chih¹

στομύλος   that is "mouthy"

ἀγοραῖος   forensic

to²⁻⁵

λάλος   babbler

chu¹

ταραχώδης   as on the East bank from Beaucaire

μὴ τῇ τοῦ ἐπάρχου ἐσφραγισμένον

not stamped with the prefect's seal βούλλη

χαμπανὸν νενοθευμένον

Ducange: στατήρ

Here, surely, is a refinement of language

> *If we never write anything save what is already*
> *understood, the field of understanding will never be*
> *extended. One demands the right, now and again,*
> *to write for a few people with special interests*
> *and whose curiosity reaches into greater detail.*

Figure 1. Ezra Pound, from Canto 96. *The Cantos of Ezra Pound.* New Directions, 1996. Page 679.

discerned by examining such fragments with a "forensic" eye. The word grid thus constitutes an ideogram of juxtaposed morsels of Byzantine and Chinese wisdom that embody some of Pound's ideas about the need for strong economic governance to curtail the exploitative and destabilizing activities of "hucksters" and "babblers."

Pound's use throughout the Cantos of fragments lifted from other texts demonstrates that for him, as for Benjamin, to write history is to cite history. Like Benjamin's dialectical image, Pound's ideogrammic method seeks out the "luminous" shards of the past and places them in a montage-like constellation with other fragments, or snippets of commentary. As for Benjamin, it is this process of decontextualization and recontextualization, and the relations set up between different elements, that reinvigorate previously dormant possibilities. Pound, like Benjamin, aims to show rather than tell; he values the concreteness of the visual image and its presumed immediacy. To draw parallels between the archaeopoetics of an American poet who fell into anti-Semitism and fascism and a Marxist Jewish German philosopher who died while attempting to flee the Nazis may seem perverse. But what this correspondence demonstrates is a powerful impulse in different modernist practices to archaeocritically rethink the philosophy and aesthetics of writing history. Pound and Benjamin forward a structure of feeling that views the history of modernity as the fragments and ruins of a calamitous present. Both seek to redeem shards of potential through processes that imagine themselves as direct and concrete. This claim to concreteness draws upon ideas of visuality presented as an alternative to the discursive logic of dominant ideologies within modernity, which have sought to represent history as continuous, progressive, and unitary. This historical sensibility structured around a visual logic, discernible in Benjamin and Pound, is extended by the work of the contemporary poets discussed in the chapters. These poets, furthermore, expand and rethink this historiographic mode in even more materially emphatic ways than their predecessors. "I wanted to write something," says Howe, "filled with gaps and words tossed, and words touching, words crowding each other, letters mixing and falling away from each other, commands and dreams, verticals and circles" (*Birth-mark* 175).

While Pound's poetry stands as a prominent formal precedent for such practices, the archaeopoetics of Howe, Cha, O'Sullivan, Brathwaite, and Philip have much more in common politically with Benjamin. Having just posited some general similarities between these two modernists, it seems just as vital to acknowledge some contrasts. While the method of citing particularly charged moments of the past is common to Benjamin and Pound, the kinds of material they seize upon as illuminating differs radically. Pound is drawn to the great men and grand monuments of history. He references these personages and monuments with the aspiration of bringing transhistorical truths to light. Conversely, Benjamin seeks among "the rags, the refuse" historically contingent glimpses of political insight (*Arcades* 460, N1a, 8). Furthermore, Benjamin's fragments and their intersecting tensions inherently resist unification into a totality, whereas Pound's ambitions are unremittingly totalizing.

Pound's *Cantos* ultimately fail to conform to the unifying vision he had for them: as the final Canto 116 famously admits, "I cannot make it cohere" (816). Finally "a tangle of works unfinished" (815) whose speaker is stranded among its "errors and wrecks" (816), *The Cantos* themselves suggest possibilities for later generations of poets that contradict Pound's explicit statements. As Charles Bernstein puts it:

> By introducing a form where dialects and languages mingle freely, where 'non-poetic' material—"raw facts," Chinese ideograms, printer's errors, slang, polylingual quotations—are given poetic status, Pound opened the flood gates for what had been left out, or refined out, by precepts such as his own "use absolutely no word that does not contribute." The undigested quality of parts of *The Cantos* gives credence to the further explorations of the unheard and unsounded in our poetry. ("Pound" 162–63)

Such archaeopoetic "further explorations," including Bernstein's, have emphasized the fragmentary and the unwhole, the irreconcilable and the unfinished, the uncertain, the indigestible, the silenced, or, as Maggie O'Sullivan puts it, "voices that are other-than or invisible or dimmed or marginalized or excluded or without privilege, or locked out, made UNofficial" ("In conversation with Brown" 159). Such an impulse to encompass hitherto suppressed presences has, in formal terms, entailed taking up and radically expanding upon the collagist, visual, and materialist techniques that *The Cantos* imply.

Charles Olson is one of Pound's immediate successors, even his "most representative and influential descendent" (Beach 84). Among the numerous post-war writers who accepted the challenge of engaging with Pound's poetics it is Olson who simultaneously extends the formal and historicist impulses of *The Cantos* furthest. As Kathleen Fraser has it, Olson's engagement with Pound, constituted a "permission-giving moment" through which later poets "gained access to a more expansive page" for the "pursuit of the unnamed" (175). In *Mayan Letters*, Olson talks enthusiastically of "the methodology of the Cantos" as "a space-field" where Pound transforms "time material . . . into what we must now have, space & its live air" (*Selected* 82). It is precisely such a spatial turn that informs the "open field" poetics of Olson's post-war "Projective Verse" proclamations. Olson's infamous "Projective Verse" essay proposes a highly physical sense of composition as an activity of arranging "OBJECTS" within "the large area of the whole poem . . . the FIELD, if you like, where all the syllables and all the lines must be managed in their relations to each other" (*Selected* 20). It is the relations between different poetic elements that generate the productive tensions, or the kinetics of the poem, and the "live air" of reinvigorated possibility. One key difference between Pound's and Olson's notion of the poem-as-field is that for all his early emphasis on the thingness of objects, Pound's ideogrammic thinking was more focused on the ideogram as a complex of ideas rather than a material thing. Conversely, Olson's poetics emphasizes the poem as a phenomenological field. As he puts it in his "Proprioception" essay, "Word writing. Instead of 'idea-writing' (ideogram etc.)" (*Additional* 20). While Olson's work participates in a spatialized mode of engaging history comparable to Pound's, and while he takes up Pound's practice of citation, he is generally more interested in the experiential rather than the conceptual dimensions of historical inquiry. His historical method is more "hands-on," so to speak. As Christopher Beach has remarked, "Pound's method is fundamentally that of the nineteenth-century cultural archaeologist; he studies the cultural archive for comparisons with, and supplements to, an unfavorable present. Olson's method, exemplified by his work on Mayan remains in the Yucatán, is in a more rigorous sense that of the on-site archaeological researcher" (87). Olson is an archaeologist who gets his hands dirty. His sense of history is much more tied to a phenomenological experience of site, and geographical and culturally specific space, than Pound's. The poem for Olson thus becomes a field that performs perceptual engagements with historical materials, sometimes in ways that transform the page into an archaeological site in strikingly literal ways, as in a poem like "Letter, May 2, 1959" in *The Maximus Poems* (see figure 2). The first and last pages of this poem represent the region of Gloucester and its local history via a number of unconventionally printed lines and arrangements of letters and numbers that resemble the visual arrangements of a map. Citations from historical documents that refer to local histories—such as the seventeenth-century peregrinations of local figures Bruen and Eveleth (150) and skirmishes with indigenous peoples (156)—are embedded into the poem's map-like contours. The poem presents itself not just as a field but a whole landscape, a landscape that is all at once geographical, cultural, historical, and perceptual.

Despite his occasional use of quite dramatic visual techniques and his frequent use of more subtle typographical arrangements, Olson's poetic statements downplay the specifically visual character of the page as space. In "Projective Verse" he scorns "that verse which print bred" as "'closed' verse"

Letter, May 2, 1959

125 paces Grove Street
fr E end of Oak Grove cemetery
to major turn NW of
road

this line goes finally straight
fr Wallis property direct
to White (as of 1707/8)

(2) 125 of curve
(3) 200 paces to Centennial

(4)
    47   90   90
                          st
       230 paces

c 300 paces
  Whittemore to the marsh

Kent's property/ Pearce

                       w to marsh
                       (hill falls off

    70
   paces   o
 hill falls   o
 S to   o
                    o   140
 marsh   o
                   o   old stonewall
        Meeting House —between Bruen & Eveleth?
 Babson   Green   (Perkins)
 house   Millet
   Ellery   fence marking

did Eveleth go to present Marsh St?

What did Bruen want? He had already shifted from Piscataqua
to Plymouth, then to Gloucester and now to New London and
would go from New London to found Newark, N.J.

Figure 2. Charles Olson. "Letter, May 2, 1959." *The Maximus Poems*. University of
California Press, 1983. Page 150.

(*Selected* 15) and associates the printed medium with fixity and stasis. His "open field" on the other hand is dominated by an emphasis on orality, on the ear and the breath. For Olson, the phenomenological "field" of the poem is above all sound based. Praising the capacities of the typewriter to "indicate exactly the breath, the pauses, the suspensions even of syllables" (22), his poetic manifesto makes the literal, visually perceptible materiality of the page subservient to the poem's oral dimensions. Opening the poetic page to an expanded spatial and visual sensibility (and this is also the case in some of his prose, as "Proprioception" strikingly demonstrates), Olson's polemical statements also place restrictions upon this impulse. Spatial arrangements must function in the service of the ear and the breath and are subordinate to these overriding oral concerns. Olson accused Pound of staying inside the "Western Box" (*Selected* 129), but Olson creates his own enclosures that limit his notion of the "open field." One of them is a phonocentric box.

However, it is sometimes difficult to see how some of Olson's own poetry adheres to such restrictive edicts. In the first page of "Letter, May 2, 1959," for example, the map-space of the page contains a crooked column of o's that run from the upward-sloping line "(hill falls off" to the very slightly downward-sloping lines "Meeting House / Green" (*Maximus* 150). The typographic trail thus appears to represent some kind of path or boundary. Indeed, as George Butterick indicates, "[t]he string of O's in this section is the printer's approximation of what in the original manuscript and first published version of the poem was drawn more clearly to represent the 'old stonewall'" (207). It is not clear how or whether this visual representation of the "old stonewall" can be rendered in the privileged oral terms of Olson's own prescriptive poetics as articulated in "Projective Verse." Rather, such elements of the work (and this is by no means an isolated example) are better understood as contributing to a multidimensional phenomenological field or, as Michael Davidson aptly puts it, "a poetry as close to perception and cognition as possible" (*Ghostlier Demarcations* 14). In such poetry, he says, the page becomes a score not only for sound but for "physical acts of writing, speaking, and walking" (*Ghostlier Demarcations* 14). The material page thus functions as a score for performance in a wider sense than perhaps even the poet himself recognized.

Olson's exploration of the poetic page as a field or space is hardly unique among post-war poets. Yet the pronounced examples of visuality found in Olson's work are rare in the work of other prominent poets of his time. Lesser-known poets such as Ronald Johnson, Dick Higgins, Emmett Williams, Bob Cobbing, Mary Ellen Solt, and Ian Hamilton Finlay, to name but a few, were influenced by the international Concrete poetry movement and experimented with visual poetics. I do not want to suggest, then, that Olson's poetry and poetics constitutes the only, nor even the primary, immediate precedent for the visually orientated poetics of the writers I discuss. However, his work does combine historical inquiry and visual techniques to a greater extent than any other writer of the time apart from Pound. Olson's work serves to illustrate some of the challenges and possibilities of combining historical inquiry with a material poetics, which later poets pick up and engage with. His archaeological poetics embody a marked emphasis on concrete particulars shared by the poetries of Howe, Cha, O'Sullivan, Brathwaite, and Philip. But Olson's compositional methods, like Pound's before him, are also circumscribed by a poetics that stakes out the field of the page in ways that can be exclusionary. Susan Howe, for example, has taken issue with Olson's masculinist assumptions and misogynistic gestures, claiming these fence in the "open field" ("Since a Dialogue" 169). Howe maintains "that the complexity of Charles Olson's writing is, for a woman, an indeterminate, sometimes graphically violent force" (168). Significantly, Howe imagines the violence of Olson's writing as functioning "graphically," as if its "despotic" activities are embedded into the material surfaces of the poetic page. Although she later revises her opinion of Olson to take a less oppositional stance, Howe's remark indicates ways in which the "open field," and the visual page more generally, has histories and political associations that contemporary poets cannot simply transcend but must, rather, acknowledge and grapple with. As Rachel Blau DuPlessis appositely puts it, "[t]he page is not neutral. Not blank, and not neutral. It is a territory" (131). To enter into this territory is to enter into a space that bears the traces of prior incursions and prior claims. Therefore, archaeologies conducted through the material page are not just investigations of history by other means; they are also investigations *of* those other means.

Materiality and Meaningfulness

To foreground the visual materiality of textual space is not only to engage with a legacy of formal experimentation spanning more than a century. It is also to stage an insurgency within a terrain long governed by a powerful aesthetic and critical regime that posits a stark separation between verbal and visual domains. "What is the relation of the visual to / the verbal? Are they not separate / realms—races—each with their own civilization?" asks Charles Bernstein, somewhat mischievously, for his work frequently challenges such an assumption (*Content's* 115). The notion of discrete areas of verbal and visual artistic endeavor reaches its apotheosis in G. E. Lessing's 1766 essay *Laocoön*, which posits a series of oppositions between visual and literary modes of signification. Lessing aligns visual signs with space and material presence, and verbal signs with time and the transparency of the medium: "we should cease to be conscious of the means which the poet uses ... that is, his words" (85). Furthermore, he asserts that the verbal and visual arts cannot and *should not* intersect: "Painting and poetry should be like two just and friendly neighbors, neither of whom indeed is allowed to take unseemly liberties in the heart of the other's domain" (93).

Despite the proliferation of avant-garde practices in both the visual and literary arts that flagrantly took such "unseemly liberties," a notion of separate domains remained remarkably powerful in the twentieth century. It was shored up by the dominant mode of mid-century modernist criticism—conducted by formalist critics such as Cleanth Brooks, William Wimsatt, and Monroe Beardsley in literary studies, and Michael Fried and Clement Greenberg in art criticism—which viewed its objects of criticism as autonomous realms defined by the specificities of their mediums. As Johanna Drucker points out, this criticism "invested seriously and intractably in the distinction between literary and visual arts practices" (*Visible Word* 228). Greenberg, in particular, enthusiastically took up Lessing's distinction between literary and visual arts in his 1940 essay "Towards a Newer Laocoon" where he argues that what is specific to the literary arts is the ideational function of language. Pure painting and pure sculpture, meanwhile, pertain to the "physical, the sensorial," the "proper" domain of the visual arts where they may find a refuge from what he decried as the "corrupting influence" (32) of literature's focus on the conceptual, on ideas, and its concomitant entanglement with bourgeois ideologies. Yet by designating the visual arts as a realm of pure physicality, divorced from the world of thought, knowledge, linguistic meaning, and especially politics, Greenberg also renders visual experience mute.[3]

This powerful discourse of separation between the verbal and visual arts operates with reference to a pervasive divide between discursively based meaning and sensuous materiality, a divide touched upon in the beginning paragraphs of this introductory chapter. This split between the verbal and visual may be traced back to Kant's account of judgment in his *Critique of Pure Reason*, which makes a distinction between the intelligible and the sensible, and to Descartes's *Meditations*, which famously rejects sensory perception as a mode of knowing in favor of rational intelligence, thereby separating the sensory from the cognitive. In aesthetic discourse, terms such as immateriality, cognitive thought, semantics, and hermeneutic exegesis thus become generally associated with the realm of language-based meaning, while materiality, sensuousness, and phenomenological experience tend to be aligned with non-verbal aesthetic forms, and particularly with the visual arts.

Poetry, especially modernist poetry, has often occupied a rather ambiguous position in discussions of relations between the verbal and visual arts because it emphasizes the sensuousness of language and has as its "primary pigment," as Pound put it, the "IMAGE" ("Vortex" 98). The very notion of the poetic image implies a fusing—or at least a collaboration—of the verbal and the visual. Even Greenberg, the purist, could not quite bring himself to place poetry as belonging properly to "literature," while Jean-Paul Sartre, who reverses Greenberg's value judgments, disparagingly positions poetry "on the side of painting, sculpture and music" (5), art forms that he sees as essentially "mute" (4) and therefore, according to his instrumentalist requirement that art be socially useful in very direct ways, politically inefficacious. Although poetry uses the same linguistic elements as prose, Sartre says poetry "considers words as things and not as signs. For the ambiguity of the sign implies that one can penetrate it at will like a pane of glass and pursue the thing signified, or turn one's gaze towards its *reality* and consider it as an object" (6). This is, of course, a generalization; much of what passes for poetry does indeed offer words as relatively transparent signs whose materiality is to be rapidly transcended in pursuit of their semantic values. But more importantly for my purposes, Sartre rather simplistically presents the sign's transparency and opacity as an either/or situation, and both he and Greenberg are anxious to position poetry on one "side" or the other of the divide between "literature" and the "mute" arts.

Nevertheless, a poetic language that emphatically "considers words as things and not [or not only] as signs" can activate tensions between semantics and materiality, and mobilize the "ambiguity of the sign" in ways that unsettle a discourse that seeks to delineate separate aesthetic realms. Pound's Imagist poetics puts such intersections into play by borrowing from the notion of a visual language, such as painting or the Chinese ideogram, which works concretely via spatial relationships. However, his notion of the image as "that which presents an intellectual and emotional complex in an instant of time" tends to move very quickly away from the physical, visual substrates that prop up his notion of the image toward its dematerialized "intellectual and emotional" effects ("A Few" 95). Despite his use of the spatial and material dimensions of the page in *The Cantos*, the visual image for Pound is really just a figure for a poetics that seeks some of the qualities long associated with visual signs. In some ways, Olson's more phenomenological poetics takes the emphasis on the concrete dimensions of language further; for him, the poem is less a domain for activating ideas and more a literal field of physical interactions. But Olson's privileging of sound and voice, which, as Derrida has pointed out, Western metaphysics has assumed to be closer to thought and thus metaphysical presence, undervalues the literal visuality of his poetic pages as merely a score for those dimensions of language that the poet sees as more expressive of being.

The discourse of separate verbal and visual aesthetic realms has rendered the visual materiality of the printed page silent even, to some extent, for poets such as Pound and Olson who have drawn on its resources. The visuality of the printed word correlates with the "muteness" ascribed to painting; but as part of a medium whose ideal state is generally thought to be its immateriality and transparency, the graphic dimension of writing is usually not even accorded the physical presence of a visual medium. To emphasize the visible materiality of the written mark, to literalize the visuality embedded in the notion of the poetic image, is to take "unseemly liberties" that confront the aesthetic regime of separate realms. It is also to contest a suppression of the concrete dimension of inscription that is not just aesthetic but ideological in the sense that the aesthetic is always also ideological. As Ron Silliman pointed out in one of the seminal essays of Language writing, the "Disappearance of the Word" is an index of the "commoditization of language" under capitalism, wherein the "commodity fetish of language" becomes its referentiality and transparency; language's means of production are concealed, while it delivers up verisimilitude for easy consumption ("Disappearance" 127, 129). (It is no accident that Lessing's dictum that the language medium ought to be absolutely immaterial comes at a key moment in the rise of bourgeois capitalism.) Silliman's notion of transactional language as a commodity fetish draws attention not only to the word's supposed transparency but also to processes of concealment; the commodity fetish hides; it puts the fact of labor and the unacknowledged laborer out of sight; it obscures the power structures that keep the laborer laboring, and it conceals this very act of repression itself. What might the commodity fetish of language hide? How might the silencing of language's visual operations on the page be implicated in wider dynamics of power and suppression? What are the political ramifications of practices that orient attention towards the material dimensions of a page "[w]here words are surrounded by and trying to fill all that white space, negative space, blank space—where the silence is and never was silent" (Philip, *Genealogy* 125)? The poetry discussed in this book makes visible the unacknowledged material dimensions of language in an effort to bring other suppressed dimensions of textuality, culture, and history into articulation. This is articulation not just as enunciation but as a point of intersection, as hinge between verbal and visual, word and blank space, cognition and perception, and semantics and materiality. As with Benjamin's dialectical image, these frictional intersections are left unresolved and active.

The aesthetic tensions and ideological questions that are brought to the surface by poetry that confronts readers with the material, and especially the visual, dimensions of writing have not, of course, gone entirely unexplored; a number of critical interventions have provided valuable insights.[4] Canadian poet and critic Steve McCaffery has drawn on Georges Bataille's notion of a general economy to argue that the physical supports of writing—its phonic and graphic dimensions—function as an excess incapable of being utilized. Because such materiality is not subsumable to the ideational function of language, it "inevitably contests the status of language as a bearer of uncontaminated meaning(s)" and in turn the socio-political structures of power invested in this linguistic "economy" (105). For book artist and critic Johanna Drucker, however, visual materiality is "never an excess, never a surplus, never an addition to the work," although influential theories of language from Saussure to Derrida have systematically suppressed the semantic contribution of textual materiality ("Visual Performance" 159). In both her creative and critical work, Drucker insists on the thorough entanglement of language's physical substance and its signifying capacities. One of her most cogent insights is that dimensions of the text such as typography and spatial organization might be thought of as functioning performatively on the page, producing an enactment that has no necessary recourse to the presence of an author or producer (unlike Olson's notion of the poem as a score for performance) but rather is "about the presence of a poem" ("Visual Performance" 131). Craig Dworkin's lively analysis of visual illegibility in contemporary poetry, meanwhile, focuses on the kinds of reading such writing provokes. Borrowing Leon Roudiez's notion of "paragrammatic 'misreading,'" he asserts that forms of literal illegibility induced by foregrounded textual materiality disrupt normative referential signification and function as a catalyst for the opening up of alternative "networks of signification" (12). Ultimately, Dworkin hopes that the practices proposed by these texts might function politically to "provide concrete models for the sort of cultural activities readers might then bring to other aspects of the world around them" (xx).

Despite their differing foci and agendas, what is at stake in these critical negotiations of visual materiality (including my own) is an attempt to broaden what we mean when we talk about meaning, beyond the rather narrow range of linguistically tied semantics that has dominated literary hermeneutics and continues to do so. I am interested in this book in exploring the epistemological implications of such an endeavor to expand meaningfulness to encompass forms of sensuous experience traditionally rendered mute. As J. M. Bernstein points out, material meaningfulness has been delegitimated in a modernity that has widely embraced a Kantian epistemological model wherein sensory experiences—intuitions that arise in the encounter with specific objects—are subsumed by concepts (*Against* 3–6). For Kant, intuition and concept are inseparable and reciprocal dimensions of knowledge, but because intuitions only have cognitive significance once they have been made intelligible by a conceptual framework, their role in producing knowledge is rendered subservient and silent: "sensory experience," says Bernstein, "becomes a mere shadow cast by (abstract) conceptuality" (*Against* 6). Nowhere is this process made more concrete than in the case of the written word, where visual materiality is positioned as a "mere shadow," a fleeting sensory experience that tends to be quickly assimilated to the "(abstract) conceptuality" of a dematerialized semantic process.

J. M. Bernstein's Adornian theory of the aesthetic as articulated in his book *Against Voluptuous Bodies* focuses on visual materiality—albeit the visual materiality of painting rather than of the written word—as the paradigmatic locus of repudiated sensory encounter. While Bernstein's focus is modernist painting, his arguments are also relevant to other kinds of aesthetic emphasis on materiality, not least because by "painting" he means something much broader than actual painting. What is significant about painting, he remarks, "is not representational but categorical, an inscription of and a way of bearing the burden of the absence of experience, the default of sensuous particulars, the excision of bodily happiness" (10). It is highly significant, in light of the discourse of "separate realms," that Bernstein selects visual art to represent modernist practices more generally, for it is visual materiality, above all, that has traditionally been accorded the status of a mute, sensory medium. Building upon Adorno's numerous discussions of the separation affected in modernity between art and discursive knowledge (especially in *Aesthetic Theory*), Bernstein argues that the arts, most especially the visual arts, "*have become the bearers of our now delegitimated capacity for significant sensory encounter: emphatic experience*" (7). Modern art functions as the dumping ground of a repudiated material meaningfulness, the embodiment of sensuous modes of engaging with and knowing the world of things. But Bernstein, like Adorno, also argues that modern art may also therefore act as a critique of modernity, not only because it epitomizes such dimensions of experience but because, like the intuitive dimension of knowing, modern art has been expelled from everyday practical life—by being positioned as autonomous—and it makes the operations of this expulsion visible. Modern autonomous art, he argues, owes its very existence to the "ever expanding rationalization of the dominant practices governing everyday life" (3), which displaces sensuous dimensions of experience into an aesthetic realm radically severed from practical life.

Bernstein thus makes an argument for the creatively critical role of the aesthetic: "[w]hat hibernates, what lives on in an afterlife in the modern arts, is our sensory *experience* of the world, and of the world as composed of objects, things, whose integral character is apprehensible only through sensory encounter, where sensory encounter is not the simple filling out of an antecedent structure, but formative" (3). Modernist art, then, offers "sensuous meaningfulness, the kind of nondiscursive meaning that material things have, material meaning" (47) as an epistemic stance that is not only expelled from practical life but that actively resists subsumption to its rationalist conceptual structures. By doing so, art proposes alternatives to discursive rational modes of understanding. It thus has the capacity to function *formatively*, generating emergent knowledge or ways of encountering the world. Bernstein sees modernist art, then, as engaged in an activity of salvaging dimensions of experience that hegemonic modernity repudiates. In this approach we may detect a distinctly archaeopoetic impulse strongly resonant with Benjaminian messianism. "The task of the arts," Bernstein asserts, "is to rescue from cognitive and rational oblivion our embodied experience and the standing of unique, particular things as the proper objects of such experience, albeit only in the form of a reminder or a promise" (7). This bodying forth of sensuous particularities induces shifts of attention that make it possible to glimpse alternative potentials, but only to glimpse them.

Such a task is perhaps increasingly urgent in an era whose dominant cultural practices tend ever more toward dematerialization. In many areas of daily life, at least for privileged Westerners, the concreteness of things is increasingly displaced by virtualities: the pixels of the computer screen, the storage "space" of the MP3 file, the dematerialized commodities of downloads and the imaginary money form that pays for them, the dislocated interactions of social media. Where is the sensory experience of things and of *thingness* when the world of objects (and of course there are still plenty of objects too) becomes mediated by such virtual experience? In what does the materiality of the page consist when it is no longer embodied in ink and paper but exists in the pixels of a screen or tablet? If, as J. M. Bernstein argues, modernism is always late, belated, *too* late, then a contemporary insistence on material meaningfulness may also be an index of its increasing delegitimation in a phase of modernity bent on numerous forms of dematerialization and disembodiment.

In the work of the five poets examined in this book, the reinvigoration of a lost relation with the thingness of the world and the recuperation of concrete particulars is carried out in the pursuit of historical latencies that have not yet been acknowledged. These archaeological poetries embody fugitive meanings and modes of knowledge that are uncannily both belated and not yet emergent. In its focus on the foregrounded visual materialities of poetic archaeologies, in its exploration of the tensions, conflicts, and collaborations between the sensuous and conceptual aspects of the printed page, the present study negotiates precisely such an articulation of the haunting "reminder" and the embryonic "promise" as the basis for poetic reflections on the possibilities and limitations of historical encounter. The chapters that follow read a range of archaeological poetries as aesthetically embodied theoretical engagements with the contemporary parameters of historical knowing. Chapter 2 considers Susan Howe's poetic excavations of American textual history and explores some of the implications of her highly ambivalent and contradictory poetics for the task of recovering silenced histories. Chapter 3 examines Theresa Hak Kyung Cha's concrete modes of negotiating the gaps and erasures of Korean history in her best-known work *DICTEE*. I also read this work the light of her wider activities as a visual artist and consider some of her lesser-known works. Maggie O'Sullivan's exuberantly visual poetry and expanded historical sensibility is explored in chapter 4. In this chapter I show how O'Sullivan's highly visceral work investigates states of voicelessness with respect to a specific Anglo-Irish heritage, but also in relation to wider social inequalities and cultural restrictions. Chapters 5 and 6 examine the poetics of two Caribbean writers by comparing and contrasting their archaeopoetic sensibilities. Chapter 5 focuses on Kamau Brathwaite's poetics of noise that seeks to body forth "submerged" dimensions of Caribbean cultural history and produce a mode of historical reflection that is highly informed by geographic imaginaries of the Caribbean. Chapter 6 in many ways extends this exploration of a geographically informed historical consciousness, investigating how M. NourbeSe Philip's poetry reflects upon the (im)possibility of recovering histories of the Middle Passage sunk within the oceanic vaults of the sea and the suffocating silences of the imperial text.

The work of these five writers conducts a process of remaking the "poem including history" in a contemporary context in which the imperative to "brush history against the grain" (Benjamin, *Illuminations* 248) has come to occupy the heart of a range of thoroughly institutionalized endeavors. And yet these poetries suggest that the politics, ethics, and methods of such a project continue to need rethinking—re-articulating—in relation to historical specificities and multiplicities, and in relation to the capacities, limitations, and ideological entanglements of available modes of representation. I hope to show how, by adopting and variously reshaping a Benjaminian model of historicism, this work performs the archaeocritical work of testing present epistemologies.

The poetries discussed in *Archaeopoetics*, then, constitute a series of materially embodied investigations into the politics and poetics of historical encounter. They collectively make a claim for the sensory dimensions of the poetic page to render palpable elements of culture, history, and experience consigned to the underside of rational modernity's dominant discourses. This poetry makes an argument for a widening of the compass of "the poetic" as a stimulus for the enlargement of knowing. In its foregrounding, above all, of the visual dimensions of the printed page, this work requires a radical shift in what we understand the activity of reading poetry, history, and culture to be. By confronting "readers" with texts that are also resolutely material, visual compositions (and often also compositions in sound, space, texture), these works invite an engagement with aspects and effects of the textual surface that normally go unacknowledged in favor of a pursuit of semantics. In so doing, this poetry tweaks "the geometry of attention" (Retallack 10), indicating ways to attend to silenced, muted, absent, or marginalized presences. Such hitherto inarticulate cultural or historical particulars cannot—and, as these works suggest, perhaps should not—be recuperated as fully intelligible. Thus this work does not in any straightforward way recover silenced voices. Rather, their traces inhere in the material strata of these poetries in the form of a palpable but not entirely articulate "reminder or promise" (J. M. Bernstein, *Against* 7).

2

"Radical visible subsurface"

Susan Howe's Frictional Histories
of the Underword

Not a derangement of the senses but yes there is an occult other sense of
meaning in all disarrangements Dis in his arranging means.

> Robert Duncan, "Poetry Disarranged"

The poetry of Susan Howe is well known for its almost obsessive preoccupation with history. Whether focusing upon the narratives of early settlers in
New England, the history of the English regicide, or the writings of Herman
Melville or Emily Dickinson, Howe's investigations revolve around a central
concern with the capacities of poetry to offer alternative versions of the past:
"If history is a record of survivors, Poetry shelters other voices" (*Birth-mark*
47). Howe's capitalization of "Poetry" and use of the lower case for "history"
here amounts to a challenge to the authority of history and a claim for the
value of a specifically poetic mode of historical investigation. Howe seeks
to unsettle the established contours of historical knowledge and render its
"subsurface" tangible or "visible" (*Nonconformist's* 98). In one of her most
widely cited remarks she says, "I wish I could tenderly lift from the dark side
of history, voices that are anonymous, slighted—inarticulate" (*Europe* 14). It
is important to note, however, that her cautious "I wish" articulates both an
impulse to recover effaced aspects of the past and a recognition of the opacity and inaccessibility of histories consigned to the "dark side." Poetry may
shelter "other voices" but may not necessarily give them lucid expression.

Howe's archaeological terrain is the American archive—whether understood as the literal spaces of libraries such as those at Harvard and Yale or the
wider body of texts that make up American literary history more generally.
As her accounts of her struggles to gain physical access to libraries evince,
Howe enters the archive both as a cultural heir to "the record of survivors"
and as a marginalized outsider, an imposter "trespassing" (*Birth-mark* 18).
For her, libraries are simultaneously places of exclusion and freedom, violence and beauty, enclosure and wildness, danger and possibility. The tex-

tual topography of the library is circumscribed by authoritarian power yet it also serves as the dwelling place of other latent potentials. Howe's characteristically ambivalent excavations of the archive yield textual fragments that she incorporates into her poetry, often without explicit acknowledgement of source. Her description of Emily Dickinson's poetic process very much echoes her own: "[f]orcing, abbreviating, pushing, padding, subtracting, riddling, interrogating, rewriting, she pulled text from text" (*My Emily* 29). Howe's acts of appropriation and redeployment are irresolvable and double-edged: they involve veneration and iconoclasm, reverence and rebellion, "collusion" and "collision" (*Singularities* 33).

The coexistence of such conflicting impulses in Howe's work has been remarked upon by many recent commentators (see especially Stephen Collis, Will Montgomery and Brian Reed). I want to examine the stakes of such tensions in this highly material poetry that proceeds to archaeologically "pull[ ] text from text." Howe sees antinomy as a primary characteristic of American textual history: "Contradiction is the book of this place" (*My Emily Dickinson* 45). Her poetics embody frictional contraries positioned both as characteristic of American history and as a mode of reflecting on the prospects of articulating its "other voices." Enacted upon the poetic page through the appropriation, "disarrangement," and redeployment of textual materials and page space, her archaeopoetics is driven by a conviction that the archive's suppressed or silenced potentials "can be reanimated by appropriation" (*Souls* 15) at the same time as it acknowledges and preserves the particularity, the opacity, and even the obdurate unintelligibility of historical residues. For Howe, the past's latencies are both tangible and unrecoverable. Through its techniques of material engagement with textual history, then, Howe's archaeopoetics investigates both the possibilities for encountering history "otherwise" and the problematics of such an endeavor. In so doing, this work also archaeocritically explores the conditions of possibility for historical knowledge in the context of a history characterized by patriarchal colonial appropriation, domination, and violence, at times entangled with nonconformity and antinomian zeal. Performing critical reflections on the foundations of the "dark wall of rule [that] supports the structure of every letter, record, transcript: every proof of authority and power" (*Birth-mark* 4), Howe's archaeocritical project acknowledges its own implication in this epistemic enclosure, and thus its own limitations and lacunae.

Howe on Historical Violence

The question of recoverability becomes particularly acute for Howe in relation to historical violence, whether understood as the violence of war, colonial appropriation, and brutal suppression, or epistemic forms of violence that silence socially marginalized others such as women and Native Americans. For this reason, this chapter focuses on three poems from Howe's "middle period" in the late '80s and early '90s that are particularly concerned with violent histories: *A Bibliography of the King's Book, or, Eikon Basilike* (hereafter referred to as *Eikon Basilike*), "Scattering As Behavior Toward Risk," and *Thorow*, the latter two of which appear in the three-poem collection *Singularities* published in 1990.[1] These works epitomize Howe's mode of archaeo-critical inquiry into the possibilities and limitations of reading history for its violently suppressed "other voices." In these poems, Howe's experimentation with the radically disrupted material page as a means for approaching violent and traumatic histories reaches a peak. Her poems of the early 1980s such as *Pythagorean Silence* tend to make use of quite subtle graphic effects such as spacing, indentation, and word grids in their negotiations of troubled historical and mythical themes, while late works such as *The Midnight* (2003) and *Souls of the Labadie Tract* (2007) attend to less obviously violent histories and have a different approach to visual elements. The works from Howe's middle period that I examine undertake quite conspicuous and distinctive visual rearrangements of the poetic page, including lines printed at unusual angles, fragmented words, and overprinting.

Howe's interest in history, and in particular the New England history that forms the nexus of her historical consciousness, stems at least partly from a sense of dismay at the forms of violent Othering evident in American society, which she describes in terms of "our contemporary repudiation of alterity, anonymity, darkness" (*Birth-mark* 89). "I feel compelled in my work to go back," she says, "I am trying to understand what went wrong when the first Europeans stepped on shore here" (175). For her, then, contemporary configurations of intolerance and social ostracization have roots in older forms of violence upon which America was established. Howe feels implicated in this cultural legacy even as she is ethically compelled to critique it.

The historicist dimensions of Howe's poetry have been extensively explored by critics. Before moving on to my own reading of this poet's materially enacted mode of historical speculation it is worth surveying a sample of the ever-expanding body of criticism that has accrued since her work began to come to prominence in the late 1980s and early '90s. Howe's poetry is now the subject of three books—by Will Montgomery, Stephen Collis, and Rachel Tzvia Back—as well as numerous book chapters and journal articles. She is often positioned as a contemporary successor to an American modernist legacy of historically orientated poetry in the tradition of Pound and Olson. Peter Nicholls, for example, rightly describes her work as "testimony to the continuing role of the poet-as-historian, though her texts also argue the need for a fundamental reformulation of Poundian principle" ("Beyond" 155). Where Pound finds a "phalanx of facts" Howe encounters history as "an indeterminate force which produces opacities and distortions within our means of expression" (155). Commentators on her work have frequently explored the ways in which such uncertainties and lacunae are bound up with questions of power. Those interested in Howe's work from a feminist perspective, such as Back, Rachel Blau DuPlessis, Kathleen Fraser, and Elisabeth Frost, have emphasized the gendered dimensions of Howe's poetry by focusing on her interest in marginalized women's voices and her search for intimations of "the feminine" in history's gaps, silences, and stutters. Many have read Howe's formal experimentation as a mode of feminist non-conformity that challenges authoritative (patriarchal) models of history and culture. Frost, for example, argues that "Howe's poetics—her fragmented, displaced lines, nonce-words and visual constructions—represent a textual form of antinomian resistance . . . [her] writing bears witness to feminist 'unsettlement' that combats conventional language and explores ways to obliterate linguistic and social constraints, including rules of gender difference" (107). Frost's stance perhaps overstates the ability of Howe's poetry to overcome power structures and limitations, but such claims have not been uncommon among some feminist celebrations of Howe's work.

Numerous critics whose agenda is not so explicitly oriented toward gender have also had much to say about the political implications of the ways in which Howe's work unsettles conventional poetic, linguistic, and typographic registers. For instance, Craig Dworkin finds in Howe's textual disruptions "points of resistance, contradiction, and the necessity—for both readers and writers—of making irrevocable ethical decisions," particularly those concerning modes of language use that violently obscure "the voices of others" (31, 38). In terms of her interest in the political potentials of poetic forms that explore and question the operations of power embedded in language, Howe clearly has much in common with the loose grouping of Language writers with whom she has frequently been aligned, particularly since her work began to be anthologized in Language-heavy collections such as Ron Silliman's *In the American Tree* (1986) and Paul Hoover's *Postmodern American Poetry* (1994). Although the poetics and techniques of Language writers are varied, the way in which Howe's poetry departs from the work of other Language writers is worth exploring. Howe's poetics does fit under a broad canopy of writing that interrogates the assumed transparency of language and aspires to "renew verse itself, so that it might offer readers the same opacity, density and otherness, challenge and relevance persons find in the 'real' world" (Silliman, *American Tree* xvi). As with many of the Language poets, the entanglements of language and ideology lead Howe to explore and challenge "the grammar of control and the syntax of command" (Charles Bernstein, *Poetics* 202). A further concurrence between Howe's work and Language poetry is her sense that "language has its own message" (Howe, "Interview" 23), that it resists a straightforwardly referential function and co-option by the restrictive limits of programmatic agendas. In a strikingly congruent vein, Lyn Hejinian, with whom Howe corresponded for many years, puts it this way: "Language discovers what one might know, which in turn is always less than what language might say" ("Rejection" 48). Indeed, it is often this frictional interplay between graspable knowledge and language's potential meaning capacities that Howe's poetry investigates.

Yet Howe's lyricism, infused with an individualism that she associates with a Puritan heritage, sets her apart from some of the main currents of Language writing, as does her abiding interest in history. Furthermore, Howe's practice has grown out of a slightly different context. Many of Language writing's key figures during its emergent years in the 1970s engaged very explicitly with the critical theory that was at that moment rapidly gaining ground in the universities. The influence of Marxism, poststructuralism, Russian formalism, and the work of the early twentieth-century avant-gardes on the thinking and practice of Language poets is well known. But Howe's lines of intellectual influence and affiliation are rather different: Emily Dickinson, Herman Melville, Henry David Thoreau, Charles Olson, and, importantly for my discussion, visual artists such as Agnes Martin, Ad Reinhardt, Robert Smithson, and the concrete poet Ian Hamilton Finlay, with whom Howe had a long correspondence in her formative years as a poet. In what follows, I shall occasionally highlight the ways in which Howe drew on some of these connections in the visual arts as touchstones for her poetics. Indeed, it was through these artists, she says, that she absorbed some of the same theoretical influences as the Language writers ("Interview" 20), though in a more indirect way.

Montgomery, one of Howe's most careful readers of recent years, emphasizes how, in particular, the theological and Romantic dimensions of Howe's poetry sit uneasily with Language poetics and its Marxist and poststructuralist frameworks. Such theoretical underpinnings have also formed the basis of much critical commentary on Howe. Montgomery, however, is keen to point to the ways in which Howe's poetry does not always fit with the critical tools so often used to read her work. He thus sounds a note of skepticism about claims made for the political radicalism of her poetry. Rather than approaching Howe's work as simply antagonistic to dominant forms of power, he traces the tensions and contradictions of Howe's engagements with authority, theology, and history, reading the poetry as "productive of combustible antinomies rather than as antinomian per se" (*The Poetry* xv). Like

Montgomery, I am interested in the ambivalences and tensions at work in Howe's poetry, especially in relation to the operations of power that circumscribe historical events and the ways in which they are known in the present. But at the same time I do want to make a general argument for the political and ethical significance of the formal strategies of Howe's poetry. It is my sense that it is in the *material* dimensions of the text, as well as the conceptual dimensions upon which Montgomery focuses, that bring these tensions into play. Howe's archaeopoetics are often performed by means of mining a "radical visible subsurface" of textual materials. Her engagement with the particulars of historical events and with wider questions of historical recovery may be fruitfully explored through her textual and visual "disarrangements." The capacity of these disarrangements for an "occult other sense of meaning" are hinted at in the epigraph above from Robert Duncan, an influential figure for Howe. To materially disarrange the textual matter of the American archive, in other words, is both to brush up against the limitations of history's epistemic "arranging means" and to intimate an alternative "sense of meaning" bound up with the sensory, physical dimensions of textuality.

Ambivalent Disarrangements

"I came to words through other visual artists," says Howe in an interview. "I just took years of moving around the edges of what was present for words to penetrate my sight" ("Speaking" 29). In this rather unusual narrative of poetic beginnings, Howe roots her formative development as a writer in her early career as a visual artist working in New York in the 1960s and early '70s. She locates her shift to writing poetry in relation to the verbal-visual explorations of other visual artists, such as Carl Andre's concrete poems and Robert Smithson's "Language to be looked at and/or things to be read" (*Collected* 61), during the development of pop, conceptual, and minimalist art. Like Theresa Hak Kyung Cha, whose work I discuss in the next chapter, Howe became involved in visual arts practice at a moment when young artists were interrogating the traditional art object, its mode of exhibition, and the borders between the language and visual arts. The printed word became more central to Howe's practice in the late '60s when she began to incorporate typewritten text in paintings and installations and produced artists' books. Even when she claims to have been "just list[ing] words" ("Interview" 5) in works comprising names of birds or flowers juxtaposed with photographic images or abstract arrangements of watercolor washes, Howe was writing poetry.[2] Her early list poems evince an acute sensitivity to visual and sonic shapes, rhythms, and semantic resonances. By the time she moved on to making word and image environments or installations such as her series "Walls" in 1969–70, she was writing paratactic poetic lines often combined in couplets or longer irregular stanzas largely devoid of capitalization and punctuation—distinctive traits of her later published poetry. Such early poems were part of verbal-visual environments in which placing, size, orientation, and word-image relationships were carefully considered. Howe's later poetry has retained a pronounced awareness of all these dimensions of the artwork; an attuned visual sensibility remains a characteristic feature of her writing practice.

Perhaps even more importantly, Howe's visual arts milieu provided key theoretical stimuli for her poetics. As Howe herself indicates ("Interview" 20), it was through the writings of artists such as Ad Reinhardt, Ian Hamilton Finlay, Donald Judd, and Robert Smithson that she absorbed ideas current during the rise of critical theory in the 1970s. Through her engagement with the work of these artists she began to articulate theoretical reflections that would later enter her poetics. In a 1974 article, "The End of Art," written for the *Archives of American Art Journal*, Howe explores works that create dialogues between poetry and painting in ways that echo her own way of moving between these practices. Faced with the radical abstraction of Ad Reinhardt's minimalist black canvases, Howe finds herself involved in "a careful search for the point where line or shape begins or ends. Forward, or back" (2). In her close encounter with concrete poet Ian Hamilton Finlay's poem *Fisherman's Cross*, she ponders the material dimensions of the poem's slippage between its two repeated words, "seas" and "ease." She proceeds to draw a parallel between the almost undecidable edges between one area of black canvas and another in Reinhardt's painting and the demarcations between Finlay's words "as close in value as two slightly different blacks are close . . . close rhythmically and visually" (6). Both minimalist painter and concrete poet, she concludes, "tell us that to search for infinity inside simplicity will be to find simplicity alive with messages" (7). There are several key points to be drawn out from these comments. First, what we witness in Howe's consideration of works by Reinhardt and Finlay is a performance of ambivalence, an unresolved oscillation between alternative possibilities in a mode that becomes characteristic of her later poetic investigations. Second, Howe's oscillations are produced in response to an encounter with indeterminacy, which she describes as an "infinite power of suggestion" or "mystery" (6) arising from the "simplicity" of non-referential work. In an illuminating discussion of this essay, Kaplan P. Harris remarks that here "Howe discovers a link between simplicity (or let us say minimalism) and the poststructuralist notion of shifting signifiers" (445). I would go slightly further than this to say that Howe developed ideas about indeterminacy precisely through her engagement with such work. She absorbs aspects of what we might retrospectively recognize as something akin to "poststructuralist theory" through her encounter with such figures as Reinhardt and Finlay. Third, it is important to note that for her, however, this indeterminacy arises out of an encounter with a non-referential materiality: the undecidability between blacks and the material (acoustic and visual) slippages between two similar words. It is the foregrounding of the signifying medium's physicality that opens the work of minimal means to potentially multiple dimensions of meaningfulness. This understanding of indeterminacy is somewhat distinct from a primarily linguistically oriented poststructuralism in which play and deferral tend to be imagined in rather immaterial, semantic terms. The foregrounded visual materiality of Howe's later poetic work can be seen as a development of such early discoveries. In particular, the kinds of uncertainties and infinites she detects in her exploration of the emphasized physicality of minimalism offers possibilities for a poetic investigation of history understood as "an indeterminate force which produces opacities and distortions within our means of expression" (Nicholls, "Beyond" 155).

Yet the material dimensions of Howe's work pose critical difficulties. While literary critics are well versed in poststructuralist ideas of linguistic play, the forms of opacity we encounter in Howe's work represent a somewhat different kind of challenge. As Craig Dworkin indicates, "we lack a sophisticated critical tradition and ready vocabulary" for talking about the visual dimensions of poetry (32). Many of Howe's unusual-looking graphic surfaces not only outstrip the vocabulary of poetry criticism, they also pose fundamental perceptual dilemmas for readers. Consider any one of the poems depicted as figures in this chapter. The visual geometry of such poetic layouts presents numerous problems. In what order are we to read the lines? Are these pages really readable at all in the usual sense? What, indeed, does "reading" become here? To what extent do factors such as the orientation and placing of words and lines affect their meanings? How do we go about interpreting the visual shapes on the page?

By engaging with such problems of reading commentators such as Dworkin, Alan Golding, Michael Davidson, and Brian Reed have made valuable contributions toward the task of constructing a "ready vocabulary" for talking about the visual elements of Howe's work (see Dworkin, *Reading the Illegible*; Davidson, *Ghostlier Demarcations* and "Palimtexts"; Golding, "Drawings with Words"; Reed, "Eden or Ebb"). These critics often make connections between her poems' visual effects and historical themes. Reed observes that "the 'exploded' pages occur at the points of maximum violence in Howe's work" (par. 9). Dworkin remarks that "Howe structures her . . . writing within a thematics of mythical and historical violence: Pearl Harbor, the colonizations of America and Ireland, pursuits and exterminations, captivities and expulsions, regicide, revenge." Her poems, he contends, "mate their [historical] themes to the visual violence . . . of Howe's disrupted folio pages" (*Reading* 36–37). But what exactly is the nature of this "mating"? Both Reed's and Dworkin's analyses assume—to some extent at least—an essentially mimetic relation between Howe's disruptions of page layout and her historical themes; chaotic page layouts echo or even mimic historical violence. But this poetry does much more than use disrupted page layouts mimetically. Howe's dramatic visual disturbances of the printed page are not entirely shaped by a principle of randomness and disarray that approximates historical violence, nor are they innocently pictorial; rather this work performs through the material embodiment of indeterminacies an excavation of the paradoxes, conflicts, and lacunae of the very processes of historical inquiry.

Nowhere in Howe's oeuvre is this aesthetic enactment of historical reflection performed with more drama than in *Eikon Basilike*. This poem derives its title and much of its source material from an obscure bibliography written by Edward Almack and published in 1896, a text which catalogues and describes the multiple editions of *The Eikon Basilike*, the book purportedly written by King Charles I during his imprisonment and trial prior to his execution in 1649. Printed on the very day of the monarch's beheading and instantly outlawed by Cromwell's government, *The Eikon Basilike* nevertheless continued to be printed and secretly distributed by royalists; as a result it became hugely popular and widely read. Due to the underground nature of its production, the relative fluidity of print culture at this time, and controversies concerning the book's authorship, *The Eikon Basilike* exists in numerous materially different versions. Howe's poem treats Almack's scholarly documentation of *The Eikon Basilike* as an archaeological site that carries in its pages traces of history's physical and textual conflicts.

Michael Davidson's notion of the "palimtext" offers a useful entry point into thinking about Howe's excavations of her source text. Characterized by intertextuality combined with an emphasis on the material forms of its own textual borrowing, the palimtext, he says, "retains vestiges of prior writings out of which it emerges" ("Palimtexts" 78). These traces are resolutely material in that they proclaim both their own physical presence on the page and their entanglement with the material world and its social forms. In Howe's poem, such "vestiges of prior writings" make a claim for their own indexical relation to historical events. According to C. S. Peirce's semiotic theory, indexical signs work by "physical connection" (159), such as when a pointing finger, a footprint, or a thunderbolt "indicates that something considerable happened, though we may not know precisely what the event was" (161). In a similar way, text appropriated from Almack's bibliography is offered as material remains that constitute a "physical connection" with the

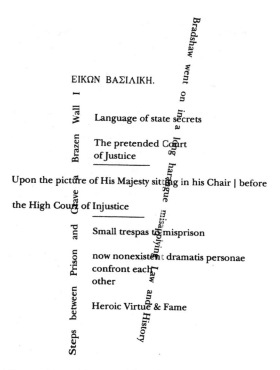

Figure 3. "Chair" page from *Eikon Basilike. The Nonconformist's Memorial* by Susan Howe, copyright © 1993 by Susan Howe. Page 54. Reprinted by permission of New Directions Publishing Corp.

modes of production, ideological conflicts, and traumas involved in *The Eikon Basilike*'s history.

Howe's poem palimtextually attempts to tease out its source text's indexical properties by radically foregrounding the materiality of the printed text, thereby bringing attention to its status as physical matter to which historical residue adheres. One way in which the work performs this move is by rendering trauma and violence in dramatically visual terms, as in the page depicted in figure 3, which comprises cut-and-pasted material from Almack's bibliography and from a version of the king's book reprinted therein. What Howe refers to as the "vertically jagged" effect of this particular textual layout is, she says, "based around the violence of the execution of Charles I, the violence of history" ("Interview" 8). Referring to a speech made by chief judge Bradshaw at the king's trial, one "vertically jagged" line slices downwards, turning this "harangue misapplying Law and History" into an assault that literally attacks the horizontal text. Meanwhile, another almost vertical line demonstrates the irreversibility of the "Steps between Prison and Grave" that the king was compelled to tread. This line, cut off immediately after the "I," suggests the severance *of* the "I": both the termination of the self who speaks here and of the Roman numeral I that forms part of this king's monarchical title. As if to emphasize the finality of this severance, the vertical line concretely forms an impermeable barrier, or "Brazen Wall," symbolizing the irreversible line crossed at death. The line's vertical arrangement and positioning makes it both an embodiment of this "Wall" and, in the upward-moving direction of reading it induces, a description of the orientation of the "Steps" that, as Bishop Juxon promises Charles elsewhere in the poem, "will carry you from Earth to Heaven" (*Nonconformist's* 59).

This mode of interpreting the page's visual drama, however, begins to imply that *any* record of historical violence could be treated in this way to register traumatic effects. But Howe's page does more than mimetically signal the violence of the king's execution. It also constitutes a particularly archaeo-poetic mode of investigation in that its aesthetic forms investigate a specific conflict between the diametrically opposed guiding principles of the textual adversaries at the center of the struggle between royalists and regicides: the king's *The Eikon Basilike* and John Milton's *Eikonoklastes* (literally, "image smasher"). Milton's counterattack, written in support of the Puritan cause shortly after the initial publication of *Eikon Basilike*, defended the regicide and cast doubt on the authenticity of the king's book, thereby initiating a debate about the book's authorship that continues today. Embedded in these warring textual factions are two ideologically saturated principles: the royalist position that elevates the visual image or icon as a reliquary for divinely ordained power, and the iconoclastic purging that pursues the systematic destruction of images in the name of the religious doctrine of Puritanism.

Howe's poem stages a scene in which these "now nonexistent dramatis personae / confront each / other," and thereby depicts the conflicts and moral dilemmas of the debate between icon worship and spiritually motivated iconoclasm, as well as bringing to attention the political stakes of this struggle over visual representation (*Nonconformist's* 51). Howe's radically disrupted page partakes of Milton's iconoclastic violence by means of a cut-and-paste collaging that literally carves up the king's book and scatters its fragments in a manner that dramatically breaks with the conventions of the printed page. And yet to describe the material on this page as "scattered" would imply a principle of randomness, whereas the layout here is actually very carefully choreographed. As Howe's remarks about the effects of this "vertically jagged" layout indicate, the visual composition of this page in one sense participates in an iconoclastic impulse and in another sense involves a highly calculated dismantling—not so much a scattering as a careful rearrangement. This is a page composed with an artist's eye for design and with an acute interest in how the reading and viewing eye perceives its object.

In Howe's aforementioned article "The End of Art," she conducts a visual reading of the shapes of letters in one of Finlay's poems, remarking that "the vertical letters l, k, and b, positioned as they are, make vertical lines that pull the eye up and down, and that pulls the o, a and c letters apart . . . The round short letters give a horizontal tug which prevents the poem from being read up and down" (7). This sensitivity to how specific shapes and visual arrangements actively "pull" and "tug" readerly attention is undoubtedly at work in the page layout of her poem *Eikon Basilike*. By a careful recomposition of textual fragments from Almack's bibliography, Howe's "vertically jagged" page embodies a potential alternative to the iconoclastic act; the same disarrangement that acts out the violence of iconoclasm also enables the pieces of text on this page to form the ghost of an image. Suggested by the central, demarcated scene-setting lines, the apparition of a sideways "Chair" seems to float upon the page, constructed from lines of text. This "Chair" is both the seat in which Charles appears as the accused "before/ the High Court of Injustice" and the throne from which "His Majesty" is unseated. According to historian Andrew Lacy, "it has to be said that Milton failed in his task of iconoclasm" because his counterattack "did nothing to stem the popularity or dissemination of the King's Book, or the 'image' of Charles presented therein" (8–9). Howe's highly iconographical page suggests, then, that Charles's image lives on as a kind of afterlife in his *Eikon Basilike*, and perhaps especially in the controversies surrounding it. The icon persistently haunts the act of iconoclasm, re-forming itself from the fragmented remains of the smashed image to hover, specter-like, upon Howe's page.

The haunting of the iconoclastic act by the icon not only references a violent historical struggle between Puritans and royalists, it also signals a conflicted stance toward the image within Puritanism itself, an attitude more complex than a straightforward repudiation of the visual image based on an adherence to the second commandment, "Thou shalt not make thee any graven image" (Deuteronomy 5.8). Howe's poem both inherits and investigates this ambivalence. According to Ann Kibbey's engaging study on this subject, Puritanical iconoclasm was the manifestation of a simultaneous fear and reverence for the image stemming from a Calvinist mimetic theory of art that invested the visual image with lifelike properties: "Protestant iconoclasts believed it necessary to attack the visual images in church sculpture, glass, and painting not because they disbelieved these images but rather because they believed quite strongly in their power" (47). Furthermore, iconoclastic rhetoric relied heavily upon verbal imagery, which was conceptualized as not entirely distinct from visual imagery. Exemplified in the poetry and prose of Milton or the sermons of John Cotton, for example, the war against the icon was often carried out, textually and verbally, in a battle that pitted word and visual image against one another. But the iconoclasts' modes of articulation were rich with verbal imagery whose appeal to the mind's eye paradoxically invoked the power of the visual icon, if not its literal form. Therefore, Puritanical iconoclasm has to be understood not simply in terms of the rejection and destruction of icons but rather as a complex and contradictory set of concepts and practices in which religious icons and visual imagery more generally were simultaneously feared and revered, renounced and reappropriated.

By staging a clash between icon and iconoclasm, Howe's poem not only investigates a specific history but also raises questions about the entanglement of aesthetic representation and political ideologies. Furthermore, it articulates a profound ambivalence about its own affiliations with the conflicting principles embodied here. The disruption of the page's visual cues and codes constitutes an embrace of an iconoclastic impulse; as a result, critics such as Rachel Tzvia Back and Craig Dworkin have read Howe as an iconoclast. But the "Chair" page in Howe's *Eikon Basilike* also powerfully signals a return to the haunting power of the icon.

A fruitful way to think through this tension between icon and iconoclasm in Howe's work more broadly is by considering her engagement with minimalism. As stated earlier, Howe's encounter with minimalism proved highly influential for the development of her poetics in the formative years of the 1960s and '70s. When an interviewer asks her to imagine how she might translate her writing into the medium of paint, Howe's response evinces a minimalist aesthetic: "Blank. It would be blank. It would be a white canvas. White" ("Speaking" 42). In a later conversation with Lynn Keller, she explains that this remark "springs from my love for minimalist painting and sculpture" ("Interview" 7), naming artists such as Agnes Martin, Robert Ryman, and her second husband David von Schlegell (1920–1992) as among her most enduring influences. Yet in this interview she adopts a critically reflective attitude towards the minimalist aesthetic that has been so influential for her. "Now I can see minimalist art of the sixties and seventies as an American movement rooted in Puritanism" (4), she says, detecting in minimalism a cultural logic with connections to the dominant cultural paradigms of early American history. While Howe does not pursue this impulse very far or expand on this intriguing statement, I would suggest that what she is doing here is reading minimalism's eschewal of representational imagery as an aesthetic reenactment of the Puritanical tradition of iconoclasm. She is not alone in making this link; Robert Morris states that "[t]he origins of abstract art lie far back in the history of the West" (475). "Minimal art," he argues, "was the attempt to recuperate transcendent Puritan values by re-encoding them via an iconoclasm of austere formal spatial purity" (480).

While Howe's work has affiliations with a minimalist sensibility, she distances herself aesthetically from minimalism's most severe forms of iconoclasm. In some respects her ambivalence toward minimalist principles echoes the aesthetics of Robert Ryman, of whose work she is surely thinking when she describes the imagined transposition of her poetry into the medium of painting as "a white canvas." Ryman's square-format white paintings might seem to fit rather unambiguously with the pared-down "iconoclastic" aesthetic of 1960s minimalism. However, as Robert Storr indicates, many of his paintings, and especially the early ones, "contain shapes that sometimes appear to have the status of pictorial images" (18). This is not pictorialism in the form of representational imagery, but rather shapes, lines, grids, or painterly marks that function suggestively rather than mimetically. These paintings bring attention to dialogues between figure and ground, or medium and context, in ways that reject representation but nevertheless subtly draw on the figurative.

Even in Howe's early visual works, when minimalist art was at the forefront of her aesthetic thinking and practice, there is also caution toward its principles. Howe's paintings from the late 1960s—cataloged on slides in the Susan Howe Papers collection at the University of California, San Diego—feature loosely applied washes or daubs of color derived from a restricted palette and thinly applied to paper or canvas, sometimes overlaid by series of lines (MSS. 201, Box 61, Folder 10). These aspects of the paintings echo the pared-down sensibility of minimalist painters such as Ryman or Agnes Martin; yet the lines and color washes of Howe's paintings are more often than not juxtaposed with photographic images of birds, trees, or landscapes. This reinsertion of the representational image into the minimalist field embodies a much more conflicted engagement with the visual language of minimalism than one finds even in the painterly "pictorialism" of Ryman's minimalism. Howe's early visual works exhibit both a pared-down "minimalist" aesthetic and a desire, or even an imperative, to retain the pictorial image. While Howe finds the "spare and infinitely suggestive" spaces of minimalist painting compelling, she also resists capitulation to what she interprets as this aesthetic's iconoclastic demand for the effacement of the image.

A similar tension is at work in the "Chair" page of *Eikon Basilike*, which resuscitates the specter of the icon even as it participates in an iconoclastic act. Howe's disrupted page is animated by the revolutionary energy of the capacity of iconoclasm to deconstruct established aesthetic and social structures; in this manner it contains an appealing transformative promise. But by invoking rather than disavowing the visual icon, this page embodies iconoclasm's reviled other. It thus critiques the destructiveness of the iconoclastic gesture, especially its tendency toward effacement and suppression. This poem undertakes a resurrection of the power of the icon by bringing to attention the signifying potential of the visual dimensions of printed text that normally go almost entirely unacknowledged in everyday reading practices. "[W]ords, even single letters, are images," says Howe. And, more importantly, "the look of a word is part of its meaning—the meaning that escapes dictionary definition, or rather doesn't *escape* but is bound up with it" ("Interview" 6). This notion of the poetic image resonates with the struggle between icon and iconoclasm enacted in *Eikon Basilike*, recasting this struggle as a debate between literal, concrete, visual imagery in the space of the page and verbal imagery directed at the mind's eye. Howe's page simultaneously invokes and defies Romanticist distinctions between a sublimated poetic image of the intellect and a denigrated poetic image of the senses. It also recalls and questions Pound's dictum that "[t]he image is not an idea. It is a radiant node or cluster; it is a . . . VORTEX, from which ideas are constantly rushing" ("Vorticism" 92). Pound's approach here aspires to move beyond the Romantic notion of the image as idea even as it continues to privilege the abstract and non-material aspects of the image, its intellectual energy. Diverging from these formulations of poetic imagery, Howe foregrounds the role of literal visual materiality in the meaning-making processes of printed language. As demonstrated by the "Chair" page of *Eikon Basilike*, her poetry insists on a sensuous, concrete dimension of the poetic image, an iconic power of the printed word, a capacity not only to carry semantic meaning but also to physically embody residues of presences that hover on the threshold of signification but cannot be entirely recuperated by linguistic or conceptual structures. As Peter Middleton so eloquently puts it, "Howe's work shows that literary experiment is not necessarily 'destructivism', but can also be an exploration of what is never clearly text nor clearly other, only a history of boundaries, captures, escapes, genocides and glimpses of something 'seen once'" ("On Ice" 93).

Howe's ambivalent negotiations of iconoclastic "destructivism" and its alternatives provide a way of approaching the question of why the history of the English regicide and its textual "aftershocks" hold such interest for this poet, given her abiding concern with American history. For her, the history of her own society's "contemporary repudiation of alterity, anonymity, darkness" (*Birth-mark* 89) has its roots in a New England Puritanism inextricably intertwined with the history of the English regicide. Speaking of a failed attempt to write an essay on "American voice" and the seventeenth-century Mather family, she states, "[t]he Mathers were over here, so they didn't actually do the killing, but they were of the killing party" (175). In *Eikon Basilike*, she claims, "the Mather essay I couldn't write is there too" (175). For Howe, the ideological convictions of Puritan settlers implicated them not only in the regicide but also in the wider patterns of violence this event crystallized.

A major source for Howe's thinking about Puritanism is Ann Kibbey's account of the forms that seventeenth-century iconoclasm took in early American culture (Howe, *Birth-mark* x). Kibbey argues that because of Puritanical iconoclasm's reliance on the classical concept of *figura*, which blurred distinctions between the figurative and literal, the graven image and living "image," "[t]he violent destruction of artistic images of people developed into a mandate for sacrosanct violence against human beings" (2). Clearly the English regicide, committed against a figure that was both a self-fashioned image and a man of flesh and blood, is an instance of this "sacrosanct violence." Kibbey argues that the translation of iconoclasm into early American society became a mode of prejudicial violence directed "especially against people whose material 'image,' whose physical characteristics, differed from the Puritan man's own" (2). She cites the banishment in 1637 of Anne Hutchinson during the antinomian controversy and the genocide of the Pequot tribe in the same year as instances of how the iconoclastic principle was extended to physically "different" human beings. This thinking clearly chimes with Howe's broader historical interests and with her poetic exploration of iconoclasm in *Eikon Basilike*. For her, the beheading of the king and the subsequent censoring of his book manifest a violent Puritanical impulse to purge. Howe sees the legacy of this impulse in her contemporary society's continuing repudiation of otherness. Yet at the same time, the iconoclastic impulse offers a model of progressive nonconformity that Howe's poetics often embraces. Rather than commit to a stable critical position, her archaeopoetics investigates by aesthetic means the struggles, contradictions, tensions, and fault lines opened up when "[d]ominant ideologies drift" (*Nonconformist's* 80).

Howe's excavations of historical and ideological "fault lines" not only investigate the configurations of historical violence embedded in American history; they also elicit traces of disavowed alterities from these conflicted terrains. By cutting, pasting, scattering, and rearranging textual history's material remains, this poetry seeks to unearth suppressed dimensions of historical "actuality" latent in its source texts.[3] Often, this activity seizes upon instabilities visible to the poet on the textual surfaces of documented history, performing a kind of radical poetic editing that seeks not to resolve but to emphasize indeterminacy and inconsistency.

The one-page poem that forms an epigraph or preface to *Eikon Basilike* (see figure 4) serves as a particularly good example of Howe's method. The poem's opening refrain "Oh Lord/ o Lord" references debates over the idolatry of King Charles and his book's questionable authorship. Like the king's last prayer on the scaffold, included in some of the early editions of the king's book, Howe's poem borrows from a pagan prayer uttered by the shepherdess Pamela in Philip Sidney's *Arcadia*. This prayer was at the center of an acrimonious debate between the royalists and revolutionaries. Milton cited the plagiarism of this "vain amatorious Poem" (qtd. in *Nonconformist's* 49) as evidence of the king's sin of idolatry and his deficiencies as a ruler. Royalists, however, accused Milton of arranging the insertion of this poem so as to discredit the king's book and cast doubt on its authorship. Notably, both of these arguments disavow and silence Sidney's pagan shepherdess. Because of its central role in the debates around idolatry, authorship, forgery, and authenticity, Pamela's prayer has been excised from and readmitted to different versions of the king's book. Almack's bibliography, the text upon which Howe's poem most extensively draws, minimizes the whole contentious issue; its author was anxious to demonstrate royal authorship, and a version of *The Eikon Basilike* subsequently edited by Almack neither contains the prayer nor makes any reference to it. Howe's epigraph poem seizes upon this evasiveness, invoking the shepherdess's supplication and thus the unresolved controversy associated with it. Furthermore, it does so on a material as well as a conceptual level. The shape of this poem, with its first section tilted forward and to the left, visually echoes the attitude of a person praying, with head bent forward at an angle from the torso. Yet in the particular context of the English regicide, this layout also suggests something else: the top section seems to topple forward as if decapitated. This inference is reinforced by the placing of the word "zeal" at the base of the poem's first section, the point at which these lines appear to have been zealously severed from the body of the text. Colliding with the upside-down word "transposed," the word "zeal" indicates the point at which a "beering" or "bearing" is "transposed" and one thing becomes another: text printed on a page becomes the suggestion of an image, an attitude of prayer becomes a decapitation, and religious "zeal" becomes murderous fanaticism. Yet a key question emerges here: how does Howe's poem achieve its own tipping point? How does its own violent, iconoclastic dismemberment of text rescue disavowed dimensions of historical actuality?

Peter Nicholls remarks that Howe's "shattering of language into bits and pieces . . . gesture[s] toward a writing that constantly courts the noncognitive in its preoccupation with phonic and graphic elements." He continues: "To write in this way is to jettison historical narrative at the same time that it is somehow a refusal to let go of the past, to give it up to 'discourse'" ("Unsettling" 597). For Howe, discursive cognition represents an appropriative force that subsumes the heterogeneity of historical actuality to a unitary logic shaped by particular interests. Howe's fragmentation of her source texts, and indeed language itself, can be read as an attempt to wrest historical traces

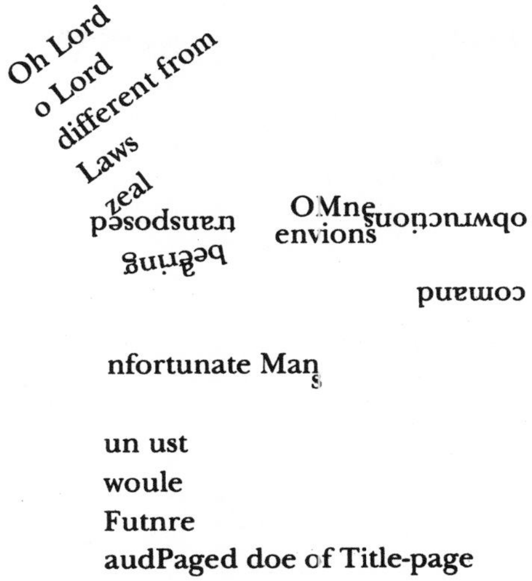

Oh Lord
o Lord
different from
Laws
zeal
transposed   OMne   obwrucuons
             envions
begusing

            comand

nfortunate Man

un ust
woule
Futnre
audPaged doe of Title-page

Figure 4. Epigraph or preface poem from *Eikon Basilike. The Nonconformist's Memorial* by Susan Howe, copyright © 1993 by Susan Howe. Page 51. Reprinted by permission of New Directions Publishing Corp.

such as Pamela's prayer from the assimilative, potentially muffling forces of logic. Howe's textual trace is an emblematic marker for "voices that are anonymous, slighted—inarticulate" (Howe, *Europe* 14). Pamela's voice comes and goes from various versions of the king's book, and while it is never able to speak for itself, it functions as a sign of uncertainty, unresolvedness, and instability that disrupts and challenges the coherence of discursive logic.

Howe's fragment of Pamela's prayer thus functions as a way of remembering historical events through an anti-narrative foregrounding of "noncognitive" materiality that retains the uncertainties, paradoxes, opacities, and fractures of history. This process continues in the "body" of the poem via a series of disjointed words, almost all misspellings and archaisms. These peculiar details testify to a process of editing that aims to concretely emphasize error, indeterminacy, and illegibility in the textual record. The "mistake"-ridden and visually non-normative opening poem of *Eikon Basilike* proposes a mode of historical attentiveness to the possibilities of reading textual and physical details for fractures and indeterminacies wherein might lie the residues or versions of the past "different from" existing narratives.

Howe's poem, then, suggests that historical texts may embody something of history's suppressed actuality as *physical detail*, and it is the task of poetry to excavate such details for what they might yield of lost realities. This constitutes a claim for the truthfulness of the material dimensions of the printed word. In Howe's poetry, the material word is the bearer of a particular kind of truth. She says, "I think there is a truth, even if it's not fashionable to say so anymore" ("Interview" 30). In her thinking, there is the possibility of "a truth," but not *the* incontrovertible truth: "the Truth a truth / Dread catchword THE" (*Nonconformist's* 68). While she is acutely aware of poststructuralist critiques of truth, Howe is committed to what Bernard Williams refers to as "truthfulness." "The desire for truthfulness," he argues, can go together (albeit somewhat uneasily) with a suspicion of the truth, because it "drives a process of criticism which weakens the assurance that there is any secure or unqualifiedly stateable truth" (1). Howe's poem proposes a way of negotiating history that recognizes a truthfulness of textual materials that provide access not to *the* truth of history but to a kind of truth replete with disparity, paradox, and uncertainty. Furthermore, Howe's *Eikon Basilike* suggests that it is sometimes in the material qualities of history's textual remains that truthfulness becomes most palpable; archaic spellings and misspellings, printing errors, editorial inclusions and exclusions, and multiple versions carry or embody a truthfulness that points to a contradictory and inconsistent historical actuality.

Eikon Basilike's often dramatic graphic surfaces, then, not only unsettle the authority of the normative textual document and mimetically register the tremors of the poem's historical theme, they also enact the tensions and ambivalences with which this history is saturated. To recall a problematic mentioned earlier, as readers and critics we have no pre-established strategy for reading Howe's dramatically reconfigured pages, nor any "ready vocabulary" (Dworkin 32) for their description and analysis. Yet this lack is absolutely key to the archaeopoetics that yokes together Howe's visual poetics and historical project. Howe's visual pages, for which we have no pre-prepared script for their navigation or interpretation, highlight an unacknowledged aspect of textual history: its material, sensory dimension. If the physical aspects of texts present readers and critics with a number of problems and uncertainties, then they also function as ways of indicating possibility—the possibility of reading history "otherwise"—for contradictions, fractures, and silences that render alternative potentials tangible, although not articulate. Howe's graphic surfaces embody an archaeopoetics that demonstrates the capacity of poetry to explore dimensions of the past for which, like the visual pages themselves, we collectively have no "ready vocabulary."

Reanimation through Appropriation

Howe's archaeopoetic excavations of historical and literary texts are part of a more or less redemptive Benjaminian project "to brush history against the grain" (*Illuminations* 248). At the same time, her work archaeocritically raises questions about the wider implications of this model of historicism. Howe's poetry adopts a Benjaminian mode of engagement with history but also self-consciously reflects upon this approach in ways shaped by the poet's ambivalent relation to American colonial history. Given that Howe's work not only critiques the violence and elisions of its cultural past but is also heir to its legacies, it cannot but be caught up in some of the very problems it investigates. Thus, in common with an Adornian "immanent critique," Howe's mode of archaeocritique reflects upon its own methods of historical investigation and their internal tensions. By being both critical and self-critical, Howe's work explores the limits of its own historiographic activities and provides opportunities for reflecting more broadly on projects of cultural recuperation that adopt a broadly Benjaminian stance.

The parallels between Howe and Benjamin have been noted before. Rachel Tzvia Back, for example, remarks that while Howe is more interested in gender and Benjamin in class, both insist that "the past must be read and written differently" (60) for the traces of those who have been "forgotten in historical documentation" (61). Paul Naylor, meanwhile, sees a correlation between Benjamin's notion of dialectical images and Howe's formal and thematic concerns (56–7). What both sidestep, however, is the redemptive dimension of these activities. To "brush history against the grain" in a Benjaminian sense is not just to read the past differently. It is also a mystically inflected project to rescue hitherto undiscovered "chips" of redemptive "Messianic time" (*Illuminations* 255). Furthermore, we may recall that Benjamin's instructions to the historical materialist are "to *brush* history against the grain": not just to read it differently but to engage with history in all its materiality. For him, cultural artifacts contain "sensory data," which might yield a kind of "felt knowledge" (*Arcades Project* 880, e, 1). As we have already begun to see in my discussion of *Eikon Basilike*, this mode of physical engagement is played out quite literally in many of Howe's poems. Howe has stated that she shares with Benjamin "his interest in the fragment, the material object, and the entrance of the messianic into the material object" ("Interview" 29). This shared interest is evident in the degree of faith her poetry invests in the materiality of fragmented textual remains as a site of hitherto suppressed potentials.

Here there are intimations of a mystical dimension that Will Montgomery finds to be such an abiding force in her poetry, and which, as he rightly points out, many critical accounts fail to acknowledge. "The mystical current in the writing, present from its beginnings in the 1970s to the present day," he argues, "is not always compatible with the elements of Marxian, psychoanalytic, and poststructuralist thought that provide the intellectual context for those who write on her" (*The Poetry* xiii). Montgomery's point is a pertinent one, and his examinations of the theological aspects of Howe's thinking are highly convincing. However, as my introductory chapter suggested, the intellectual contexts that form the backdrop for both Howe's poetry and its criticism are not entirely free from theological structures of feeling. This is particularly evident in the widespread critical endorsement, whether implicit or explicit, of a Benjaminian model of "brushing history against the grain," even if the mystical undercurrents of this model of historicism go largely unacknowledged. A recognition of these aspects of Howe's historicist poetics as they are entangled with a poststructuralist impulse that seeks out indeterminacy and ambiguity reveals a broader interplay, although certainly not a comfortable fit, between such seemingly incompatible elements of thought.

The messianic dimensions of Howe's poetics may be explored through an examination of two important poems published in the early 1990s that typify the poet's longstanding concern with the occluded elements of a specifically American history. The poems in question—"Scattering As Behavior Toward Risk" and *Thorow*—both appear in *Singularities*, a collection that appropriately enough, given the line of inquiry I want to pursue here, bears as one of its epigraphs a quotation from a short story by D. H. Lawrence: "She was looking for the fragments of the dead Osiris, dead and scattered asunder, dead, torn apart, and thrown in fragments over the wide world." The allusion to the myth of Isis and Osiris, in which Isis gathers Osiris's scattered body parts, reassembles them, breathes life back into him, and then conceives Horus, powerfully resonates with Benjamin's deployment of the Kabbalistic account of the shattering of the *sefirot* and the quest to recover the resulting fragments. The dialectic of destruction and salvage suggested by both of these tales encapsulates a redemptive impulse that Howe's archaeopoetics both embodies and critically reflects upon. I will explore her negotiation of fragmentation and revivifying recuperation further in relation to "Scattering As Behavior Toward Risk," while my discussion of *Thorow* will investigate Howe's reflections on the limitations of her own poetry's historicist ambitions.

The dynamic of fragmentation and regeneration is evident from the first line of "Scattering As Behavior Toward Risk" (hereafter referred to as "Scattering"). The first line is a fragment gleaned from American literary history, derived from "The Genetic Text" of Herman Melville's *Billy Budd*. Melville's novel was unfinished at the time of his death in 1891; the manuscript he left was a draft rather than a copy ready for publication. As a result, differing editions of the text were published, until 1962 when Melville scholars Harrison Hayford and Merton M. Sealts produced what is now accepted as the "authoritative" version. Hayford and Sealts acknowledged and documented the problem of editing a definitive version by producing two texts: a "Reading Text" for general readers and also a "Genetic Text" that shows the process of the novel's composition and includes Melville's corrections and revisions. The "Genetic Text" upon which Howe draws, then, is *Billy Budd* in its unresolved state. The extract that makes up the first line of Howe's poem embodies this instability:[4]

"on a [*p*<suddenly . . . on a > was shot thro with a dyed→<dyed→a soft]"*
(*Singularities* 63)

Peter Quartermain has remarked upon how this line brings attention to its own status "as written rather than spoken language . . . Voiced or not, it proceeds in bits and pieces, stops and starts, repeats. Problematic, and emphatically for the eye" (184). The line stutters, verbally and visually. As Howe has explained in an interview, "I hear the stutter as a sounding of uncertainty. What is silenced or not quite silenced" (*Birth-mark* 181). The first line of "Scattering," then, aspires to embody something "silenced or not quite silenced." The problem with which this line immediately confronts us is how to negotiate its stuttering surfaces. Quartermain helpfully provides a translation by using Hayford and Sealts's code, but I am not sure (and nor in the end is he) whether this is really the point. This borrowed textual material and its editorial marks are highly suggestive on their own terms. Rich, in Benjaminian terms, with unrealized meaning potentials, this extract's diacritical marks non-verbally indicate a compositional activity of bracketing off, erasing, and inserting.

Notably, this line comes at the point of climax in Melville's story, the moment when Billy Budd is hanged. The reading text proceeds thus: "At the same moment it chanced that the vapory fleece hanging low in the East was shot through with a soft glory as of the fleece of the Lamb of God seen in mystical vision, and simultaneously therewith, watched by the wedged mass of upturned faces, Billy ascended; and, ascending, took the full rose of the dawn" (Melville 124). Compare this version with the stilted, stuttering line from the genetic text that Howe appropriates as the first line of her poem. Interestingly, one of the things that the genetic text makes visible in quite literal ways is a kind of corporeal violence erased from the reading text. The serene scene of Billy's execution depicted in the reading text is in its "genetic" form a site of struggle and inferred brutality suggested by the combination and juxtaposition of verbal and non-verbal material. Most notably, the sequence "was shot thro with a dyed→<dyed→a soft]" verbally and visually suggests the piercing and killing of something "soft." In this context, the word "dyed" reads equally as a misspelling of "died" and as the past participle of "dye," and the word's repetition reinforces this semantic doubleness. In any case, "dyed" points simultaneously to a death and to something stained,

both of which connect associatively with the imagery of "a soft" body having been "shot thro."

As well as intimating an act of violence, Howe's line evinces another kind of violence—that of making a text conform to standards of coherence and lucidity, an activity that entails the suppression of indeterminacy and multiple inferences. For Howe, this process is an analogue and even a symptom of a wider cultural and historical process of containment and erasure. In Quartermain's eloquent analysis, it is a trope for a history in which women are silenced and restricted, Native Americans exterminated, and the Irish repressed by the English, a history "of the hegemony of an intellectual and economic power which would, by revising and acculturating the texts it recognizes as central, marginalize and even abolish the actual texts as written because it seeks, by stabilizing the world so that its processes are arrested or invisible, to manage it" (191). For Howe, the climactic line borrowed from the genetic text of *Billy Budd* affords a glimpse of a text as it is being shaped, acculturated, and managed; it makes visible these processes. Moreover, in its unresolved state, Howe's line is also teeming with multiple traces of possibilities that have not yet been erased or contained. To return to the genetic text, then, is to at least partially retrieve the "stutter" of American literary history and to gesture toward the otherness it presents.

The rest of Howe's poem takes its cue from the radical stumbling and faltering suggested by her first line. Careering from line to paratactic line in a fashion that leaves large conceptual gaps and requires huge cognitive leaps, "Scattering" moves rapidly away from *Billy Budd* and proceeds "on wild thoughtpath" (64) to question the discourses, processes, and structures of thought that make up the "Violent order of a world" (65) as embodied in the editing of Melville's novel. The poem is centrally concerned with tracing the "Birth of contemporary thought" in which "Counter thought thought out" (65) by intuitively ranging across and combining a host of references to various historical, literary, and philosophical moments, eschewing the teleological marching of "the old army / Enlightened rationalism" (64) in the movement of its lines. In its final pages, the poem also explodes the strictures of the "Rules," the "guards and fences" (67) of the page in a literal act of "Scattering."

The penultimate page of the poem (see figure 5) returns to the textual material of *Billy Budd*. Here, Howe appropriates words from Melville's novel that evoke the drama and the naval setting of the tale. Visually resembling a structure in the process of overbalancing, this page performs a response to the title's imperative to practice "Scattering As Behavior Toward Risk." Mimetically enacting a physical toppling of text, the poem "blasts open the continuum of history" (Benjamin, *Illuminations* 254). Howe's poem wagers

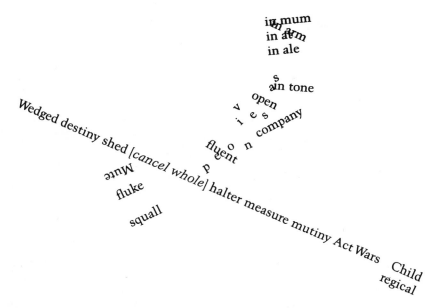

Figure 5. Penultimate page of Howe's "Scattering As Behavior Toward Risk." From *Singularities* by Susan Howe, © 1990 Susan Howe. Page 69. Reprinted by permission of Wesleyan University Press.

that unfulfilled and previously muffled semantic energies may be recovered from the wreckage (or shipwreck, given the nautical theme). The inverted word "Mute" somewhat clumsily suggests a literal overturning of muteness, enacted as part of a scattering of textual material that opens phrases, words, and single letters to a multiplicity of chance encounters, thus engendering opportunities for a recuperation of latent possibilities. The separated letters "p e o n" embody a state of inarticulacy attributable to the condition of a "peon," a term denoting a range of marginalized, disempowered, or expendable positions such as "unskilled worker," "very poor person," "messenger," or "foot soldier," for example (*OED*). Cutting across these disaggregated letters, "fluent" symbolically silences this unstable entity. And yet by its very disaggregated nature "p e o n" links up with a "company" of other scattered letters, "v i e s" and "a s," to suggest a process of resistance. The fragmented word archaeopoetically enacts the process of struggle indicated here by means of another kind of conflict: the conflict between the semantic drives of reading and the material qualities of its letters, emphasized here by their scattered status. Indeed, it is precisely this physical dimension of printed text that is the "peon," the unacknowledged ground of textuality that "vies" with a "fluent" semantic functioning of the printed text. These dimensions of the text signify "in mum": both silently (as in "keeping mum") and gesturally (as in a mummers play). The text on this page does enact a kind of mime by putting the meaning potentials of its visual dimensions in relationships of dynamic tension with the more abstract linguistic resonances of the material.

"Scattering" articulates an aspiration to recover the traces of presences edited out of American cultural history via a strikingly Benjaminian revolutionary-redemptive activity. Howe is certainly not alone in adopting such an approach to the investigation of lost or suppressed pasts. Indeed, as Vincent Pecora points out, a Benjamin-inspired model of historicism has been such a characteristic feature of cultural criticism in the humanities since the early 1970s that it warrants further scrutiny (92–3). Pecora, a cultural critic interested in, among other things, religion, philosophy, and modernity, directs his critical attention toward philosophical discourses by figures such as Jürgen Habermas, Michel Foucault, and Jacques Derrida. His arguments are also highly pertinent to parallel poetic activities such as Howe's. His thinking is particularly useful for the ways in which it identifies problems with the Benjamin-inspired historicist impulse; as we shall see, the challenges he identifies resonate with Howe's self-reflective archaeocritique. Pecora points out that "[t]he difficulty . . . is not simply that the past must be rigorously sifted to cull semantic energies that will lend enduring significance to an ever more disenchanted present. The problem for contemporary cultural criticism is that the true diversity of the past actually yields an excess of these redemptive moments" (96). Benjamin's "now time," Pecora points out, "is not simply a correspondence between the present and any number of lost opportunities for transformation rescued from the past," it "is itself irreducibly plural and contradictory, and so is its messianic promise" (96). Contemporary cultural projects that aim to rescue forgotten or suppressed dimensions of the past, he worries, tend to fasten on very particular "special histories" (97). Pecora links this to rationalist paradigms that, paradoxically, limit and contain the very notion of plurality in order to be made coherent. Thus while such recoveries of alternative histories by their very existence depend on a plural notion of history, at the same time, by privileging a particular aspect of the past, they inevitably fail to embrace the "irreducibly plural and contradictory" character of Benjamin's "now time."

Because the "true diversity of the past" offers a surfeit of unfulfilled potentialities, the impulse to recover forgotten or suppressed pasts is necessarily selective, insisting on the perceived special resonances of particular "redemptive moments" that tend to serve "present interests" (96). Pecora argues that such "semantic energies" are too easily used to fuel particular calls for "memorial justice" (96) produced by specific, competing cultural agendas of the present. Consequently, any historical project aimed at recovering "lost" moments of the past risks "a certain exclusivist particularism" (94) that works against an acknowledgement of the irreducible plurality of history even as it is rooted in this very claim for history's multiplicity. Pecora points out that the political consequences of such "an exclusive rather than inclusive vision" are potentially disastrous; forgotten moments of the past co-opted to "present interests" are often used to justify "so-called ethnic cleansing," "religious violence," and "militant communal aggression" (96–7). Although it seems to me that Pecora moves too swiftly between philosophical recuperations of lost pasts and political action in the name of memorial justice (a conflation that a critic like Habermas is careful not to make), the note of caution he sounds is nevertheless salutary. While critical and aesthetic modes of thinking and political action do constitute different kinds of representation, they are linked, albeit in complex ways. Pecora's argument suggests that even when the consequences are not so visible or extreme in concrete political terms, contemporary attempts to recover forgotten or suppressed pasts always involve suppressions, and thus paradoxically run the risk of disavowing "true" plurality even as they necessarily invoke it.

In what ways might Howe's historical project be susceptible to the pitfalls Pecora identifies? By sifting through textual history in search of stutters, gaps, silences, and fragments whose latent potentials might transform the meanings of the past and of cultural configurations in the present, does her poetry partake of an "exclusivist particularism" (Pecora 94)? How far are Howe's activities motivated by "present interests"? To what extent does the obliqueness of her poetic "recovery" of lost moments of the past—with its reliance on textual materiality and embrace of a Benjaminian mysticism— complicate these issues? Certainly, Howe's archaeology of American culture relies upon a quite specific sense of history. She tends, for example, to focus on a particular, dominant version of the American past: the settling of New England by the Pilgrims, an event that shapes her cultural roots as a New Englander and has undoubtedly become the privileged "Mythology of the American Frontier" (*Birth-mark* 181). This focus undoubtedly suppresses other versions of American history that contain alternative marginalized histories; for example, while Howe has frequently expressed an interest in the elided voices of women and Native Americans, her historical investigations are entirely silent on the history of slavery, a history that seems central to any inquiry into "what went wrong" (*Birth-mark* 164) in the early years of American history. Furthermore, one might question the nature of her poetry's engagement with the histories of America's indigenous peoples. Howe often mentions the literal and cultural oppression of Native Americans in the making of America, but how exactly do their lost histories figure in her wider project and in her poems themselves? And what bearing do Howe's aesthetic strategies have on such questions?

These many complex questions may be investigated in relation to *Thorow*, a poem explicitly concerned with American colonial history, its traces in contemporary reality, and with the barely discernable vestiges of Native Americans in this history. While *Thorow* aspires to recover a sense of the "irreducibly plural and contradictory" (Pecora 96) past of a particular geographical locale, the poem actually constitutes a reflective investigation of its own limited capacities to do so, and its own complicities in the very structures it critiques. As Montgomery points out, this poem cannot help but "embody some of the problems it wishes to expose" (*The Poetry* 103). It thus constitutes an apposite example of the self-critical dimension of Howe's archaeocritique, which both embodies and thinks through the possibilities and problems of historical recovery.

Thorow begins with an introductory passage that locates the poem's beginnings in the poet's stay at Lake George in upstate New York where she was a writer in residence in 1987. She describes the town, "or what is left of a town" (*Singularities* 40), as an embodiment of the consumer capitalist "travesty" of late capitalist American culture "grafted" onto a landscape previously rich with "spirits" and the traces of "once-upon" (40). Turning away from the specious materialism of her present, the poet positions herself "on the shores of a history of the world where forms of wildness brought up by memory become desire and multiply" (40). The poem seeks the "primal indeterminacy" (40) of this landscape even while it investigates the ways in which it has been "appropriated" by a colonial history whose legacy, Howe suggests, is manifested in the superficial "graft" of the poet's contemporary landscape. Lake George is represented as a kind of palimpsest in which primordial "wildness," a history of colonization, and the empty materialism of contemporary capitalism form a spatiotemporal mesh. The poem itself sifts through layered textual residues comprising material gleaned from the papers of Sir William Johnson, the eighteenth-century colonialist who led the British at the Battle of Lake George and built Fort William Henry, the writings of Henry David Thoreau, and Howe's own meditative communing with the landscape.[5] What this process seeks, the poem's introduction claims, is what Pecora calls "the uncertain plurality of history" (93).

Howe's introductory prose section invokes a multiplicity of competing and contradictory histories by exploring the processes of naming and renaming. Pointing to the role of naming in the project of European expansionist imperialism, she describes how Lake George is "spelled . . . into *place*" by the early European settlers who appropriated it, and has been "renamed . . .

several times since" (*Singularities* 40). From the Iroquois appellation "An-diatarocte," to the French "Lac du Saint Sacrament," to the English "Lake George" (Brodhead 422), these name changes evince a history of colonization and battles over possession of territory between the British and the French. In this imperialist history, naming functions as a way of fixing a space in "*place*," a way of constructing it as property and making it knowable, manageable, and exploitable. But the multiple names of Lake George also testify to moments of contestation within these colonial processes, and the shifting status of this place in various, different, histories. Thus Howe's introduction also offers an alternative perspective on names and naming. Quoting Gilles Deleuze and Félix Guattari, she proposes that "[t]he proper name is the instantaneous apprehension of a multiplicity" (41). The poem's title is a proper name of this sort. A homonym for Thoreau, the (mis)spelling "Thorow" also represents an archaic or idiosyncratic rendering of "through," as in Howe's quotation of Sir Humphrey Gilbert's assertion that "there is no thorow passage" (41) and her lines "thorow out all / the Five Nations" (46). In this second instance, "thorow" also suggests "throw," as in "throw out," a reading that emphasizes the expulsion of the Five Nations, or Iroquois, from their ancestral lands. Furthermore, "Thorow" might be read as a lisping rendering of the word "sorrow" and thus a lament for losses attributable to the violence of colonial history, losses that the poem sees as manifest in the hollow and pernicious "graft" (*Singularities* 40) of the contemporary landscape.

Just as the stutter is made central to "Scattering," the lisp is the primary verbal metaphor of *Thorow*. As the multiple possible readings of the signifier *Thorow* suggest, the slipping, lisping activity of the poem is allied to its pursuit of multiplicities, palpable in the history of Lake George. Consider the following, for example:

To be sent in slays
if we are not careful
To a slightly place
no shelter
(48)

As in the poem's title, lisping is not simply a primary trope for the poem's activities but a foregrounding of sound-based textual dimensions. Lines slip alliteratively from "sent" to "slays" to "slightly" and assonantly from "slays" to "place," for example. Such sonic dimensions perform in parallel ways to the visually foregrounded materiality discussed earlier in relation to *Eikon Basilike*: as a way of emphasizing sensory dimensions of writing that open texts to alternative modes of meaning.

Garrett Stewart, in his book *Reading Voices: Literature and the Phonotext*, understands sound as functioning in a series of sensory tensions and dialogues with the graphic surfaces of the text; "the acoustics of textuality" he declares, constitute "a malleable 'signifying' energy floated upon the counterplay of phonemes against graphemes within the order of signification" (11). This positioning of "phonemes against graphemes" suggests a dialectical tension that generates "'signifying' energy": "graphic and vocal patterns intersect each other, cross and discompose the text" (Stewart 15). For Stewart, this frictional "play" between different sensory dimensions forms "the alternating resistances that get in the way of reading, the energies that reading as we know it must for the most part override" (27). The invocation of lisping sounds in "Thorow" deploys such "resistances" and their "energies" as a way of "discompos[ing] the text" and in so doing approaching the multiplicities of language, history, and landscape upon which the poem meditates. The acoustic slippage in the lines quoted above, such as "to be sent in slays," for example, make of this text "a slightly place," a domain that embodies a migratory drift into a liminal terrain. Archaic spellings produce semantic slippages; "slays" works most obviously as a misspelling of "sleighs," which might carry the "we" into exile, but "slays" also works as a correct spelling of the present participle of "to slay," suggesting a violent threat associated with banishment to a dangerous domain. The ambiguous phrase "slightly place," meanwhile, operates on the margins of meaning in ways that nevertheless manage eloquently to designate a site that is itself both peripheral and nebulous. In this stanza, acoustic and semantic lisps and slippages enact a "wildness" of verbal articulation that moves to the fringes or the "shores of a history" (Howe, *Singularities* 40).

By means of its meditations on naming and the sound-based and semantic lisping, drifting activities of its poetic lines, *Thorow* seeks to recuperate traces of "primal indeterminacy" (*Singularities* 40), to open textual material to a multiplicity analogous to the history of Lake George's landscape. This avowed embrace of multiplicity would seem to enable Howe's poem to transcend Pecora's charges of exclusivism leveled at the quasi-Benjaminian tendencies of postmodern cultural criticism. But the relation of this work to a truly plural vision of history is more troubled than the poem's declared pursuit of multiplicities might at first suggest. The poem's route to the plurality of the past, via the historical and literary texts of European colonists, makes any attempt to recover the true plurality of the histories of Lake George rather limited. Howe is anxious to reveal the traces of these histories in the absences and appropriations of her source texts, in the citing of Native American place names, for example, or in references to "Indian shoes" (*Singularities* 43) and canoes. But these indexical markers tend throughout the poem to become part of the landscape. As Montgomery puts it, "the non-European, Native American presence is swept into a category of inarticulate otherness that assimilates it to the wilderness of the surrounding land" (*The Poetry* 101). Furthermore, this "wilderness" is approached only via the "we" of the poem. As Nicky Marsh points out, in Howe's wider investigation of American history, "the decimation of [the] first peoples by American colonization is given only the meaning that colonization gave it." She appositely points to "Howe's complicity, ironical as it may present itself as being, with the absence of narrative for Native Americans . . . The retention of such absences jars against the ostensible purpose of much of Howe's political agenda to discover presences within the scission of American identity" ("Out of My Texts" 132). By retaining the absence of Native American histories *as* absence, *Thorow* runs the risk of presenting them as part of an "exotic" otherness that is only knowable by means of colonial textuality.

Howe's poetry, then, is often at least partly complicit with the restrictive viewpoints of the history it critiques. As Marsh indicates, Howe is well aware of her own complicity with narratives that negate certain histories. Yet in *Thorow* the acknowledgement of this collusion is not so much an "ironical" nod to the poetry's immanent position as it is a knowing investigation of its own historicist methods, and by extension an archaeocritical reflection on the limitations of contemporary paradigms for historicist inquiry that aspire to recover the pluralities of the past. The line "Complicity battling redemption" (55) at the end of the poem's second section neatly describes a conflict in the poem itself between a compulsive kind of complicity with the configurations and power relations of a discourse that excludes, contains, and marginalizes, and an aspiration to redeem the pluralities negated by these very processes. And yet Howe's particular mode of redemption—the recovery of quite specific traces of the past—may also be seen as complicit with exclusivist forces that constrain history's surfeit of plurality. The placing of the line "Complicity battling redemption" at the very end of the second part of the poem is, I think, instructive in relation to the short third section of the poem, which performs a radical visual disruption of normative printing conventions. If this line is an acknowledgement of a partial failure of the poem to rescue history's multiplicities, then its final section stages a last-ditch gesture toward such multiplicity.

The first opening of part 3 of *Thorow* (see figure 6) contains one of the most dramatic instances of textual disarrangement to be found anywhere in Howe's work. Shrugging off the constrictions of discursive language, the conventions of the poetic line, and the rules of the page, this textual material aims to function something like an "apprehension of a multiplicity" (Howe, *Singularities* 41). These page layouts challenge the grid of the page as a way

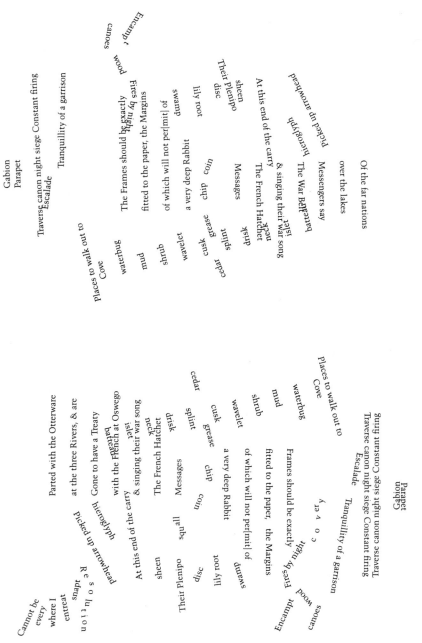

Figure 6. Penultimate opening of Howe's *Thorow*. From *Singularities* by Susan Howe. Pages 56–7. Reprinted by permission of Wesleyan University Press.

of critiquing the "European grid on the forest" (45), a central symbol for Howe of the instrumental rationality that shaped American colonial history. *Thorow* thus draws a parallel between the "grid" of the page, coded to manage and control the printed text along with its possible readings, and wider processes of ordering, managing, and controlling at work in the early European settlers' imposition of a "grid on the forest."

The prescriptive set of framing instructions placed at the center of these visually disrupted pages foregrounds the parallels between page layout and the logic of the wider "European grid." There is a notable concern in these instructions with "Margins." The depth of the "Rabbit," presumably a variant spelling of the framing term "rabbet" (the rebated part in the back of a picture frame in which the artwork and the glass sit), determines how much of the edges of the contained artwork are consequently covered by the frame. The instructions' proscription against "a very deep Rabbit" evinces a process by which "Margins" are made as narrow and constrained as possible. However, the misspelling itself undermines these dogmatic instructions, and they thus become entangled in a momentary foray into nonsense that unsettles the "grid" of rationality that underpins them.

Significantly, this challenge to the "grid" of the page occurs via instructions relating to practices associated with visual images. While the linguistic unsettling of the framing instructions points to a disruption of the usual rules of the page, it is primarily by visual means that this disturbance is physically performed. Much of the text on these pages comes from Howe's two main sources for *Thorow*; the references to warfare are derived from Sir William Johnson's papers, and those pertaining to the natural world from Thoreau's writings.[6] Textual fragments from these sources are dispersed across the page, creating a verbal-visual palimpsest that interlaces references to processes of framing, eighteenth-century colonial battles, and nineteenth-century encounters with nature. This arrangement performs physical entanglements of textual material in which, for example, a list of nouns pertaining to elements of the natural world interlaces with fragmented notes on the French and Indian wars of the eighteenth century with which Johnson was involved. These physical intertwinings spark semantic connections; the archaic "snapt," for example, concretely disrupts the components of "Resolution," suggesting an aborted process of negotiation, settlement, or, indeed, *irresolution*, the term's binary opposite. The intersection of "French" and "batteau," meanwhile, brings about a more harmonious meeting in which the words seem to mutually reinforce one another, creating an "islet" of Frenchness, as another nearby term suggests, in a sea of predominantly English words.

This visual disruption of printing conventions turns the page into a field or constellation of plural semantic potentialities. This multiplicitous effect is heightened by the repetition, inversion, and variation of textual material on either side of the opening. Both semantically and visually, these pages constitute a graphic approximation of the forms of "primal indeterminacy" Howe's poem pursues. Visual thickets and clearings suggest a terrain imbued with residues of history's layers accreted in the landscape. It is perhaps here, on the material surfaces of these disrupted pages, that the poem comes closest to the multiplicitous excess of suppressed and marginalized pasts. However, even in its most revolutionary disarrangements of the "European grid," Howe's poem retains an acute critical consciousness of its own entanglement with the language and ideologies of that "grid," which constrain its pursuit of inarticulable pluralities.

This ambivalence is perhaps most apparent in Howe's stance toward her source texts. For her, these texts hold traces both of the "other voices" her poetry yearns to recover, and also the dynamics of power and elision by which they are silenced. It is most especially through an engagement with her source texts' contradictory moments and impulses that her poetry often seeks to make such traces palpable. But the poet also knows that her own work inherits these very tensions, even as it investigates and critiques them.

So *Thorow*'s appropriation and disarrangement of material from its homonymic precursor Thoreau, for example, seeks to animate its source text, hitherto dormant potentials as well as acknowledge that its ability to do is inevitably constrained; even in its most aesthetically radical moments it cannot transcend its cultural legacy, just as its predecessor could not. Indeed, Thoreau's writings and way of life, which strove to connect with the American landscape's "primal" pre-colonial diversity, offer a precedent for Howe's own encounter with the landscape and history of Lake George. For all his renowned veneration of the land and its inhabitants, Thoreau's vision was unavoidably informed by the paradigms of his time and culture. As Lawrence Buell points out, his "notion of land apportionment," for example, "follows the European settlers' practice of assigning explicit titles to specific parcels of land" (*Environmental Imagination* 213). This is the very process by which the land is "spelled . . . into *place*" (*Singularities* 40) by its early European "discoverers," as critiqued in Howe's introduction to *Thorow*. Concomitantly, despite his admiration for America's indigenous peoples, Thoreau's writings frequently portray Native Americans in terms of a naïve, childish simplicity that romanticizes their way of life and strips them of agency, cultural specificity, and sophistication. In *The Maine Woods*, for example, Thoreau is provoked by his guide's singing to imagine "the period of the discovery of America, to San Salvador and the Incas, when Europeans first encountered the simple faith of the Indian. There was, indeed, a beautiful simplicity about it; nothing of the dark and savage, only the mild and infantile" (179). For Montgomery, Howe's poem partially inherits the tendencies of her source texts, following Thoreau in her "sweeping" of "the non-European, Native American presence . . . into a category of inarticulate otherness that assimilates it to the 'wilderness'" (*The Poetry* 101). Yet it is also the case that Howe is drawn to Thoreau's writings precisely because of the tensions they exhibit between a mythology of the American frontier that seeks to conquer and manage the "wilderness" and an often flawed quest to imagine ways of approaching the natural world and its inhabitants beyond those structures of thought dominated by the "European grid" of instrumental rationality.

That Howe's poem inherits these tensions as well as reveals them may be discerned, I think, in the precise ways in which it selects and disarranges material from Thoreau's work. Two vertical lists of Thoreauvian nouns, gleaned from *The Main Woods* and *Walden*, make up part of the tangle of printed text in the pages depicted in figure 6. By printing lists of Thoreauvian words upside down or at unusual angles and by untidily entangling the methodical list with other printed matter, Howe's poem both invokes and unsettles her source material and its itemization of the American landscape. In one such dismantling, the list "sheen / disc / lily root / swamp" is printed upside down on the recto side of the opening and unraveled on the verso side, with its separate components printed at odd, disturbed angles rather than parallel to one another. Meanwhile, the disjointed series of letters "c o v e r y" toward the bottom of this page suggest that one of the terms in this list, "disc" has been severed from its remainder and should read "discovery." Indeed, whereas "disc" appears nowhere in Howe's most likely source texts, Thoreau's *Walden* and *The Maine Woods*, the word "discovery" and its variants make frequent appearances, particularly in "Allegash and East Branch" where most of the other listed terms on Howe's pages can be found. Howe's appropriation and physical *détournement* of this word performs a critique of the notion of discovery so central to the imperialist explorations of the "New World" and to Thoreau's less avaricious contribution to the mythology of the American frontier. European claims to "discovery" could only be made by disavowing the presence of indigenous cultures or by viewing those cultures as part of the "discovery" itself. By disaggregating this word, Howe points to the ways in which processes of discovery are always also engaged in a "covery," a covering over or veiling of previous presences and claims. Perhaps, this dismantled word suggests, this process also applies to processes of *re*covery, and to the retrievals Howe's poem hopes to make; every recovery also entails a "covery" that elides other presences.

In this way, *Thorow* archaeocritically reflects on its own work of historical inquiry. Howe's visually disrupted pages not only embody a process of

"Complicity battling redemption," they also indicate the ways in which processes of historical recovery risk complicity with principles that limit, restrict, and silence. *Thorow* does at times achieve an aesthetic approximation of "multiplicities," as in the "thickets" of its most radically unsettled pages or in its lisping language. But this poem is in the end rather ambivalent about the possibilities of such a move and doubtful about whether its aesthetic embodiment of the principle of multiplicity can be translated into an apprehension of historical multiplicity. In its recourse to less radically disrupted page layouts in its final opening, the poem signals a sense of uncertainty by means of a partial return to the principles of the "grid" of the page. The poem's final page visually references the figure of the grid, a layout that recurs throughout Howe's oeuvre. Yet this is a skewed grid, its second line misaligned with the words above and below. Its final three lines, each comprising a single word, abandon the grid formation altogether, following instead a slightly different logic that aligns each word physically with some of the terms in the grid but also introduces irregular gaps and varying line spacing. This simultaneous visual invocation of the grid and mutation of its regimented formation works as an allegory for the larger problem that Howe's poem both embodies and critically reflects upon.

Thorow articulates a yearning toward multiplicities and the recuperation of thwarted possibilities that make up a thoroughly plural sense of history. Yet the poem also recognizes its own complicity with rather selective and constricting parameters of thought and representation that hinder an "apprehension of a multiplicity" (*Singularities* 41). In short, *Thorow* archaeocritically thinks through the very difficulty Pecora points to when he remarks that neo-Benjaminian projects to redeem the semantic sparks of "special histories" often quell the "uncertain plurality of history" (Pecora 93), thereby repeating at some level the very structures of suppression that such recuperative histories seek to contest. For all its pursuit of multiplicities embodied in its strategies of drifting, lisping, and unsettling the grid of the page, *Thorow* recognizes the limitations and selectiveness of its vision and its own inability to entirely shake rationalist, colonialist legacies of thought and representation. In its sifting of very particular fragmented historical remains, *Thorow* in the end looks very much like a knowing enactment of the very problems that Pecora's analysis of counter-memory highlights. As its last page suggests, Howe's poem is more a reshaping of the "European grid" than a dismantling or transcendence of it.

Yet in its radically "scattered" textual thickets and skewed grid formations, Howe's poem offers a sensuous encounter with a struggle that at the very least physically brushes up against the possibilities of a plural history. To recall the thought of J. M. Bernstein, the foregrounding of the material dimensions of the printed page in *Thorow* points to "the *orientational significance of sensory encounter, sensory experience as constitutive of conviction and connection to the world of things,*" a kind of "*significance*" that in modernity has been "excised from the everyday" (*Voluptuous* 3). The poem's aesthetic embodiment of principles of multiplicity cannot be fully translated into an "apprehension of [the] multiplicity" of history because the kinds of "significance" it offers, tangled up with the physicality of printed language and the material page, constitute "meaning beyond or without discursive redemption" (J. M. Bernstein, *Voluptuous* 120). While the kinds of "redemption" the poem offers cannot be fully realized in discursive terms, they nevertheless perform an "*orientational*" function, shifting attentions and pointing to an unarticulated plurality of presences and a sense of "*connection to the world of things*" as a form of encounter with "primal indeterminacy."

3
"The word. The image"

THERESA HAK KYUNG CHA'S FRACTURED FORMS

The book, I have to admit, is closer to an anthology than to an epic.
Edmond Jabès, "The Light of the Sea"

When Theresa Hak Kyung Cha's *DICTEE* was first published by a small
avant-garde New York press in 1982, its front cover depicted a black-and-
white wide-format photograph of some nondescript ruins in a geographically unspecific desert landscape. The image shows a crumbling pyramid-
like structure standing against a featureless sky; in the foreground a large
eroded boulder occupies a raised mound of stony ground, one of a line of
such shapes that stretch into the distance. The cover gives no information
about the photograph's source or about the geographical location or cultural
origins of the ruins. Nor is there any intimation of their relevance to the Korean diasporic history with which *DICTEE* is centrally concerned. Indeed,
in its original printing, the book's external coverings contain few clues that
would bring this history to the attention of the casual browser. The back
cover features no blurb or textual material whatsoever, only another un-
explained photograph of Korean schoolgirls. In spite of the old adage about
books and their covers, the inscrutable photograph of crumbling monumental structures that adorned the original jacket of *DICTEE* indicates something vital about this work's mode of historical inquiry. As a concrete trace
of a people and history long since disappeared from living memory, the ruins embody a process of memorialization. However, Cha's radical decontextualization of her cover image renders this memorial gesture anonymous.
Although the photograph articulates a desire to recoup traces of a particular
past, it functions at the same time not to offer knowledge but, conversely, as
an artifact that fails, or even refuses, to provide lucid information about its
historical referents. It resists connection to the personal and to established
historical narratives (in stark contrast to the cover of the re-released 2001
edition that features a photograph of Cha's mother and describes the text as
a "work of autobiography"). The first edition's cover image refuses assimilation to a knowable past. Facts, figures, names, and dates are withheld; in-

stead, the photograph mutely documents a process of material disintegration and a concomitant sense of abandonment and forgetting. It also points to a series of disjunctions: between seeing and knowing, apprehension and understanding, concrete particulars and overarching epistemological frames. Such disarticulations are invoked variously but recurrently within the larger project that this cover enfolds.

DICTEE eschews a straightforwardly epistemological relation to its cultural past in favor of a more sensory mode of encounter with the gaps, dislocations, and erasures of Korean diasporic history. The text proposes an archaeological mode of knowing that privileges the tangibility of material particulars over abstract generalities. Emphasizing the concrete specificities of Korean historical experience, Cha's text offers the various documents and "found" materials within its pages as palpable traces of a traumatic history. Often characterized by a fragmented materiality, the very fabrics of these documents evince physical deteriorations analogous to those displayed by the structures depicted in the cover image. Cha's text embodies an archaeopoetics of disintegration and fracture, whose aesthetics of wear and tear are invested with very particular kinds of historical resonance. It is the material meaningfulness of these documents, their decompositions, and their often disjointed juxtapositions that constitutes a primary means of bodying forth the ruptures of a past for which the very notion of epistemological recovery, the text suggests, would amount to a misapprehension of this history's irresolvably fractured character. In Cha's work, as in Howe's, the gaps, fractures, and silences of the past are not to be "filled in" or compensated for in some way by the artwork but rather made hauntingly, provocatively present. Entwining its aesthetic dimensions with historical questions informed by the very specific configurations of a Korean diasporic consciousness, *DICTEE* performs archaeocritical reflections on broader questions about the ethical quandaries of historical recuperation, and the connotations of both retrieval and healing associated with ideas of such "recovery."

To carry out these forms of investigation and reflection, Cha's archaeopoetic mode draws on her wider practice as a visual artist with interests in film, performance, and conceptual art. While *DICTEE* is by far her best-known and most-discussed work, it constitutes only a small part of her oeuvre. In this chapter I will examine examples from her wider body of work alongside *DICTEE* to demonstrate how much the formal qualities of this text owe to her engagement and involvement with video and film as well as specific developments in the visual arts during the 1970s and early '80s. Cha's wider practice shaped the aesthetic strategies and techniques that are vital to *DICTEE*'s historical inquiry.

DICTEE's Histories

DICTEE raises the question of what a "poem including history" might look like, or feel like, when ruptures, erasures, and gaps are the characteristic features of the history under investigation. In many respects, this work's historical reach is epic. Cha's book references a long history of imperialist interventions involving a suppression of specifically Korean cultural practices. Her references range from the Catholic missionary projects beginning in the nineteenth century to Japan's more aggressively military colonization in the first half of the twentieth century to the thinly veiled imperialisms of the Cold War superpowers that brought about the partitioning of Korea and the Korean War in 1950. It was in the wake of the bloody border disputes and during the subsequent waves of migration that Cha's family moved to the United States in 1962.

In response to a history of cultural suppression, violent division, and displacement, *DICTEE* presents itself as a fragmented archival collection of poetry, prose, letters, photographs, citations, diagrams, and maps. In its incorporation of found materials and its juxtaposition of different genres and discourses, this work has clear affiliations with the modernist epic. Josephine Park, the critic who has explored this connection most fully, argues that from its outset, *DICTEE* invokes the most prominent work of this genre, Pound's *Cantos*, to create "a new instantiation of the American epic" that "expands a genre famous for its openness while at the same time exposing its limits" (226). Park demonstrates how Cha rejects key dimensions of Pound's poetics, such as his search for the ideal state and an "authoritarian voice" (231) that strives (but ultimately fails) to hold the poem's constellation of materials together. *DICTEE* also embraces "the elements of epic that Pound took for granted and scorned" (228) such as the figure of the mother, bodily acts of speaking, and, centrally for Park's argument, epic's "generic other" in the form of "the fragile, lyric self" (232). This new mode of the American long poem "including history," in other words, activates possibilities neglected or marginalized by its precursors. Most interestingly for my purposes, Park notes how *DICTEE*'s collage method "goes one step further than Pound's grab bag of letters, conversations, and histories: Cha shows us the documents themselves" (231). This strategy foregrounds the physical qualities of the text's archival objects, their often fractured or degraded qualities, and also the affective disjunctions between different kinds of materials and modes of representation. As discussed in the introductory chapter of *Archaeopoetics*, Pound's ideogrammic method was often more interested in performing concrete juxtapositions as a way of "heaping together the necessary components of thought" (*Selected Prose* 209) than in inviting attention to the physical particulars of materials. Cha, however, is alert to historical and cultural residues that may offer ethically viable modes of inquiry into a history of silencing, violent conflict, and dislocation. Furthermore, while Pound was interested in presenting diverse materials in order to "suggest some fundamental relation between them" (Fenollosa 46) that would comprise "an intellectual and emotional complex" (Pound, "A Few Don'ts" 95), in Cha's work such relations are often highly ambiguous or even inscrutable. And where Pound sought to create a "useable past," Cha's collage poem formally enacts failures of recall, connection, and identification. In so doing, it radically reshapes the epistemic ambitions of the modernist epic.

This sensibility is evident at the outset of any encounter with *DICTEE*. As with the image of enigmatic ruins on its original cover, the text itself offers few navigational signposts. Readers are cast adrift among a miscellany of juxtaposed documents, many of which, in a similar way to the cover photograph, are severed from their contexts; other materials are downright unreliable or misleading, such as the book's epigraph, which is attributed to Sappho but is nowhere to be found in the corpus of works normally associated with the ancient Greek poet. It is precisely this refusal to function as "an object of revelation" (Cheng 120) that has often been at the center of critical commentary on Cha's text, which has accrued since it belatedly came to attention on a rising tide of postcolonial, diaspora, and women's studies in the 1990s. Before embarking on my own discussion of this work's complex engagement with history, it is worth glancing at the broad outlines of these debates because of what they begin to reveal about the political and aesthetic stakes of Cha's archaeopoetic project.

During the decade following its first publication in 1982, and its author's untimely death in the same year, *DICTEE* was largely ignored by the academic world, attracting the attention of only a handful of commentators involved with East and West Coast avant-garde circles. It was the seminal collection *Writing Self, Writing Nation* (ed. Elaine Kim and Norma Alarcón) that in 1994 galvanized critical interest in *DICTEE* within Asian American and postcolonial studies; Cha's text quite quickly acquired canonical status. Contributors to this volume such as Kim and L. Hyun Yi Kang openly admit an initial frustration with *DICTEE*'s "incongruous juxtapositions" (3), its oblique references, and the "crisis of inaccessibility/ incomprehension" (76) these strategies induced. Motivated by a perceived need to rescue the text from what Kim sees as its depoliticization by those who emphasize its aesthetics of fragmentation and indeterminacy at the expense of its Korean contexts, both Kim and Kang surmount the challenges posed by its formal techniques to offer readings frequently aided by the kinds of contextualization that the text itself withholds.

For other commentators, however, an overcoming of *DICTEE*'s intransigence is not really the point. For Lisa Lowe, it is precisely the text's "aesthetic of infidelity" (37) to mimetic conventions of representation that constitutes its most productive intervention. "[I]n disturbing the function of representation as reconciliation," she persuasively argues, *DICTEE* "returns us, as readers, to the material contradictions of lived political life" (62), most especially to unresolved tensions within identity politics. More recently, Anne Anlin Cheng has argued that "the form of Cha's text offers a critique of [the] documentary desire" (121) that motivates the recuperation of texts such as hers for projects that hope to offer "corrective re-readings" (120) of suppressed pasts. In common with Lowe and Cheng, critics working in the context of experimental poetics regard *DICTEE*'s resistant form as "the place to dwell" (Spahr 125). Reading Cha's text alongside a number of Language writers, Juliana Spahr argues that by denaturalizing or "decolonizing" the very activity of reading, *DICTEE* "addresses domination in many forms" (123). As part and parcel of a critique of patriarchal, colonial, and neo-colonial power, "we need to examine works that challenge how we read to categorize, conquer, penetrate, and settle" (127). Spahr demonstrates how, far from depoliticizing the text, a focus on its experimental form can politicize reading to offer ways of interrogating the assimilationist demands of dominant cultures. Her notion of "colonial thinking" (127) is, however, somewhat general. Michael Davidson offers a more specific materialist grounding of *DICTEE* as a work that engages with an evolving Pacific Rim discourse. He sees Cha's foregrounding of the resistant materiality of her various documents as a mode of bringing attention to "the inscripted form of historical representation" ("Hunting" 198), or the mediation of historical knowledge by representational modes that are themselves implicated in specific and shifting regimes of power.

Such discussions of Cha's text have negotiated tensions between a critical recuperation of the text that privileges its Asian American and postcolonial credentials and approaches that foreground Cha's experimentalism and affinities with European and American avant-gardes. Kim puts it rather strongly when she describes what she sees as an inherent conflict between "Asian Americanists who believe that Cha's identity as a gendered and racialized Korean American is crucial to the understanding of her work" and (implicitly "white") "historians of avant-garde art who . . . fear that brainless advocates of 'identity politics' will flatten and reduce her work with their 'disheveled,' 'mawkish,' 'bumper sticker'-level readings" ("Interstitial Subjects" 47). It is clear where Kim's affinities lie; this polarized view of the reception of Cha's work implies that critical attention to its formal aspects and aesthetic contexts not specifically Asian American betray its political import.

This discursive split between "Asian American" and "avant-garde" modes of understanding *DICTEE* has occurred in relation to a wider context within which "minority literature" and "experimentalism" have, until quite recently, been assumed to be at odds with one another (I shall touch on this assumption again in chapters 5 and 6). Some of the most recent discussions of Cha address themselves explicitly to this issue, and in so doing, move the debate on, even as they offer nuanced accounts of the cultural politics of this very divide. Josephine Park's aforementioned essay focusing on *DICTEE*'s engagement with specific European and American modernist poetic traditions has been part of this current. She argues that Cha's text crosses the boundary between Baudelairian lyric and Poundian epic modes as a way of framing numerous other boundary crossings: between mother and daughter, subject and object, North and South Korea and, implicitly, the categorizations of "Asian American" and "avant-garde." It is precisely "*[t]hrough* its avant-garde strategies" (214, my emphasis), Park argues, that *DICTEE* is able to perform interventions into both its aesthetic and cultural-political legacies. In another important contribution, Joseph Jonghyun Jeon's compelling book *Racial Things, Racial Forms* begins with a consideration of Cha's work as exemplary of an Asian American avant-garde practice. Revolving explicitly around questions of intelligibility, his book opens by remarking on the dangers as well as the possibilities of a discursive correlation between "the figure of the inscrutable Asian" and the "difficult" avant-garde art object. He proposes that works like Cha's, rather than capitulating to essentialist notions of Asian unintelligibility, provide opportunities for exploring how "the perceived strangeness of the avant-garde art object might function as a way of interrogating the way in which Asianness gets racially coded and visualized in contemporary American discourse" (xvii). Jeon compellingly demonstrates that Cha and other formally experimental writers engage the politics of race in ways that challenge the assumptions of more conventional paradigms of identity politics. "What might seem to be avoidance of social issues," he writes, "is actually the avoidance of their more conventional forms in hopes of gaining significant interpretive advantages by adopting more oblique approaches" (xxxvi).

A further welcomed dimension of reading Cha as part of an Asian American avant-garde is a broadening of attention beyond *DICTEE* to her wider— emphatically experimental—activities as an artist. While critics such as Spahr and Davidson have readily acknowledged Cha's involvement with performance art and film, the specifically *visual* forms of materiality deployed throughout *DICTEE* received relatively little extended commentary, until quite recently. Exemplary here is Jeon's chapter on Cha in *Racial Things, Racial Forms*, which focuses on her artist's book and film works to make provocative and fruitful connections between the visual materiality of these media and the visual materialization of race. Jeon's argument parallels my own, in many ways. But whereas he is interested in how Cha's work crucially reflects on the epistemologies and ontologies of race, my own emphasis is on how *DICTEE*'s materially emphatic formal moves investigate the possibilities, limitations, and politics of historical encounter in a specifically Korean diasporic context. I share with Jeon and a small but growing number of recent commentators, though, the conviction that Cha's mode of aesthetic engagement with such matters is highly informed by her wider artistic activities and milieu.

Cha spent her formative years as an artist in the early 1970s at the University of California, Berkeley at a time when the campus was a center of student protests and political activism as well as a hothouse for artistic innovation. In this highly charged atmosphere, she studied comparative literature, film, and art; she encountered modernist poetry, film theory, feminist criticism, and performance art along the way. These formative influences had a significant bearing on her own practice, including the writing of *DICTEE*. Alongside her studies, Cha worked at the Pacific Film Archive from 1974 to 1977 in its exciting early years as an important venue for experimental film, international cinema, and video art. Interested in the work of filmmakers such as Carl Dreyer, Jean-Luc Godard, Chris Marker, Stan Brakhage, and Michael Snow, she subsequently pursued film theory. In 1976 she studied with Christian Metz, Jean-Louis Baudry, Monique Wittig, and others in a year abroad at the Centre d'Études Américain du Cinéma in Paris. Cha's time at Berkeley coincided with a flourishing of conceptual and performance art in the Bay Area where, along with Berkeley's University Arts Museum and the San Francisco Museum of Modern Art, alternative art spaces proliferated. Cha not only exhibited her work at many of them but also encountered the performances, videos, and installations of influential practitioners of the time including Bay Area conceptual artists such as Linda Montano, Tom Marioni, and Terry Fox, whose work had a particular influence on Cha (Lewallen 6), and more widely known artists such as Eleanor Antin, Paul McCarthy, Bruce Nauman, Vito Acconci, and Chris Burden. When in 1980 Cha moved to New York and began working for the small press Tanam, these experiences shaped her activities in publishing. In 1980 she edited an anthology of essays on film for Tanam entitled *Apparatus: Cinematographic Apparatus: Selected Writings*; her contributed piece, "COMMENTAIRE," was a film-like visual essay or concrete poem that incorporated stills from Dreyer's film *Vampyr*. In the same year her visual poem "EXILÉE," a piece also realized elsewhere in film form, appeared in *Hotel*, an anthology of commissioned text works by artists including Jenny Holzer, Laurie Anderson, and

Reese Williams, the press's founder. So too, the influences of film, film theory, performance, and conceptual art can be seen in *DICTEE*. Filmic dimensions are evident in the cinematic aesthetic of *DICTEE*'s original cover, with its two photographs printed on a dark maroon backdrop, and its montage-like composition and its use of camera directions and stills. The documenting practices of performance and conceptual art, meanwhile, have had a profound impact on Cha's consideration of the relationship between an event and its record, a concern that resonates throughout her exploration of the possibilities of historical anamnesis in *DICTEE*. Cha's work of historical investigation into the fractures and erasures of her cultural past is shaped not only by her position as a Korean American immigrant woman but also by her engagement with aesthetic questions relating to photography, film, and inscribed language and their capacities and failings as bearers of historical knowledge.

A Poetics of Wear and Tear

If the enigmatic ruins depicted on *DICTEE*'s original cover raise wide-ranging questions about the knowability of the past, then the work itself scrutinizes the adequacies of available means for representing the specific traumas of Korean history. Such issues are most explicitly highlighted in the section "CLIO HISTORY," where an early and oft-cited passage declares:

> Unfathomable the words, the terminology: enemy, atrocities, conquest, betrayal, invasion, destruction. They exist only in the larger perception of History's recording, that affirmed, admittedly and unmistakably, one enemy nation has disregarded the humanity of another. Not physical enough. Not to the very flesh and bone, to the core, to the mark, to the point where it is necessary to intervene, even if to invent anew, expressions for *this* experience, for this *outcome*, that does not cease to continue.
>
> To the others, these accounts are about (one more) distant land, like (any other) distant land, without any discernable features in the narrative, (all the same) distant like any other.
>
> This document is transmitted through, by the same means, the same channel without distinction the content is delivered in the same style: the word. The image. (32–33)

Emphatically underscoring the gap between history and "History's recording," this account critiques "the document" delivered by means of "the word" and "the image" whose role as distancing device allows the bracketing off and non-acknowledgement of a troubled and troubling history. In this mode, historiography violates the corporeality of historical actuality and its specificity, erasing the particularity of "*this* experience . . . this *outcome*," and abstracting it to a formulaic and generalized form of discourse "about (one more) distant land." Serving to categorize, contain, and dismiss that "distant land" as "other," this process ensures that its distress can be "[n]eutralized to achieve the no-response" (*DICTEE* 33).

An opening some pages later, at the end of "CLIO HISTORY," once more questions the capacities of "the word. The image" when a text and a photographic image on facing pages signal their own inadequacy as representations of a specific historical experience. This text and image, however, differ from "History's recording" in that rather than claiming to transparently deliver a formulaic form of historical knowledge, they work to emphasize their own unfathomability, their own failure to capture "*this* experience." The image depicts three human figures, tied, blindfolded, and standing in a line with outstretched arms on raised mounds of earth, faced by six other figures, some in uniform (see figure 7). This seems to be the scene of an execution; references to summary executions on previous pages and the phrase "[t]he decapitated forms" on the facing page reinforce this supposition. But beyond this, the text offers no specific context, articulating only "a longing in the face of the lost," reflexively suggesting that its own words may only gesture toward "the missing, the absent" rather than fill this gap with the fullness of an explanation. Who are these tied and blindfolded men? Why are they apparently about to be executed? Where and when is this event taking place? Without a caption or framing commentary, the photograph's connections to historical events are tenuous and imprecise to say the least. Like *DICTEE*'s cover image of archaeological ruins, this is a document of a historical reality that remains radically uncertain; it is, above all, this gap that is highlighted here.

Such a questioning of the representational adequacy of text and image bears comparison to related explorations in many works of conceptual and post-conceptual art. Cha's meditation on the problematic relations between text, photograph, and historical actuality resonates with works such as Joseph Kosuth's infamous *One and Three Chairs* (1965), a work that comprises a chair, a photographic image of that same chair, and a dictionary definition for the word "chair." By bringing attention to relations between text, image, and referent, this work might superficially seem to echo some of Cha's concerns because it puts the referentiality of its representations under

Misses nothing. Time, that is. All else. All things else. All other, subject to time. Must answer to time, except. Still born. Aborted. Barely. Infant. Seed, germ, sprout, less even. Dormant. Stagnant. Missing.

The decapitated forms. Worn. Marred, recording a past, of previous forms. The present form face to face reveals the missing, the absent. Would-be-said remnant, memory. But the remnant is the whole.

The memory is the entire. The longing in the face of the lost. Maintains the missing. Fixed between the wax and wane indefinite not a sign of progress. All else age, in time. Except. Some are without.

Figure 7. From *DICTEE* by Theresa Hak Kyung Cha, © 2001 The Regents of the University of California. Pages 38–9. Page 38 reprinted by permission of University of California, Berkeley Art Museum.

question. But Kosuth's allusion to Plato's theory of forms (neither the text, nor the image, nor the object are presented as the "real" chair) and his privileging of the transcendent art idea over the concrete realization of the work is clearly odds with Cha's desire to find a language that may provoke an affective rather than a "neutralized" abstracted response to a highly material history. Furthermore, Kosuth's more general insistence on the self-referring task of art, typified by his declaration "art's only claim is for art" (170), contrasts sharply with Cha's urgent need for an aesthetic mode capable of engaging wider social and political issues. Indeed, Cha's questioning of the referential capacities of text and image in *DICTEE* interrogates assumptions and preoccupations of early conceptual art such as Kosuth's. Her practice shares more with the work of a figure such as Martha Rosler, whose work sometimes appears in the same group exhibitions as Cha's because of these artists' Californian context and their shared interest in gender. Rosler's critique of documentary photography and the descriptive claims of language in a work such as *The Bowery in Two Inadequate Descriptive Systems* (1974) might be better described as post-conceptual (Alberro, "Reconsidering" xxviii). Rosler's work questions the ideology and power in its own means of representation in ways that many earlier conceptual artists such as Kosuth barely registered, let alone reflected upon.

The series of 45 panels that make up *The Bowery* juxtaposes lists of words and phrases connoting drunkenness with photographs of storefronts and shop doorways where itinerants and drunks have spent the night, leaving behind the detritus of drinking and drug taking. Rosler describes *The Bowery* as "a work of refusal" ("In, around" 322) because while it references a history of documentary photography, the absence of the drunks themselves in the pictures acknowledges and critiques the power relations at stake in the act of subjecting a victim to the camera's gaze. Interestingly, then, like Cha's overall project, these images revolve around absences and the concrete traces of past events. The list form adopted by the texts, meanwhile, eschews syntactical cohesion while the proliferation of terms points to their collective failure to adequately capture their subject, while also suggesting that such a plethora of synonyms locates the phenomena of drunkenness and destitution firmly within cultural and social relations (rather than as somehow exterior to "normal" society, as traditional social documentaries often imply). "If impoverishment is a subject here," states Rosler, "it is more centrally the impoverishment of representational strategies tottering about alone than that of a mode of surviving" ("In, around" 322). Both the photographs and the texts "are powerless to *deal with* the reality that is yet totally comprehended-in-advance by ideology" (322), and both are implicated in this ideology.

Anne Anlin Cheng has appositely described Cha's text as following an "anti-documentary" impulse, in that it critiques the epistemological assumptions of documentary and also its role in the "cultural 'rescue mission[s]'" so prevalent in minority discourse (120). As the example of Rosler's work suggests, Cha's reflections on documentary operated contiguously with those carried out by her contemporaries in the visual arts. Cha's project is, however, more personal and more pressing than Rosler's in *The Bowery*. *DICTEE* moves beyond the act of refusal to ask whether text and image can indeed be rendered "physical enough" to resonate with the visceral actuality of the history they investigate. As Shu-Mei Shih indicates, Cha's text seeks ways of addressing a history whose "materiality . . . escapes linguistic signification" (150). She goes on to suggest that *DICTEE*'s photographic images supply a "visual eloquence" (150) that counters the "impossibility of historiography (words) to capture history's concrete, material, physical, and above all bloody reality" (150). However, Shih's reading of Cha's images as somewhat transparent depictions of a historical reality misses their intransigence; the execution photograph, for one, demonstrates how the image as documentary evidence is no more "eloquent" than words. Yet Shih is right to detect in *DICTEE* an impulse toward an often visually manifested physicality that attests to a concrete historical actuality; however, this materiality is not necessarily pictorial and is often just as much a quality of printed language as of images.

In this respect, too, Cha's work resonates with the tenor of her aesthetic milieu and in particular with the work of Robert Smithson, another figure associated with the complex and diverse practices of conceptual art. In particular, Smithson's work, and especially his understanding of language, puts under pressure the definition of conceptualism as a "dematerialization of the art object" (Lippard). While, like other conceptual artists, Smithson emphasized process over product and interrogated institutionalized conventions of exhibiting, for him the process and placing of the work were still utterly material practices. When Cha was just beginning her studies at Berkeley, Smithson was in the process of constructing his famous *Spiral Jetty*, a work that as Craig Owens points out, is both "a graphic document, inscribed on the surface of the Great Salt Lake" (128), and a monumental sculpture, constructed out of "mud, salt crystals, rocks, water" (Smithson, *Spiral Jetty*). This is a work born out of Smithson's sense of an underlying affinity between writing and geological matter, language as "earthwords" (qtd. in Owens 120). In contrast to the view of language held by Kosuth, Smithson declares "My sense is that language is matter and not ideas" (*Collected* 61). Accompanying this 1967 statement is Smithson's exemplary work, *A Heap of Language*. In this work a series of handwritten lines, inscribed upon a piece of graph paper that measures their spatial dimensions, are piled up to resemble a pile of rubble. In a similar vein, his "Strata: A Geophotographic Fiction" (1972), interleaves blocks of fragmentary capitalized text, whose lines resemble the strata of the title, with horizontal photographic strips of fossils and rocks. In this manner the work presents printed language as an equivalent to geological matter. As Smithson puts it elsewhere, "Words and rocks contain a language that follows a syntax of splits and ruptures. Look at any *word* long enough and you will see it open up into a series of faults, into a terrain of particles each containing its own void" (*Collected* 107). For Smithson, printed language is primarily concrete and visual: something to be looked at. A shift of perceptual attention that acknowledges the physicality of printed matter might "open up" language to multiple alternative significations beyond the straightforwardly linguistic. It is precisely such a process of offering both words and images to be literally looked *at*, rather than seen *through*, that *DICTEE* proposes as a means of approaching the materiality of modern Korea's traumatic history.

Furthermore, Smithson's work brings into focus issues of documentation, representation, and reference pertinent to Cha's explorations of the knowability of history through its material remains, and the work's capacities to address this history. As Gary Shapiro indicates, Smithson's work in general, and *Spiral Jetty* in particular, raises the issue of "the difficulty of access" (5). *Spiral Jetty*, the earthwork, is built in a remote location only accessible by dirt tracks with the aid of an all-terrain vehicle and a detailed map. Furthermore, because of fluctuating water levels it has sometimes been underwater (especially in its early decades) and is only visible when water levels drop. The work, however, exists not only in the jetty itself but in the film *Spiral Jetty* (1970), made during the process of its construction, in photographs, and in the essay "Spiral Jetty" (1972), now published in Smithson's *Collected Writings*. Indeed, because the earthwork is so inaccessible, it can largely *only* be known through its documentation, so the essay and film are just as much the work as the earthwork. Moreover, they function not just as records but as parts of the work that are also, at the same time, reflections on this very process of documentation. The film, for example, ends with a shot of its own editing room in which hangs a photograph of the *Spiral Jetty*, drawing attention to the multiple acts of mediation that do not just record the work but actually constitute it.

One of *DICTEE*'s primary concerns is a related "difficulty of access," albeit to a traumatic and marginalized history rather than to a piece of land art. The text emphasizes the document's inadequacies for the task of conveying the reality of historical actuality. But in foregrounding the mediated nature of that history—and the failings of its documentation—the work reflects upon the very processes of representing this history. Many of its own documents make visible—often in very literal ways—the fault lines and lacunae of historical documentation; in so doing they offer reflections on the specific character and significance of these scissions and gaps for the particular history of modern Korea.

Fracture and fragmentation recur as historically oriented formal principles in numerous different ways throughout *DICTEE*. A midden heap of various documents, the text has much in common formally with a work like Smithson's "Strata" whose verbal and visual elements are piled upon the page like so many sedimentary layers, crosscut with syntactic and visual "splits and ruptures." But where Smithson's sensibility is geological, Cha's archaeo-poetic mode evinces close formal ties with filmic structures. Indeed, one of the ways in which Cha's long poem reshapes the collage form of the modernist epic is through its engagement with film. As Michael Davidson rightly points out, *DICTEE* is structured like a montage ("Hunting" 211), a formal technique rooted in her practice as a filmmaker and informed by an engagement with contemporary theoretical debates. Christian Metz, for example, with whom Cha worked in Paris, was interested in constructing a structuralist theory of "film language" based on the premise that the process of editing shots could usefully be compared to the process of constructing a linguistic structure like a sentence or, perhaps more accurately, a larger narrative. Such endeavors built on theories of montage such as those developed by early twentieth-century filmmaker Sergei Eisenstein, who saw montage as *the* defining feature of the art of film. For Eisenstein, montage was characterized "[b]y collision. By the conflict of two pieces in opposition to each other" (133). Eisenstein's emphasis on "collision" and "conflict" engendered characteristically tension-filled and frantically paced films such as his infamous *Battleship Potemkin*. The violent cuts and conflicting energies he both theorized and practiced resonate powerfully with the abrupt juxtapositions evident throughout Cha's book.

As shown in figure 7, Cha's text cuts between one montaged fragment and the next. The movement between these elements is made all the more abrupt by virtue of a shift between the different materialities of verbal and visual means of representation and the different kinds of attention they demand. This arrangement contravenes the conventional text-image relationship in which either words explain the image or the image illustrates the text; image and text are simply juxtaposed. While Smithson's "Strata" performs a similar move, the geological logic of his composition presents word and image as equivalent to one another. In contrast, *DICTEE*'s filmic "cut" places text and image on facing pages in an uneasy, even conflictual relationship. Such juxtapositions might be read as "collisions" of word and image in which, to deploy the words of Michel Foucault, "[w]e must . . . admit between the figure and the text a whole series of intersections—or rather attacks launched by one against the other, arrows shot at the enemy target, enterprises of subversion and destruction, lance blows and wounds, a battle" ("Pipe" 26). As Foucault's deliberations upon word/image relationships suggest, this "battle" stages a conflict between the activities of reading and seeing, or as W. J. T. Mitchell puts it, "between the (speaking) self and the (seen) other; between telling and showing; between 'hearsay' and 'eyewitness' testimony; between words (heard, quoted, inscribed) and objects or actions (seen, depicted, described); between sensory channels, traditions of representation, and modes of experience" (*Picture* 5). *DICTEE*'s text/image juxtapositions put such tensions into play. In the opening of the execution scene, for example, the process of reading the text from left to right and top to bottom and then viewing the image "at a glance" almost acts as a vindication of G. E. Lessing's dictum that verbal signs unfold in time and are experienced as a sequence while visual signs are spatial and experienced in terms of simultaneity. Furthermore, the text in this opening apparently reflects on its own capacity for temporal unfolding: "Time, that is. All else. All things else. All other, subject to time. Must answer to time, except" (38). Thus the text implicitly launches an "attack" on the image of the facing page, which can only capture a frozen moment of time; the photograph cannot relate, for example, whether its tied and blindfolded subjects were actually executed—it cannot indicate what happened next. At the same time, the image's capacity to show, to bring the likeness of a scene materially before the viewer, points to the text's inability to depict. Indeed, this particular piece of text is especially inadequate in this respect; its fragmented, frequently "Aborted" (38) sentences embody writing's constant pursuit of "the missing, the absent," the referents that words may gesture toward but never make present even in the form of an illusory likeness.

It is at sites of word/image intersection such as these that the principles of discord at the heart of Cha's collage technique are most palpable. As in Eisenstein's thinking, such a structural "battle" enacted between juxtaposed pieces has political as well as formal implications. Eisenstein saw the conflicts of montage as an embodiment of a Marxist dialectical process by which the energies of colliding elements not only ultimately combine to form a synthesized totality, but also "serve as impulses driving forward the total film" (134) in a process which echoed a progressive view of social history. But *DICTEE* repeatedly insists on its own status as a collection of fragmented "remnant[s]" (38) that resolutely refuse to cohere into a unified or coherent whole. Furthermore, any notion of a dialectical process "driving forward" the narrative of the work is repeatedly thwarted by *DICTEE*'s "cuts," which frequently diffuse any sense of momentum. As if to declare such a refusal of a forward-moving dialectical process, the text with which the execution scene is juxtaposed announces: "Fixed between the wax and wane indefinite not a sign of progress." As the ambiguous and jolting "indefinite" dropped into the center of this statement intimates, one of the most unsettling features of Cha's text/image juxtapositions and "cuts" more generally is an "indefinite" relation between the different elements and the absence of a sense of progression or dialectical resolution. Cha's technique constitutes a more radically disjunctive and anti-narrative form of montage than Eisenstein's model of collisions, or indeed Metz's notion of montage as an essentially narrative "film language." Having more in common with Benjamin's notion of the dialectical image, her text/image juxtapositions resist the developmental process of dialectical progression. Between the text and the image of the execution scene opening of *DICTEE*, both tenuous linkages and Eisensteinian "collisions" occur, but on the whole, the text and image seem simply to miss one another. The conflicts of the text/image battle are perhaps more glancing blows than the head-on collisions Eisenstein had in mind.

Just as Benjamin's notion of the dialectical image is a model for his historical thinking, Cha's disjunctive aesthetic method is intimately connected with *DICTEE*'s historical project. By cutting between fragmented narratives and uncaptioned photographs for example, between different modes of representation and different kinds of materiality, this work *embodies* the fractures of modern Korea's traumatic history: the oppressive Japanese occupation and colonization between 1910 and 1945; the post-war partition of north and south that placed an "incision" (*DICTEE* 79) across the country; the bloody Korean War fueled by Cold War agendas; the violent social unrest in South Korea during the 1960s, '70s and '80s under oppressive regimes; North Korea's continuing political isolation; and the ruptures of diaspora. In the wake of these events that are "not a sign of progress," *DICTEE* offers a kind of "cut-up" cultural memory of disjointed scraps, many of them "found texts" purloined from the rubble of this history. Like Benjamin before her, for Cha, "[t]o write history . . . means to *cite* history" (Benjamin, *Arcades* 476, N11, 3).

But *DICTEE* is just as interested in citing the gaps and disjunctions within and between its documents as in citing the documents themselves. The work's juxtapositions of text and image epitomize and dramatize a sense of fracture and dislocation endemic to Korean history. As the text facing the image of the execution scene puts it, "[t]he present form face to face reveals the missing, the absent." The literal "face to face" confrontation of text and image here opens up a gulf or rupture that might approximate a sense of "the missing, the absent" with which Cha's book is recurrently concerned. In the discomforting stuttering jumps between one montaged piece and another, and especially between one medium and another, inhere the ruptures, losses, and absences that—somewhat paradoxically—form the vital core of *DICTEE*'s sense of history.

Cha's text, then, returns time and again to confront the problems of representing a history characterized by "the missing, the absent." An important dimension of this project is the issue of historical silencing and the difficulty of articulating from a "subaltern" position (in Gayatri Spivak's sense). One of the ways in which Cha's archaeopoetics performs its work of archaeo-critique is by exploring the "epistemic violence" (Spivak, "Subaltern" 76) in which any attempt to articulate a colonial history is grounded. She does so by obsessively revisiting the problems—the impossibilities even—of speaking from a disempowered minority position; in common with Spivak, Cha is alert to the prohibitions placed on subaltern speech by colonial and patriarchal dynamics of power. One of *DICTEE*'s recurring tropes is that of "broken speech" (75); as has been commonly noted, this is a work characterized by a lack of fluency, and many of its pages record symbolically freighted struggles with verbal inarticulacy intimately tied to Cha's sense of her own position as an immigrant within American culture and as a woman in relation to the patriarchal cultures of both the United States and Korea. But the struggles with speaking repeatedly enacted in *DICTEE* also have very specific historical resonances; during Japan's colonization of Korea, the native language, Hangul, was suppressed as part of an aggressive project of cultural assimilation. During the latter stages of Japan's colonial project, Korean-language newspapers were banned, instruction in Hangul was abolished in schools, and Koreans were forced to adopt Japanese names (Nahm 192). The Korean subaltern subject, then, was quite literally silenced by colonial "epistemic violence."

In *DICTEE*, the multiply silenced Korean subject is embodied by the female figure of the section entitled "DISEUSE." This French term for a woman skilled in the professional performance of monologues is clearly an ironic title for this passage; the female figure here is hardly an articulate *diseuse*. Despite her desperate attempts, she fails to produce "speech," uttering only "Bared noise, groan, bits torn from words" (3), thwarted articulations that function as an analogue for the historical silencing during the Japanese occupation of Korea. Cha's text gestures toward the imposition of harsh penalties on those who dared break the colonial restrictions on Hangul: "The tongue that is forbidden is your own mother tongue . . . To utter each word is a privilege you risk by death. Not only for you but for all" (46). The inarticulacy of Cha's *diseuse* is an embodied reminder of the traumatic silencing embedded in Korean history.

If *DICTEE* represents processes of speaking as problematic, the relationship between the speaking subject (or perhaps more properly the subject struggling to speak) and the printed text is hardly untroubled. The text's persistently "broken speech" not only represents a multiply inscribed voicelessness, it also forms a critique of phonocentric models of writing. As Derrida has argued in *Of Grammatology*, dominant Saussurian models of semiotics based on a "metaphysics of presence" posit writing as a derivative of speech and thereby conceive of writing as an inscription that marks the presence of a speaking subject. This is an assumption that underpins much "minority literature"; for example, the *bildungsroman*, which charts a teleological process of "coming to voice," is prevalent in literatures that emerge from marginalized or disempowered communities. Henry Louis Gates Jr. has demonstrated that African American literature has been characterized by an "urgent need to make the text speak" (64); early slave narratives, for example, were attempts by their authors to write themselves individually and collectively into being as speaking subjects. But Gates usefully points out that underlying the "figure of the talking book" is a fundamental paradox. Because black people were positioned as "the 'lowest' of the human races" without a political voice, "[t]he trope of the talking book is not a trope of the presence of voice at all, but of its absence" (64). This absence of the black subject, Gates argues, is embedded in the English language, which aligns blackness with non-existence and lack, making "the attempt to represent what is not there, to represent that which is *missing* or absent" somewhat "untenable" (65).

DICTEE emerges from a quite different socio-historical context than that of the slave narrative. Although Cha's text positions its struggle with speech in relation to a literal historical prohibition of the native Korean language rather than a racially inflected metaphysical logic of presence and absence, it nevertheless labors under a comparable imperative to "make the book speak" at the same time that it is haunted by a history that makes "the presence of voice" problematic. For Cha, the imperative to acknowledge the untenability of a textual "coming to voice" is equal to the need to "make the book speak," because the failure to acknowledge the multiple inscriptions of voicelessness on its cultural history would amount to a failure to acknowledge its specificity: a suppression of some of its defining features. Here lies one of the central dilemmas of Cha's book: how does a writer articulate a cultural history in which both marginalization and literal silencing play such a large part? How does a book "speak" this history when a "coming to voice" would imply a transcendence of that history in ways that would too easily resolve and smooth over its haunting silences? *DICTEE* embodies an ethical obligation *not* to perform such a "coming to voice."

Like Spivak's famous essay "Can the Subaltern Speak?" then, Cha's text seems pessimistic about the prospects of recovering subaltern histories. But Spivak's notion of the epistemically suppressed subaltern "voice" is useful not only for the ways in which it points out the difficulty, or even the unfeasibility, of recovering suppressed histories, but also for the ways in which it indicates possibilities for their detection. In the course of her "Subaltern" essay, Spivak quotes Pierre Macherey on how one might identify a literary work's ideological workings:

> What is important in a work is what it does not say. This is not the same as the careless notion "what it refuses to say," although that would in itself be interesting: a method might be built on it, with the task of *measuring silences*, whether acknowledged or unacknowledged. But rather this, what the work *cannot* say is important, because there the elaboration of the utterance is carried out, in a sort of journey to silence. (qtd. in Spivak, "Subaltern" 81–82)

Going somewhat "against the grain" of Macherey's argument, Spivak proposes that something like the process of "measuring silences" and scrutinizing "what [the social text of imperialism] refuses to say," might constitute a methodology for a critique of imperialism. It might also, she obliquely suggests, provide an opening in which subaltern presences could be discerned: "When we come to the . . . question of the consciousness of the subaltern, the notion of what the work *cannot* say becomes important" (82). The subaltern might be "heard," Spivak implies, but only in a kind of speaking silence, as an almost spectral presence that manifests itself in what the text cannot say. The subaltern articulation can be looked for in the gaps and silences of history where it makes itself apparent in indirect ways, but it must not be subsumed to modes of articulation that threaten to symbolically perpetuate its oppression by smoothing over the difficulty of this articulation (hence Spivak's "difficult style" of writing) (Spivak, "Interview" 33).

In ways that are pertinent for Cha's project, Spivak's thought highlights some of the ethical questions involved in the recovery of suppressed histories and advocates a process of seeking submerged presences in absences, ruptures, and unspoken moments of resistance. This thinking proposes a mode of registering these indexical traces indirectly rather than subsuming them into already constituted discursive frameworks of knowledge and representation. Cha's engagement with the problems of speaking in *DICTEE* might be read as an aesthetic manifestation of a practice of "measuring silences," or perhaps more properly, the cracks and fissures of "broken speech." These fault lines and failures, breaks and inarticulacies, amount to a form of subaltern utterance that in Cha's book is embedded in the materiality of the written word. For Cha, the written word is a visually manifested presence of print that embodies a different kind of verbal-visual relation to the text/image juxtapositions deployed by *DICTEE*'s larger montage form. As W. T. J. Mitchell puts it, "Writing, in its physical, graphic form, is an inseparable suturing of

Aller à la ligne   C'était le premier jour   point
Elle venait de loin   point   ce soir au dîner   virgule
les familles demanderaient   virgule   ouvre les guillemets   Ça c'est bien passé le premier jour   point
d'interrogation   ferme les guillemets   au moins
virgule   dire le moins possible   virgule   la réponse
serait   virgule   ouvre les guillemets   Il n'y a q'une
chose   point   ferme les guillemets   ouvre les guillemets   Il y a quelqu'une   point   loin   point   ferme
les guillemets

Open paragraph   It was the first day   period
She had come from a far   period   tonight at dinner
comma   the families would ask   comma   open
quotation marks   How was the first day   interrogation mark   close quotation marks   at least to say
the least of it possible   comma   the answer would be
open quotation marks   there is but one thing   period
There is someone   period   From   a far   period
close quotation marks

Figure 8. First page of *DICTEE* by Theresa Hak Kyung Cha, © 2001 The Regents of the University of California. Reprinted by permission of University of California, Berkeley Art Museum.

the visual and the verbal, the 'imagetext' incarnate" (*Picture* 95). With the notable exception of some reproduced letters, handwritten notes, and Chinese characters, *DICTEE*'s printed language rarely strays too far from the norms of the conventional printed page. Yet Cha's subtle manipulation of printed language physically makes palpable the fissures that enable silences to be measured. In many of her textual manipulations we can detect close affinities with Smithson's notion of language as matter that, like geological matter, "follows a syntax of splits and ruptures," a material that, once engaged on a concrete level, might "open up into a series of faults, into a terrain of particles each containing its own void" (Smithson, *Collected* 107). For Cha, though, the physicality of language, and the making-palpable of its fractures, has very culturally and historically specific resonances.

A recurring technique in *DICTEE* is the physical "breaking" of the written word or sentence; it is through this technique that the text raises the possibility of "speaking" visually. The potential of such a graphically embodied "voice" is raised in the book's very first page, which presents itself as a record of a simultaneous dictation and translation exercise (see figure 8). Most immediately noticeable here is the "mistaken" rendering of punctuation marks as printed words, pointing to the transcriber's unfamiliarity with the rules of dictation and also to the gap between spoken words and graphic marks. The act of translation from French to English also emphasizes the incommensurability of languages, indicating what is lost in linguistic and cultural translation. The explicit gendering of the French disappears in the English version; the recurring rhymes between "point," "loin," and "moins" vanish, too. Throughout this page, double spaces between phrases and punctuation commands evince the ubiquitous presence of such gaps and losses, making this a visually perforated text. In this way, the graphic surface of the text "speaks" in a fractured graphic "voice" of the non-equivalence of voice and writing and of the stubborn non-translatability of languages. Furthermore, this graphic voice acts as an index for the experience of the "She" who "had come from afar," the stranger struggling to find her way through "the first day" in a new cultural situation. The textural textual surface of this page with its errors, approximations, non-equivalences, and gaps makes visible a sense of loss and disjunction by embodying these principles in its material form on the page.

Cha's technique of using visual gaps as a way of bodying forth inarticulacy and unfamiliarity owes much to her earlier work with film. In the performance piece "Pause Still" (1979), a work comprised of slide projections, narrative, and a series of bodily movements, Cha uses blank frames, what she calls the "specific, isolated time and space between two images," as a means of investigating "certain 'states,' 'holes in time,' memory—the ability and inability to recall, to reminisce." She writes, "[w]hile working with projected still images (slides), my concern has been the specific, isolated time and space between two images" ("Pause Still" n. pag.). The gap between slides or frames becomes a way to investigate memory, its capacities, and its "holes." As the large white space in the title "Pause Still" suggests, Cha's use of the blank frame in the earlier work finds its counterpart in the use of blanks and white spaces on the printed page, a technique that she employs throughout *DICTEE*. Like the blank frames of the film piece, visual gaps in the printed text function as "holes," failures of recall, cognition, and articulation, concrete manifestations of loss and absence.

Consider these lines from the verse section entitled "ALLER/RETOUR":

Day receding to dark
Remove light Re move sounds to far. To farther.
Absence full. Absence glow. Bowls. Left as they are.

Fruit as they are. Water in glass as beads rise to the rim.
Radiant in its immobility of silence.
As night re   veils the day.
(124)

The broken words "Re move" and "re   veils" here physically enact the all-pervasive occurrences of "Absence" and "silence" woven into these pages of stilted verse. The shared prefix "re" indicates a return or repetition that brings to mind processes of recovering some element of the past, while the interruptive visual gaps suggest a fissure or elision in these processes. The white spaces in "Re move" and "re   veils" literally evince what the writer Henri Raczymow, writing on memory and the Holocaust, has described as "Memory Shot Through With Holes" in an essay of that name. Despite its different cultural history, *DICTEE* shares this sense of a personal and collective memory whose "holes" do not just represent the wear and tear of time but rather indicate a past which violence and oppression has "shot through." Moreover, these holes are not consigned to the past but rather return to haunt the present of the "Memory less" (*DICTEE* 45). The gaps of "Re move," "re   veils," and "Memory less" embody an "Absence" or "silence" that returns from history to haunt the text of Cha's book.

Furthermore, the haunting that *DICTEE's* broken words physically enact generates a semantic haunting: the spaces between stems and affixes open particular words to a linguistic ghosting by which alternative meanings suggest themselves. "Re move" comes to indicate not only a taking away but also a renewed motion. "Memory less," broken apart, suggests not so much total amnesia as memory minus something. Meanwhile, "re   veils," which features a particularly large gap in its midst, accrues supplementary meanings almost in proportion to the size of the space inhabiting its center. This fractured word suggests most obviously an action of veiling again, but as "reveils" is neither a familiar word, nor to be found in the dictionary, it is perhaps just as easy to read as "reviles." This suggestion of verbal abuse, when read in relation to the "immobility of silence" (124) in the poem's previous line, corresponds to the sense of oscillation and power struggle between night and day, dark and light, going and returning, silence and enunciation in this page of verse. In addition, "re   veils" invokes the French *reveil*, meaning awakening or recovery, a possibility that would amount to a reversal of the implications of the line as a whole. Instead of describing a recurring cycle in which night falls, extinguishing the day, this last line of the page would designate a process by which night awakens the day, suggesting dawn rather than dusk. Furthermore, the invented word invariably invokes the term "reveals," which once again stands counter to a process of "reveiling." Ultimately, however, "re veils" and the line in which it occurs resist being read definitively in any of these ways. Instead, the fissure in the word's midst holds multiple possibilities in suspension, insisting on a sense of uncertainty and a refusal of resolution. The gap thus engenders a supplementary logic by which each empty white space indicates an absence while at the same time intimating something more, something extra in the processes of signification, a state that cannot be resolved.

The alternative and even contradictory meanings produced by the fractures of *DICTEE*'s broken words reveal the trace structure of language, the *trace* in Derridean parlance being the "presence" in every signification of that which is absent. Certainly, these aspects of Derrida's thought seem particularly apposite for an exploration of the ways in which Cha's "broken speech" negotiates a "Memory Shot Through With Holes" (Raczymow), although with more of an emphasis on the materiality of the trace than Derrida allows for. The multifarious gaps in Cha's text act as markers for what is absent or missing while also generating a proliferation of meaning. I do not want to simplistically suggest, however, that the supplement, the "something extra" in Cha's text acts as consolation for that which is missing, that the proliferation of meaning would compensate for the "holes" that haunt the work. Rather, as Derrida's notion of the supplement suggests, the "something more" in the text is always in play with a lack and thus unravels the dichotomy of presence and absence. *DICTEE*'s many broken words both embody the absences and silences that haunt Cha's version of Korean diasporic history and at the same time they "speak" visually via a graphic voice that concretely manifests speaking silences and invokes absent presences.

By the time Cha wrote *DICTEE*, she had already spent many years exploring in her performance and film works the possibilities and problems of investigating voice through visual materiality as well as the difficulties of articulating a fraught cultural history. This body of work shows Cha experimenting with formal disjunctions, fractures, and gaps in ways that parallel many of *DICTEE*'s techniques. But she was also frequently interested in the muffling effects of a degraded materiality; in this respect it is useful to examine an example of Cha's earlier work that helps to illuminate similar strategies adopted in her later work. In an eight-minute black-and-white video entitled *Mouth to Mouth* (1975), Cha experimented with the capacities of the new medium of video, particularly its propensity toward static and interference, in ways that correspond with some of her visual tactics in *DICTEE*. *Mouth to Mouth* is one of the few works in Cha's oeuvre in which she explores her native language, Hangul, a language with a very specific history and guiding philosophy. Conceived as a phonetic alphabet, Hangul was created under King Sejong in the fifteenth century with the intention of creating a system that was better able to express not only the spoken language but also the feelings and thoughts of Koreans than the Chinese script in use at the time. The letter shapes of Hangul are designed around the physical act of speaking and with the relationship between the self, the world, and the divine in mind; the consonants mimic the shapes of the speech organs used to pronounce them, namely the tongue, lips, teeth, and throat, while the vowels consist of differing configurations of three elements: a vertical line signifying the upright figure of the human, a horizontal line signifying the earth, and a dot (which evolved into a short line) signifying the round heaven (see, for example, Sohn 13). The written form of Hangul, then, is not only intimately connected to the act of speaking, claiming a mimetic relation to the corporeal act of producing sound, but also has embedded within it the idea that language is a quite literal description of the human in relation to the earth and the divine. Furthermore, Hangul has as its very *raison d'être* the belief that a Korean way of being in the world could not be represented in a "foreign" script such as Chinese.

Cha's video begins by panning across nine Hangul vowel graphemes. The various combinations of the three elements indicating the human, the earth, and heaven suggest particular ways of speaking one's presence in the world.[1] This is followed by close-up shots of a mouth carefully and painstakingly forming six different sounds in succession; presumably these are the sounds of Hangul vowels, but the shots are accompanied not by the sounds of a voice sounding them but by birdsong and the sound of running water, fading in and out. However, the overriding visual and acoustic dimension of this video is the incessant, although fluctuating, presence of video static (see figure 9). This unremitting white noise overlays the image of the speaking mouth and the sounds of the natural world, a combination that might otherwise work to posit the vowel phonemes as speaking a state of nature and Hangul as a "natural," unmediated expression of a pure, authentic Korean culture.

The intrusive force of these effects recall practices of physically painting on, scratching, and marking film in many of Stan Brakhage's works and also in Carolee Schneemann's sexually explicit *Fuses* (1965), both of which bring attention to the materiality of the film medium, denaturalizing it. However, Cha's video deploys the medium's properties in a manner more akin to Joan Jonas's *Vertical Roll* (1972), which uses an interrupted electronic signal to render the frames of the film visible. This "vertical roll" unremittingly thumps across the image (accompanied by a harsh rhythmic banging sound), interrupting the process of viewing the female body depicted in the film and highlighting the symbolic violence of its normally naturalized cultural mediation. In Cha's film, the overwhelming static at times completely blots out the speaking mouth and the sounds of birdsong and trickling water, signal-

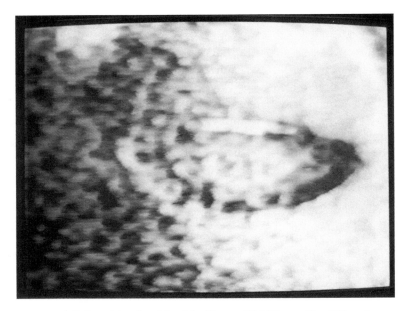

Figure 9. Still from *Mouth to Mouth* by Theresa Hak Kyung Cha. Video, © 1975 University of California, Berkeley Art Museum/Pacific Film Archive. Reprinted by permission of University of California, Berkeley Art Museum.

ing an erasure of language and culture as well as recalling once more the historical suppression of Hangul under Japanese colonial rule. In this way, Cha presents the ideal of a fullness of being in language as always already lost. Indeed, it is video static rather than the sounds or shapes of Hangul that very quickly becomes the central defining feature and primary medium of this work. Cha's preparation materials for *Mouth to Mouth* show that she had initially entitled this work *White Snow*, a working title that points to the primacy of the video medium's particular form of interference ("*Mouth to Mouth* Documentation"). In the fully realized work, the very processes of interference and muffling by the materiality of the medium become the means by which the work articulates processes of linguistic, cultural, and historical loss.

The physical motions performed by *Mouth to Mouth*'s disembodied mouth recall the struggles of *DICTEE*'s "DISEUSE." Indeed, when in the section of *DICTEE* entitled "ELITERE LYRIC POETRY," the *diseuse* is invoked once more, the text quite explicitly makes a pun of *diseuse* and "*disuse*" (133). What suffers "*From disuse*" in the processes of foreign language acquisition and in the efforts to "mimick[ ] the speaking" (3) in French and English, and is conspicuously largely absent from the pages of *DICTEE* itself, is Cha's own

Figure 10. Hangul inscription: Frontispiece of *DICTEE* by Theresa Hak Kyung Cha. University of California Press, 2001.

"mother tongue" (46). Hangul itself appears only once in Cha's book, in the form of an image facing the title page (see figure 10). The Hangul characters inscribed in this image appear without translation or explanation. Yet even if the inscription is understood or translated, the characters remain, in a sense, *"Dead words"* in a *"Dead tongue . . . Buried"* (*DICTEE* 133). According to Shelley Sunn Wong, the inscription reads "Mother. I miss you. I am hungry. I want to go home" (107) and was taken from a coal mine in Japan to which Korean workers were forcibly imported during the colonial period. Not only is this inscription literally "Buried" within the earth, but because of the restriction of Hangul under the Japanese it is also a written representation of a "forbidden tongue" (*DICTEE* 46) that had to remain submerged within the muteness of the "tongue tied" colonized Korean subject.

DICTEE's image of Hangul characters testifies to processes of muffling and loss on many levels, but it is the image's material qualities that signal these processes most powerfully. Firstly, as Rosalind Krauss indicates, the graffiti mark is characterized by its concrete, indexical, and elegiac qualities:

With the graffito, the expressive mark has a substance made up of the physical residue left by the marker's incision: the smear of graphite, the stain of ink, the welt thrown up by the penknife's slash. But the form of the mark—at this level of "expression"—is itself peculiar; for it inhabits the realm of the clue, the trace, the index. Which is to say the operations of form are those of marking an event . . . even at the time the marker strikes, he strikes in a tense that is over. . . . He delivers his mark over to a future that will be carried on without his presence. (259–60)

The graffiti depicted as *DICTEE*'s frontispiece belongs precisely to this "realm of the clue . . . trace . . . index." The slanting lines of hurried inscription materially evince the furtiveness and urgency of this dangerous act of graffiti when, if to speak Hangul "is a privilege you risk by death" (Cha, *DICTEE* 46), then to etch it on the walls of a Japanese mine is undoubtedly a risky enterprise. These marks also indicate the absence and anonymity of the inscribing hand, the hand that "strikes in a tense that is over." But in Cha's rendering of the Hangul inscription, this indexically signified sense of loss is heightened by the reproductive medium's physical qualities, which almost entirely eclipse the forms of the inscription's scratched words. Resembling an overexposed photograph or a bad photocopy, this high-contrast printing renders the scratches, scrapes, and fissures of the writing surface as blobs of white whose signifying potential is as powerful as that of the written characters, particularly for readers unfamiliar with Hangul. Comparable to "the smear of graphite, the stain of ink, the welt thrown up by the penknife's slash," these marks of poor quality reproduction are the "physical residue" left not by the "marker's incision" but by the processes of this document's transmission. Nevertheless, "the operations of form are those of marking an event." Like the white noise of the video medium in *Mouth to Mouth*, the high-contrast blobs, scrapes, and splashes of the reproduced image become a central part of the document's signifying processes, literally enacting a muffling of Cha's own "mother tongue" (*DICTEE* 46). In this way, the deteriorations of the medium perform physical acts that in themselves indexically register a process of disintegration and distancing that materially amplifies the effect of this articulation of loss.

Elsewhere in *DICTEE*, the degraded image embodies other kinds of suppression. The first opening of the section entitled "CLIO HISTORY" (see figure 11) contains a photograph of a young woman, Yu Guan Soon, facing a text that reports the bald facts of her short life. The narrative following this opening indicates that Soon was an activist involved in the Korean independence movement who was arrested following her participation in a wave of uprisings, the most notorious being a mass demonstration held on March 1, 1919. This demonstration was suppressed by military force, resulting in a massacre and tens of thousands of arrests. The material quality of Soon's image, though, signals an anxiety about the memory of this martyred child revolu-

YU GUAN SOON

BIRTH: By Lunar Calendar, 15, March 1903
DEATH: 12, October, 1920. 8:20 A.M.

She is born of one mother and one father.

Figure 11. From *DICTEE* by Theresa Hak Kyung Cha, © 2001 The Regents of the University of California. Pages 24–5. Reprinted by permission of University of California, Berkeley Art Museum.

tionary. The image's heavily pixelated surface suggests that it derives from a reproduced and much-enlarged newspaper cutting. The resulting grainy mechanical quality flattens out the young woman's features, making them seem hurriedly sketched, while flaws and high-contrast blobs introduced by reproduction interfere further with the clarity of the image. These marks function like Roland Barthes's *punctum*, that aspect of the photograph "which pricks me (but also bruises me, is poignant to me)" (27). For Barthes, the *punctum* is often held in a material detail, more particularly in an accidental or incidental detail that holds an affective charge though its meaning cannot be entirely explained. The *punctum* thus performs an archaeopoetic function, embodying in aesthetic form a charge or spark of recognition that also raises questions about the processes involved in recovering the past. Resonating strongly with Cha's archaeopoetics of fractures and gaps, Barthes's notion of the *punctum* as "sting, speck, cut, little hole" (Barthes 27) foregrounds incision, fracture, and loss encountered both as physical detail and affective response. For Barthes, there is a process of memorialization at work but it cannot appropriate the inscrutable detail to a broader conceptual schema or code: "[w]hat I can name cannot really prick me" (51). The *punctum*'s affect operates outside of established frames of reference. In the image of Soon in Cha's book, the ragged definition of the young woman's features and the printing errors that invade the picture act collectively as the *punctum*, signaling in very literal and physical ways not only the erasure of the specificities and potentials of this woman's life with her execution but also her elision from official narratives of Korean history. The material qualities of the image testify to what is not and cannot be known of her. Like the *punctum*, this image suggests, Soon herself is a lacuna in historical cognition.

The reproduced mass media feel of the photograph suggests that Soon's image occupied—however briefly—the public domain of media circulation, but its degraded material qualities evince a collective forgetting, or a failure of acknowledgement. Indeed, Soon's name is largely absent from historical accounts of the independence movement, which are generally dominated by male names. She is pictured here in the process of disappearing into the graininess and the ephemerality of a newspaper cutting. Like the "5,000 years of [Korean] history . . . lost . . . to the Japanese" (28) referred to in the section's following narrative, her memory is caught in the process of vanishing beneath the tumult of Korean history: the Japanese colonial occupation, Cold War partition and the subsequent disastrous war, emigration, and exile. Moreover, the tale of this young woman is muffled by male-dominated Korean nationalist narratives, and she is all but invisible, Cha feels, to an unconcerned global community for whom Korea itself, despite being so deeply affected by world affairs and by the policies of superpowers such as the United States, largely remains an unrecognized corner of the world and a forgotten chapter of history.

The affective "prick" of the *punctum* also occurs in the relation on these pages between text and image. The placing of Yu Guan Soon's image facing the token summary lines that sketch her life and death induces an experience like that described by Barthes on observing a photograph of a young man in a prison cell waiting to be hanged: "the *punctum* is: *he is going to die.* I read at the same time: *This will be* and *this has been*; I observe with horror an anterior future of which death is the stake. By giving me the absolute past of the pose (aorist), the photograph tells me death in the future. What *pricks* me is the discovery of this equivalence" (96). We might detect here a parallel with Benjamin's dialectical image, "wherein what has been comes together in a flash with the now" (*Arcades* 462, N2a, 3). What Barthes's notion of the *punctum* reveals, however, is the affective charge of this "flash" of recognition. *DICTEE*'s presentation of Yu Guan Soon's life also "tells . . . death in the future." The combination of text and image on these pages unavoidably becomes a "discovery" of the death that the text tells us has already happened even though it has yet to happen in the photograph.

However, despite Barthes's claim, neither text nor image can claim "equivalence" to the death they purportedly record and foretell. Indeed, the combination of text and image point to the glaring inadequacy of "the word. The image" to the task of articulating the historical specificities toward which Cha's text refers a few pages later. This image/text composite is as close as

Cha comes to providing a caption for one of her images, but here image and text grate against one another. The text both provides too little information and too much apparently extraneous detail, mostly of a familial, personal nature. The disintegrating image, meanwhile, especially in its material details, tells a different story of a public and political if largely unacknowledged and forgotten life, which jars with the personal statistics on the facing page. As in the badly reproduced image of Hangul that makes up *DICTEE*'s frontispiece, the degraded materiality of the image of Soon indicates the capacity of the photograph not just to embody traces of memory but also to lay bare as tangible fact failures of historical recall. Cha redeploys the intrusions of mechanical means of production to make these processes of simultaneous remembering and forgetting indexically tangible. The aesthetic qualities of these images, and their relations and non-relations with textual inscription, perform processes of muffling and interference that physically resonate with specific losses and scissions of Korean history.

Strata of Semantic Potentials

Cha's archaeopoetics of gaps and disintegration both tests the capacities of her aesthetic materials and transforms their failings into tangible traces of the fractures and silences of Korean history. In so doing, the work performs a critique of quite particular power relations and their legacies in contemporary modes of knowing and representing that history. A further dimension of *DICTEE*'s archaeocritique may be discerned in the way this work raises even wider questions about the activity of historical recovery. Cha's text correlates with a Benjaminian messianic stance that seeks out the potentials for new kinds of meaningfulness within the fragmented ruins of the past. In so doing, it also investigates the possibilities, limitations, and nuances of such a "redemptive" model of history in the light of the particular traumatic past it negotiates. This dimension of the work has particular relevance for the fields of Asian American and postcolonial studies, which have readily adopted Cha's text. As Cheng points out, "[t]he desire to know and bear witness as some kind of 'redemptive' act has fueled much of the recent academic moves to recognize and understand the various histories and forms of colonization" (120). Cheng argues that *DICTEE*'s formal strategies resist this redemptive "desire," which she correlates with the documentary mode. I want to suggest, however, that Cha does participate in a redemptory activity if we understand this in Benjaminian terms, but she does so in ways that also offer critical reflections on the recuperative impulse.

One way in which this dimension of Cha's historicist project might be productively explored is through a focus on her technique of palimpsestual layering. Her film work of the late 1970s became increasingly interested in various kinds of palimpsest. In works such as *Other Things Seen Other Things Heard (Aillures)* (1978), she mixed slide projection with performance, moving her own body in and out of the projected image, while in *Exilée* (1980) Cha combined video and film by embedding a video monitor in the film screen, thus producing a composite layered image. Many of Cha's films of this time consisted of a series of still images combined by lap dissolves rather than single moving images, a technique for which a work such as Chris Marker's *La Jetée* acts as a ready point of reference. One such work, *Passages Paysages* (1978), is made up entirely of dissolves arranged as three different series of still images shown simultaneously on three monitors, accompanied by two different soundtracks, emitted from the far left and far right monitor and comprising interwoven voices, music, and spells of silence.[2] *Passages Paysages* is, then, a multiply layered piece; not only are there three series of images played simultaneously, but sounds often overlap and images create a palimpsestual effect when each dissolves into the next. As the title indicates, the constantly shifting images and acoustic effects of this work explore migratory processes, passages from one terrain or landscape (*paysage*) to another. Images of rooms, crumpled sheets, landscapes, bundles of letters, and typeset and handwritten French and English words succeed, superimpose, and play against one another, describing different kinds of cultural spaces and objects. The work's multiple voices, meanwhile, speaking in English and Hangul, enact a similar process of formal and cultural layering, and often meditate on the very processes of moving between languages as well as on memory and forgetting.

While a sense of fracture, loss, and displacement infuses *Passages Paysages*, this filmwork also articulates an aspiration to form a "memory bond," as a voice in the work itself puts it, by combining "layer upon layer" the material "embers" (*Passages Paysages*) of lives lived in transition across cultures, languages, and eras. As these snatches of speech from the film suggest, the palimpsestual form of this work enacts a process of recomposition and rearticulation, forging new forms from the scraps of a fragmentary diasporic existence. While Cha's work seems to refuse consolatory gestures, it exemplifies a Benjaminian model of redemptive history in its recovery and redeployment of cultural fragments. Benjamin sees history in terms of an Adamic fall, an ongoing "catastrophe" that leaves behind a "wreckage" of cultural ruins (*Illuminations* 249) whose remains must be sifted through to recover shards or "spark[s] of hope in the past" (247). In *Passages Paysages*, the physical layering of multiple such "embers" aims at a combining or accretion of the "spark[s] of hope" held within the fragments of a broken history. By means of such palimpsestual strategies, Cha hopes to "retrouver les passages—of memory" ("Preparation Materials for *Passages Paysages*"), to open up lost pathways to the past and thus enable history's latent and fragmented possibilities to infuse the present moment of viewing with potentially transformative sparks of promise.

Cha's recuperation of cultural "embers" resonates with what Jürgen Habermas refers to as Benjamin's rescue of "semantic potentials" or "semantic energies" (120, 112). An emphasis on the physicality of these traces, though, works to extend the notion of "semantic energies" to include forms of material meaningfulness that resist incorporation into straightforwardly linguistic notions of semantics. *DICTEE* aims to recover, then, "energies" that are perhaps not uncomplicatedly "semantic" in the usual sense of the term but carry unfulfilled potentials that extend what we might understand as meaningful. The attempt to make these "semantic energies" (Habermas 112) and their redemptory promise visible can be discerned, for example, in Cha's frequent meditation upon slippages between languages, most particularly the printed forms of English and French that occur throughout her oeuvre, including *DICTEE*. These languages, implicated in the operations of imperialism and the experiences of migration and exile, are sites of rupture in her work. And yet such fractures play a key role both in Cha's particular sense of cultural memory and in a Benjaminian project of seeking the past's thwarted potentials precisely in its fissures. Furthermore, Cha's French/English wordplays participate in an activity of layering comparable to that in *Passages Paysages*, whose palimpsestual principle aims at an accretion of "semantic energies."

Consider an example from *DICTEE*'s "ERATO LOVE POETRY" section, where the influence of filmic works such as *Passages Paysages* is very much in evidence. This section layers and interweaves multiple narratives. Many of its scenes focus on cinematic experience and are narrated as if viewed on the screen or through the lens of the camera. In one scene echoing the "Mouth moving" of the earlier video work *Mouth to Mouth*, a female speaker "shapes her lips accordingly, gently she blows whos and whys and whats. On verra. O-n. Ver-rah. Verre. Ah. On verra-h. Si. S-i. She hears, we will see" (97–99). The promise "On verra"/ "we will see" corresponds to the expectation of literal seeing provoked by the filmic narrative, but it also hints at the possibility of a visionary experience articulated by the overlap of languages. The homonymic wordplay between "verra" and "Verre. Ah" invokes the association between vision and understanding; the combining of "Verre" (glass) with the exclamatory "Ah" suggests transparency, clarity, and sudden comprehension. By means of language's affinities and happy accidents, this play on words heralds a forthcoming moment of lucidity that seems to inhere precisely in the "semantic potentials" (Habermas 120) of this layering of languages. Performing a series of linguistic slippages that are structurally similar to the lap dissolves in *Passages Paysages*, the speaking mouth shifts from "On verra" through "Si"—both affirming and announcing the contingency of the initial statement—to an English phrase containing a homonym of "Si" and a translation of "On verra," "we will see." Semantic sparks arising from these movements between languages gesture toward the presence of what Benjamin, in his essay "The Task of the Translator," calls "pure language" (*Illuminations* 74) or the "one true language" (76). This "pure language," for Benjamin, emerges in the processes of translation, in the simultaneous "kinship" (73) and "foreignness" (75) of languages that reveal "the hidden seed" (75) of "that which is meant in all languages" (80). This "hidden seed" is similar to the "spark" or "chip" of messianic possibility that dwells in the ruins of history—both Benjamin's view of language and his view of history being highly influenced by Kabbalistic thought—and is similarly charged with redemptory potential. Indeed, Cha's layering of language seems to pursue something very like this "hidden seed," an irreducible something glimpsed in the slippage of languages that cannot be assimilated to existing symbolic structures but which might, like a seed, generate something new. This spark hints at a kind of understanding that transcends language, a redemptory moment of visionary insight.

The Benjaminian model of historiography with which Cha's archaeological activities have such strong affinities is not, however, without its critics. Considering such reservations in relation to Cha's text thus offers opportunities to reflect on the wider stakes of such redemptive aesthetic projects, even when their mode of "redemption" is to be understood in complex and qualified terms. For example, literary theorist Leo Bersani critiques Benjamin's contribution to what he calls "the culture of redemption." Literary art in the modern period, he says, has been commonly ascribed a compensatory function for a historical sense of "damaged or valueless experience" (1) emerging from the traumatic shock of "the apocalyptic nature of our own modernity" (48). He is highly critical of "apparently acceptable views of art's beneficently reconstructive function in culture" based on a Benjaminian messianism because they "depend on a devaluation of historical experience and of art. The catastrophes of history matter much less if they are somehow compensated for in art, and art itself gets reduced to a kind of superior patching function" (1). Bersani certainly has a point; as his vocabulary powerfully indicates, to suggest that art may act as a salve to historical trauma both implies that history's catastrophes may be compensated for—and thus resolved and ultimately dismissed as "past" and "over"—and it risks instrumentalizing art, turning it into a tool for historical repair. To what extent does the redemptory impetus of *DICTEE* fall prey to this danger?

While a messianic impulse is part of *DICTEE*'s project of cultural recuperation, the work also reflectively emphasizes the limitations of its own redemptory impulses. A central way in which *DICTEE* performs this move is precisely through its treatment of implied moments of transcendent vision, such as in the scene of linguistic exchange in "ERATO." The notion of redemptory visionary insight appears again, in a different form, in *DICTEE*'s epiphanic ending where the promise of visionary enlightenment accompanies a narrated imminent moment of literal seeing. Set at "early dusk or dawn" (179), this scene represents a moment of change when shifting light symbolizes a process of transformation. Throughout the passage, a child repeatedly demands "Lift me up to the window," anticipating the prospect of visually witnessing a moment of change that not only promises to bestow "vision" upon the beholder but also to "lift[ ] the immobile silence" (179) that recurrently haunts *DICTEE*. The narrative moves impressionistically toward a final long sentence in which the child's desire to see "the picture image" also becomes a command to "unleash the ropes" that bring forth the sound of "bells." This sound not only forms "a peal" but also an "a[p]peal" to the possibility of transformative change, when the hidden may be perceived and the silenced may gain a voice.

Significantly, this passage constitutes a metaphorical "window" that offers a moment of illuminating vision; it also physically embodies the shape of a window on the page. The shaping of the text into a perfect square appears so vital to its articulation of visionary promise that it overrides grammatical concerns; in order to achieve the precise alignment of the final period with the right-hand margin, the expected "the" of the phrase "a peal to sky" is dropped. Yet, throughout this passage is hardly a smooth, grammatically correct articulation of imminent enlightened vision; in its last lines especially the narrative falters as it approaches the moment of "vision" so that the particularly conspicuous absence of the expected definite article at the passage's end is only really the culmination of a radical stumbling in the face of the expected climactic moment. Furthermore, this block of writing visually resembles not so much a "pane" as a semi-opaque screen or veil. Thus *DICTEE*'s final testimonial fragment both proffers and withholds a redeeming moment of transformative vision by means that are simultaneously linguistic and material, verbal and visual.

Through moves such as these, *DICTEE* materially resists reduction to "a kind of superior patching function." Indeed, as I have argued throughout this chapter, this is a work that leaves its gaps, fractures, and wounds unresolved and unhealed. But this text also offers ways of revealing some of the problems of Bersani's polemic against the redemptory claims made for art. A central difficulty with his argument is that it hinges on a splitting-off of art from any kind of cognition. Bersani ascribes the redemptive role of art not to the works themselves but to a critical culture of redemption. "[*T*]*he corrective virtue of works of art,*" he asserts, "*depends on a misreading of art as philosophy.* Art, as Plato rightly saw, cannot have the unity, the identity, the stability of truth; it does not belong to the world of perfectly intelligible ideas" (2). Bersani thus disavows the possibility that art might be capable of functioning as a mode of thinking. True, a work of art such as *DICTEE* "does not belong to the world of perfectly intelligible ideas," but does this necessarily mean it cannot constitute a form of cognition or philosophy? My broad claim in this book that poetry performs the work of archaeocritique refutes such a notion. Indeed, I would argue that to position art and cognition as mutually exclusive is to perpetuate just the sort of excision of art from rational modernity described by J. M. Bernstein in a move that delegitimizes art—and its forms of "sensory encounter"—as a mode of cognition (*Against* 7). Art, Bersani asserts, cannot legitimately function as a corrective to history because it exists in its own autonomous domain. But by trying to rescue art from its "devaluation" as a redemptive tool, he strips it of any capacity for cultural and historical critique. Yet work like Cha's *DICTEE* does indeed function as a mode of cognizing not only a traumatic history but also the problems of articulating it. Furthermore, it embodies and reflects upon the very problems of redemption that Bersani discusses by means of a sensuous materiality and a concomitant investigation into the politics of sensory encounter that his argument would consign to an autonomous and mute realm of art.

Cha's simultaneous offering and withholding of redemptive vision in her epiphanic last page is one instance of such an aesthetically embodied critical reflection on a messianic stance. These issues are investigated further via a more complex move in *DICTEE*'s "ERATO LOVE POETRY" section. This section splices together a number of different narratives across a particularly intricate page layout. The main narrative, concerning the visual pursuit of a woman as an object of the filmic gaze, is printed only on the verso (left-hand) side, while the recto (right-hand) pages contain other scenes and narratives. Despite thematic correspondences and even textual repetitions across facing pages, reading this section is unarguably a fragmentary experience. Whether following a conventional reading pattern that tackles each page in numbered sequence and moves across the pages from top to bottom through the alternating chunks of text, or tracking one narrative across the verso pages before turning back to follow the recto side sections in sequence, the process of reading and the flow of narrative are invariably interrupted by the textual layout, the large white gaps on each page, and the constant splicing of storylines. Recall Cha's palimpsestual and multi-channel filmworks and the logic of this layout becomes clearer. The two sides of the opening function like a split screen, with each side moving along a separate narrative trajectory. Meanwhile, the relation between facing pages echoes the lap dissolve. The two sides of each opening are connected in a visual dialogue: text on one side is "answered" by white space on the other side; in a sense, each opening describes the fading in and out of a dissolve. However, the dissolve only literally occurs when the pages are closed, when the "split screen" of the opening physically becomes the layered text with one page overlaying the last. In this position, text and white space would interlace to create one solid block of text with no overlaps or gaps, but when the pages are opened to be read, the invisibly interwoven text pulls apart to form two related but disjunctive and fragmented bodies of text. This visual dialogue gestures toward an imaginary plenitude, a wholeness of vision or a vision of wholeness that could only occur when the writing is removed from sight by closing the book or in the mind's eye as an imaginary process in which visual language floats free from the page. Furthermore, as Joan Retallack points out in her reading of these pages, "this text will never be one. When the book is closed the interfacing type will always face in opposite directions" (125). As a result the imaginary "image" of wholeness is haunted by fragmentation, and its intimations of plenitude touch only "the emptiness of the other (opposite) page" (Retallack 125).

Importantly, both *DICTEE*'s final epiphanic passage and its "ERATO LOVE POETRY" section tie the promise of a redemptive visionary moment to literal activities of seeing. Like Benjamin, Cha links the promise of new forms of knowledge to the "flash" of the image and its potential to produce a "now of particular recognizability" (*Arcades* 463, N3, 2). Also like Benjamin she draws on an obvious fascination with film and photography; but Cha's involvement not only with the practices of image-making but also with contemporary theories of the image constitutes a much more circumspect treatment of optical experience. What the "ERATO" section makes clear are the operations of power and domination in processes of seeing. Cha's familiarity with French film theory and semiotics as a student in the 1970s and her later editing of *Apparatus*, which collected together cutting-edge essays of film theory of the time, demonstrate an awareness of critiques of the gaze and "scopic regimes" conducted by theorists such as Barthes, Baudry, and Metz with whom she worked in Paris. The narrative of a voyeuristic pursuit of the female subject by a cinematic gaze in "ERATO" suggests that she was also well-versed in the gendered dimensions of these debates. A feminist engagement with the status of the female body in Western art and the power relations of the "scopic regimes" within which this body functioned was a prominent dimension of performance and post-conceptual art of the 1970s. Well-known examples include Carolee Schneemann's performance *Interior*

Scroll (1975), Joan Jonas's aforementioned video *Vertical Roll* (1972), Martha Rosler's photomontage *Hot House, or Harem* (1967–72) constructed entirely from images found in *Playboy* magazine, and Eleanor Antin's project *Carving: A Traditional Sculpture* (1972) in which she photographed her naked body every day during a 45-day regime of strict dieting. Similarly, Cha's narrative about the pursuit of a woman in "ERATO" is conducted with an acute sense of the power relationships between the gaze of the camera and its feminine object; as Laura Mulvey notoriously put it, "In a world ordered by sexual imbalance, pleasure in looking has been split between active/male and passive/female. The determining male gaze projects its fantasy on the female figure which is styled accordingly" (750). "ERATO" knowingly charts these processes of projection and styling; "One expects her to be beautiful," the narrative announces, before stalking its female quarry, building up the "anticipation" of her visual image, tracking her presence "through her things, that are hers," tracing her absent body in her "dress," which "hangs on a door," constructing her image "without actually seeing, actually having seen her" (98, 100). The moment of "actually seeing" is recurrently deferred, though, and when the narrative does "catch sight" of a "her" (the same "her"?) the anticipated pleasure of seeing is absent. Furthermore, references to "whiteness," "white mist," and "snow" (94–119) signal an increasing impediment of sight and prefigure the eventual disappearance of the woman pursued by the camera's gaze. Cha's narrative both makes visible and refuses the power structures at work in the processes of looking, eventually enabling her female character to "leave[ ] the frame . . . leave[ ] them empty" (114) and escape the intrusive gaze of the viewer in a symbolic assertion of agency.

Cha's "ERATO" section also critiques the power relations of the gaze by pointedly enacting a failure of filmic suture. Defined by Kaja Silverman as "the procedures by means of which cinematic texts confer subjectivity on their viewers" (195), techniques of suture mask the mechanical operations of the camera, inviting an identification between viewer and the (invariably masculine structured) gaze of the film's characters. By including such camera directions as "Extreme Close Up shot of her face" and "camera begins to pan" (96), *DICTEE* foregrounds the mechanics of the camera's gaze, declining to suture its readers into an approximation of visual fantasy. Furthermore, as this section visually demonstrates, *DICTEE* also literally fails to physically suture its own various parts together. Just as the camera directions of "ERATO" remind us of the apparatus of the filmic eye, the split narratives and visually fragmented page layouts return us time and again to the materiality of the unwhole page, the visually broken text. This fragmented text refuses to cohere into any kind of transcendent vision of wholeness that would not only smooth over the gender inequalities that Cha's focuses on but might also problematically suggest a healing or transcendence of the ruptures of the history with which this work is centrally concerned.

There is yet more to Cha's negotiation of the politics of seeing in "ERATO"; if processes of literal looking and visual suture are put under pressure in this section, so is the messianic promise of visionary enlightenment. The female figure's evasion in "ERATO" of the reifying gaze functions as an analogue for a moment of enlightening vision that is implied but never wholly realized because to fully grasp this vision would be to fix, trap, or capture it and thereby strip it of its transformative potential. However, the redemptive impetus of this simultaneously offered and withheld visionary experience is not negated by this frustration of attainment but is, rather, ever more active because it is figured as ongoing, always in process, its redemptive promise not actualized but left as potential. In common with Benjamin's "dialectical image," Cha's text keeps oppositional tensions alive. In "ERATO," *DICTEE* aspires not to restore a unity of vision by a piecing together of fragments but rather to reenergize possibility by means of materially embodied "semantic energies," which are all the more active precisely because they are never aesthetically resolved and thus exhausted; they gesture continually toward a state of plenitude only tangible to the "mind's eye" while persistently and concretely negating a vision of completion.

DICTEE's fragmented forms keep the multiple tensions of "the word. The image" unresolved and thereby also active. Presenting itself as an archaeological site strewn with the decontextualized debris of a past whose traumas and inassimilable specificities elude contemporary recuperation, this is a text that is often more eloquent about the difficulties of historical anamnesis than it is about the traumatic history to which the work bears witness. Yet it is this very lack of eloquence and intelligibility that renders *DICTEE* a faithful witness to the elisions and ruptures of modern Korean history. The text proposes that traces of this past and of the fractured processes of their transmittal might be affectively apprehended rather than epistemologically comprehended. To be confronted with the disjunctive relations between the book's multiple documents, their gaps and mistake-ridden textual surfaces, or the degraded materiality of a much-reproduced image is to glimpse the suppressed potentials of this history. But the potency of these materials remains stubbornly resistant to recuperation into a coherent epistemic framework, instead subsisting in the work and in the acts of its reading as "Seed, germ, sprout, less even . . . Would-be-said remnant, memory" (*DICTEE* 38).

4
"Haemorrhage of uns –"

MAGGIE O'SULLIVAN'S CORPOREAL SALVAGINGS

the stuff and the blob
articulate fissures within
Bob Cobbing, *Shrieks and Hisses*

In conversation with Charles Bernstein as part of his Studio 111 poetry radio series, British poet Maggie O'Sullivan remarks that "writing is a body-
intensive activity . . . the whole body is engaged in the act of writing" ("A
Conversation"). This poet's processes of working involve an exceptionally
high degree of manual and physical labor, including "writing by hand, re-
drafting the words by hand—bending, sticking, cutting, shaping marks, shaping sounds into the recorder, pain(t)ing and building—all inscriptions of
my body's breathing" ("Writing / Conversation" par. 21). Through such processes her work also foregrounds the corporeal dimensions of language itself. O'Sullivan's is an especially somatic multi-medial poetry that melds
textual, oral, visual, sculptural, and performed dimensions of language. Performances of her poetry over the years have often involved slide projections,
recordings, collaborations with other readers or musicians, movement, and
manipulations of vocal sound. On the page, her work is also performative,
staging processes that dynamically unfold through shifting verbal and sonic
landscapes, striking visual layouts, typographic experimentation, colored
inks, collage, and drawings. O'Sullivan's work makes the word flesh in quite
a literal and palpable sense.

By enlarging the field of the poetic through such means, O'Sullivan's work
formally embodies openness to numerous forms of otherness and proposes
expanded realms of experience and knowledge. Her poetry mines multiple
strata of meaningfulness, revivifies archaic vocabularies, investigates "unofficial" aspects of history and culture, and journeys toward the unknown.
While her work is less focused on specific cultural histories than the other
poets discussed in this book, she nevertheless draws on her own Irish heritage as a rich repository of poetic resources and as a departure point for a
historical consciousness oriented toward a multiplicity of unacknowledged

dimensions of language, history, and culture. O'Sullivan's archaeopoetics is less concerned with the kinds of historical documentation that engages a writer like Howe than with language as corporeally inhabited and inhabiting. Her work proposes a sense of cultural memory as incorporated materially in language as it is lived, with an emphasis on the *corps* of this incorporation, both upon the page and beyond it. Although she shares much with the other poets discussed so far, her sense of the cultural past is more diffuse and visceral than theirs. She sees her archaeological task as a process of "excavating *language* in all its multiple voices and tongues, known and unknown" (*Out of Everywhere* 10). This process involves stretching the body of language beyond parameters of the "known" in response to what the poet feels very acutely as a violent restrictiveness of dominant cultural forms. Language, for her, is both complicit with hegemonic coercive imperatives and at the same time a fecund means of engendering alternatives. Her poetry's particular mode of archaeocritique, or broader philosophical activity, directs itself toward reflection upon and active intervention in the tension between language's constricting enclosures and its fertile potentials. An exploration of this dynamic, understood in the emphatically corporeal terms that O'Sullivan's poetry adopts, archaeocritically raises wide-ranging questions concerning language, power, epistemology, and the implications of lost connections to the sensory world in modernity.

This chapter will explore the ways in which O'Sullivan's work enlists the palpable materiality of the poetic page in its archaeopoetic and archaeocritical activity. While my primary focus will be the poet's poetic experimentation with the visual dimensions of language, it has to be recognized that her work is always sensuously *multi*dimensional, enacting a violent struggle as well as a productive transformation that renders language as a living body. O'Sullivan's poetry conducts a viscerally performative archaeopoetics. Comprising somatic language forms highly resistant to epistemic closure, her poems encompass multiple traces of alterity and explore the potentials and limits of a poetic modeling that creates expanded ontologies and epistemologies. In the process, this work necessarily and exuberantly embraces states of incoherence, error, and inarticulacy.

Histories of VOICELESSNESS

O'Sullivan's emphasis on the embodied dimensions of cultural memory means that she turns not so much to libraries and historical records to furnish source material for her poems but to the cultural heritage of what she calls the "Celtic fringes" ("Interview") of the British Isles. Her poetry very often draws on Celtic mythology, folk tales, oral and material culture, symbolism, and cultic ritual rather than text-based sources. Her poetic excavations of such cultural forms are always highly sensitive to the dynamics of power and marginalization, which she connects with her own Anglo-Irish heritage and "sense of the ancestral self" ("In conversation with Brown" 156). In conversation with Andy Brown, she expands upon the formative influence of her upbringing: "My background undoubtedly has shaped who I am / how I am in the world / my work. My father and mother had little schooling and my father worked as a laborer in and out of work all his life. We were brought up on the edge, locked out, without any voice" (159). It is, she declares, her parents' "oral culture / struggle for voice despite centuries of repression which I feel has a lot to do with my poetics" (qtd. in Rothenberg and Joris, *Poems for the Millennium* Vol. 2 835). This narrative of an inherited "struggle for voice" reveals an "ancestral self" disempowered by a history of diasporic and class-related oppression, a legacy which is at the core of a broader concern with suppressed utterances:

> Particularly I have always been haunted by issues of VOICELESS-
> NESS—inarticulacy—silence—soundlessness—breathlessness—how
> are soundings or voices that are other-than or invisible or dimmed or
> marginalized or excluded or without privilege, or locked out, made
> UNofficial, reduced by ascendant systems of centrality and closure,
> configured or Sounded or given form and potency: how can I body
> forth or configure such sounds, such tongues, such languages, such
> muteness, such multivocality, such error—and this is perhaps why the
> non-vocal in mark and the non-word in sound or language—make up
> much of the fabrics and structures of my own compositions. ("In con-
> versation with Brown" 159)

The sheer length of O'Sullivan's list of inarticulate entities here is especially striking; this listing enacts her interest in investigating a multiplicity of exclusions and silenced utterances rather than a specific history. Furthermore, she aligns this multiplicity of inarticulate forms with the "non-vocal" and "non-word," implicitly positioning such negatively defined dimensions of language as possible archaeopoetic modes of materialization for elided articulations. But rather than confidently asserting such a claim, her statement frames this pursuit of "lessness" and muteness via "non" forms as a problem central to her archaeopoetics: How might excluded forms of otherness be articulated? How might negatively defined poetic dimensions such as the "non-vocal" and the "non-word" endow presence and form on states of voicelessness? To use the terms of my epigraph, in what ways can "the stuff and the blob" of language "articulate fissures within" (Cobbing, *Shrieks* n. pag.)?

To address such questions, this chapter examines three of O'Sullivan's poetic works in detail and traces a trajectory from her interest in a specific cultural history—that of her Irish heritage—to a wider concern with multiple forms of voicelessness. This poetry attends to a multiplicity of marginalities and the mechanisms of exclusion and othering in language as they pertain to a broad range of "UNofficial" dimensions of culture. The poet's Irish ancestry informs her broader interest in conditions of liminality. The poem in her oeuvre that most explicitly deals with Irish history is *that bread should be* (1996, reprinted as part of *Etruscan Reader III* in 1997 and again as part of *WATERFALLS* in 2009), which investigates the Irish famine of 1845–52. My discussion of this poem leads to a consideration of O'Sullivan's archaeopoetics in two other poems that deal with wider questions of voicelessness but in which the legacy of an Irish diasporic history is still palpable: *red shifts* (2001) and *murmur* (2011), a poem which has been available online for some years and has also recently been published in paper format with Veer Books. These latter two works extend O'Sullivan's experiments with the visual and synesthetic dimensions of her writing practice, making extensive use of color, texture, and collage. O'Sullivan's multi-media poetry draws on such techniques to foreground corporeal dimensions of language forms. In so doing, this work constitutes a language body that pushes at the limits of established epistemic frames.

Historiographic concerns are not commonly highlighted in the corpus of critical work that is now beginning to accrue around O'Sullivan's poetry (although it is worth noting that her work has not as yet received nearly so much critical attention as Cha's or Howe's). Critical accounts of this work have tended to focus on the present-and-future-oriented dimensions of its reshaping of language forms. The many excellent essays anthologized in *The Salt Companion to Maggie O'Sullivan*, for example, examine topics such as her poetry's shamanism, its implications for metaphysics, its use of neologism, its engagement with gender politics, and its relations to Language writing. Such perspectives also locate O'Sullivan within a field of British and Irish "innovative poetry," where the stress on *innovation* is one of the primary characteristics of the tradition within which she writes. While it is certainly the case that O'Sullivan does not investigate particular histories with quite the degree of focus displayed by other poets discussed in this book, in its excavations of her Anglo-Irish inheritance and its fascination with the cultural traditions of the "Celtic fringes" her work has a significant historiographic dimension intertwined with a sensitivity toward questions of epistemology and articulation.

O'Sullivan's poetry suggests a sense of the cultural past comparable to that outlined by social anthropologist Paul Connerton, who argues that social or collective memory is embodied. For him, "images of the past and recollected knowledge of the past . . . are conveyed and sustained by (more or less ritual) performances" (4), from commemorative ceremonies in which large collectives participate, to the shared bodily practices of individuals. Studies of collective memory, he says, rooted in a hermeneutic tradition that takes textuality as its primary domain of inquiry, have tended to focus on inscribed forms of memory. Connerton aims to show that memory or tradition is also "passed on in non-textual and non-cognitive ways" (102–3) by means of what he calls incorporating practices, performative modes of communication rooted in a "bodily substrate" (71). By scrutinizing such practices, he wants to show how "memory is sedimented, or amassed, in the body" (72). This model of memory is highly resonant with O'Sullivan's invocation of the lived experiences and social practices connected to a working-class life lived "on the edge . . . without any voice" and her sense of a cultural heritage silted into the "ancestral self."

While Connerton's study of incorporated memory concerns itself largely with the hegemonic practices of dominant cultures, it also has implications for investigations of unofficial or marginalized versions of the past. If, as he asserts, "[i]nscribing practices have always formed the privileged story, incorporating practices the neglected story, in the history of hermeneutics" (100–101), then O'Sullivan's poetry suggests that incorporating practices might also form ways of remembering those "neglected" dimensions of history and culture that have not been part of canonical traditions of inscription. In the same way that, as Connerton points out, "[o]ral histories seek to give voice to what would otherwise remain voiceless even if not traceless" (18), so might incorporated practices harbor hitherto "voiceless" elements of the past. Certainly, a conception of a corporeally based memory that might give shape and form to the voiceless informs O'Sullivan's poetry. However, her reliance on the poetic page, on the word made flesh, complicates the distinctions Connerton makes between inscribing and incorporating practices. Clearly the books, pages, writing, and drawing that form the core materials of O'Sullivan's excavation of embodied memory are all forms of inscription. Yet while Connerton's notion of embodied memory largely depends upon differentiating between—and even opposing—inscribed and incorporated forms of memory, he does admit overlaps: "it is certainly the case that many practices of inscription contain an element of incorporation, and it may indeed be that no type of inscription is at all conceivable without such an irreducible incorporating aspect . . . . It is certainly true that writing, the most obvious example of inscription, has an irreducible bodily component" (76).

Connerton wants to minimize the importance of this sort of crossover and to demonstrate that writing is predominantly an inscribing practice.

But it is precisely at the intersection between the inscribed and the bodily, the textual and the material, the cognitive and the non- or extra-cognitive that O'Sullivan's archaeopoetics performs its excavation of cultural memory. O'Sullivan's highly corporeal sense of writing and her emphasis on the physical substrates of language proposes an understanding of the written and sounded word made flesh in a very visceral sense. By foregrounding the "irreducible bodily component" of inscription, her work taps into the multidimensional "incorporated" dimensions of writing and language practices which, for her, hold traces of the "neglected" stories of the voiceless and of a struggle for articulation, a sense of cultural memory "amassed, in the body" (Connerton 72) of material language.

Corporeal Excavations in the Expanded Field

O'Sullivan's aesthetic strategies for her especially physical mode of cultural excavation emerged from the British Poetry Revival of the 1960s and '70s. This heterogeneous flowering of experimental poetries provided fertile ground for practices that went beyond the traditional boundaries of the poetic medium. A key figure for O'Sullivan's practice is Bob Cobbing and his multi-medial—and emphatically somatic—intertwining of sound poetry, performance, and visual experimentation. An emphasis on the materiality of sound and the visual qualities of the printed word linked Cobbing's work to the international movement of Concrete poetry in the 1960s. Such affiliations are evinced in a poem such as his "W OW R OM WRO RMM," included in Emmett Williams's 1967 *Anthology of Concrete Poetry*, in which lines of overprinted words associated with decay wriggle, wormlike, down the page, enacting a disintegration of print that resonates with the poem's overall focus on decomposition. Some of his later works, such as *Shrieks and Hisses* (1999), do away with legible words altogether, consisting instead of a series of photocopied experiments in which textual materials are crumpled, hugely magnified, over and under exposed, and moved around during the process of copying. Cobbing considered works such as these not just as books but as embodiments of a process. He also treated them as scores for performance; for him, even a text containing no legible words could be sounded.

Such a foregrounded physicality of sound, text, and performance, along with an interest in crossovers between media, have tended to be more characteristic of the loose London collective of experimental writers associated with Mottram and Cobbing than some of the other regional groupings that emerged during the 1960s and '70s, in particular the poets centered around J. H. Prynne and Cambridge University. In poetry such as Prynne's, investigation of the ideological workings of language is conducted through careful syntactic experimentation, for example, rather than through such flamboyant cross-medial gestures as Cobbing's. While O'Sullivan's work broadly shares Prynne's suspicion of the authority of linguistic structures, its emphatically material and corporeal modes of excavating language evince closer ties with the activities of London Revival poets. Her work also emerges from a quite specific moment in the history of British poetry. The early-to-mid 1970s were relatively optimistic years for the experimental poetry scene due in no small part to the involvement of Revival poets in the Poetry Society and its publication *Poetry Review,* which afforded some modicum of visibility and financial backing. This all changed in 1977, when prominent figures such as Eric Mottram, Bob Cobbing, Allen Fisher, Lee Harwood, Robert Hampson, and Barry MacSweeney collectively left the Poetry Society after the Arts Council criticized the alleged esotericism of their contributions. These "poetry wars" (Barry) produced a cultural geography of British poetry characterized by a schism between an institutionally sanctioned and subsidized "mainstream" and a marginalized strand of alternative experimental activities.

These were formative years for O'Sullivan, whose work developed in a post-1977 atmosphere in which experimental poets felt embattled and sidelined, "almost totally excluded from both popular and academic awareness" (Barry and Hampson 3). Yet the British Poetry Revival in general, and the activities of poets such as Cobbing in particular, prepared the ground for expansive intermedial poetic practices. Cobbing advocated the view that "[i]t is a mistake to think of poetry as just a branch of literature; it is also a branch of the performing arts and has much in common with music, dance and the graphic arts. There is, therefore, so much more to poetry than is normally 'allowed' for in the publishing and broadcasting media" (Cobbing and Upton eds., *Word Score* n. pag.). A younger generation of poets continued to explore the possibilities of multidimensional poetries, many of them in directions which deployed visual media; Paula Claire's sound, performance, and visual experiments, Allen Fisher's interrelated activities of poetry, painting, and installation, and Tom Raworth's visual collages stand as particularly notable examples.

O'Sullivan's poetic sensibilities were shaped in no small part by her participation in the Writers Forum workshops in the 1970s, where such intermedial practices were encouraged. She also worked with Cobbing making and printing books at the Writers Forum press, and in so doing she established a very physical relationship with the printed word as stuff—as paper and ink—and with the book as a made, material object. In an interview with Dell Olsen, she recounts the experience of printing the handmade version of her *A Natural History in 3 Incomplete Parts*:

which I brought out from my own Magenta press in 1985 when I lived in London and which Bob Cobbing and I made together at his place—(we constructed the entire book going from xeroxing my original pages, collating, binding, gluing, trimming the A5 pages, etc. and it took us a 5-day working week—Monday—Friday—to do this—working intensively from 10 till 5 every day and getting to grips with the brand-new binding machine Bob had just bought!). We'd planned to launch it on the Saturday, so it simply had to be done that week! ("Writing / Conversation" par. 52)

This is publishing as a physical, improvisatory, and collaborative activity, a process of manually "getting to grips" with the equipment and skills involved in bookmaking, an "intensive labour" ("Bob Cobbing") of constructing the material poetic artifact. Such direct involvement with the actual labor of bookmaking produces an acute awareness of the processes of producing and disseminating poetry, and of the social and cultural configurations with which poetry's own forms, materials, and means of production are entangled.

While O'Sullivan's involvement with Cobbing and the Writers Forum has shaped her attentiveness to the physicality of poetry as material making and her expanded sense of what poetry can be, she also cites visual artists as influential forces, including Eva Hesse, Doris Salcedo, and her life partner, the painter Antony Cook (1936–2005). Perhaps the most important point of reference here for her archaeopoetics is Joseph Beuys. O'Sullivan worked on a BBC *Arena* documentary (dir. Tisdall 1987) on Beuys in the 1980s, an experience she describes as "transformative" (*Palace* 67). Like Cha and Howe, O'Sullivan practiced as a visual artist as well as a poet; throughout the 1970s and '80s she made large colorful collages and wall-hung assemblages (some of which can now be viewed on her website) while also writing and performing poetry. Certainly, some of her visual pieces of the late 1980s, resembling ceremonial garments made up of streamers, found objects and materials, drawings of animals or animal-like forms, and objects such as feathers, resonate strongly with Beuys's shamanic ritualistic practices and costumes as well as his practice of collecting plant and animal remains to use in his work and his drawings of human and animal bodies. Indeed, one of her visual works, *In the House of the Shaman #2*, draws its title, as does the poetic work of the same name, from a drawing by Beuys. Beuys's work is also resonant for her wider sense of an expansive materialist poetics and for her mode of historicist reflection.

Beuys's emphasis on performance as well as his notion of "social sculpture" and his associated infamous statement "everyone is an artist" in many ways echo the participatory, inclusive, and boundary-crossing aspirations of O'Sullivan's Writers Forum milieu. Beuys's interest in particular materials is also a provocation for O'Sullivan's aesthetic. Of most immediate concern, however, are Beuys's investigations of the past and the archaeopoetic mode they suggest, which are perhaps most divergent from contemporaneous discourses of innovative poetics and most distinctively instructive for O'Sullivan. Of particular relevance is Beuys's 1974–75 installation piece *Show Your Wound*, originally located in an underpass in Munich and comprising a series of objects, including two mortuary tables, two blackboards, and paired sets of agricultural tools. The doubling of these objects suggests the repetitive structure of trauma. In an echo of such recurrence, Beuys returned time and again in his work to the notion of "the wound." This concept gestures toward the artist's own personal history, including his traumatic experiences during the Second World War, when the warplane he was piloting was shot down over Crimea and, according to Beuys, he was rescued by Tartars. But Beuys's notion of "the wound" also refers to the profound scars of recent German history. Few other German artists of the post-war period were as committed to addressing this history as Beuys; Irit Rogoff goes as far as to say that "Beuys alone attempts to come to terms with the experience of the war and its consequences and to find a new visual language which would combine past, present and future" (273). This "visual language" often entails presenting eclectic arrangements of objects that function as somewhat enigmatic relics, nevertheless imbued with historical resonance. Beuys's entry for a Holocaust commemoration competition held in 1955, and later reassembled in a somewhat altered form as *Auschwitz Demonstration, 1956–64*, addresses a central trauma of modern German history in precisely this way. The work consists of a vitrine containing various objects, including several moldy rings of blood sausage, two blocks of wax on a portable electric hot plate, a panoramic photograph of Auschwitz, and two garden sieves lined with dried grass, one of which contains a desiccated rat corpse. Objects such as the sausages, wax, and the dead rat are suggestive of the corporeal atrocities inflicted upon Jewish victims. However, as Matthew Biro remarks, collectively these objects induce "a hermeneutically undecidable experience when spectators attempt to assemble the vitrine's elements into larger, more overarching interpretations" (120). Beuys's objects resist assimilation into resolved meanings or narratives, confronting viewers instead with a simultaneously hermeneutically open and resolutely opaque thingness. As we shall see, O'Sullivan's language forms often perform a parallel move, offering a phenomenological encounter with aesthetic materials that cannot entirely be incorporated into more abstract modes of conceptualization.

For Beuys, "the wound" is more pervasive than personal history, but it also goes deeper than the events of Germany's recent history to encompass a sense of mourning for a loss of intuitive and sensuous forms of knowledge in modernity. O'Sullivan's historical consciousness enacts a similar process in the linkages and transitions she makes between her familial history on the cultural margins and a concern with much wider issues of voicelessness and inarticulacy. Like O'Sullivan, Beuys was attracted to particular cultural traditions made peripheral in modernity. His response to the traumas of modern history was to revisit archaic or pre-modern cultural practices and traditions that he saw as having a closer, more intuitive and more ethical relationship with the material world of elemental nature. Beuys's veneration for the tribal cultures of the Tartars is evident in his narrative of his own rebirth under these people's care and his subsequent adoption of the Tartar materials of felt and fat. In his notorious "action" (or performance piece) *I Like America and America Likes Me* of 1974, Beuys had himself transported by ambulance to a New York gallery where he spent several days cohabiting with a coyote, an animal persecuted by white settlers but revered and respected in a variety of complex ways by Native Americans. This performance with the coyote was simultaneously a recuperation of these lost symbolic meanings, an acknowledgement of Beuys's own animality, and an enactment of a healing process. Beuys was also fascinated by Celtic cultures, which he understood as pan-Eurasian: "They seem to have emerged from the east; then, for almost a thousand years, they dominated the center of Europe, stretching from the Black Sea to Iberia and from the Mediterranean to the North Sea and Ireland. Two thousand years later they survive on the western periphery of Europe, having been pushed to the extreme edge" (qtd. in Rainbird 52). For Beuys, Celtic cultures have not been entirely superseded by Western capitalist modernity but cling to its geographic and cultural margins.

For this reason, Beuys frequently visited Scotland and Ireland in the 1970s and '80s, where he staged actions, gave lectures, and got involved with community projects. He also adopted Celtic symbols, such as the spirals and zigzags he saw carved into the stone at Newgrange in Ireland, which he incorporated into his drawings and actions. The shepherd's crook-like staff he famously wielded in performances such as *I Like America* was, for him, a Celtic object, its crook symbolizing a return to pre-modern modes of relating to the world. Beuys's engagements with such peripheral cultural traditions were often problematic and contradictory. Nevertheless, O'Sullivan has found it instructive that this prominent visual artist accorded such value to the cultures of the "Celtic fringes" (O'Sullivan, "Interview"), that he materially integrated their remnants into his practice and perceived their traditions as embodying alternative, transformative, and redemptive modes of knowledge in the face of a catastrophic modernity. Beuys's engagement with Celtic cultural artifacts has acted as a galvanizing force for O'Sullivan's excavation of such marginalized cultural legacies.

Connerton's theory of embodied memory along with the aesthetic legacies of artists such as Cobbing and Beuys offer theoretical and contextual frames for an exploration of O'Sullivan's archaeopoetic methods. The first poem to consider, *that bread should be*, performs what is perhaps O'Sullivan's most emphatic turn to the modern history of the "Celtic fringes" of Ireland. This work's investigation of a defining event in Irish history explores the relationship between people, land, and capitalist-colonial power by drawing on the resources of folk culture, song, and oral history. The poem begins, uncharacteristically for this poet, with a few introductory paragraphs that outline the area of its historical investigation, the Great Irish Famine of 1845–52, which killed an estimated one million people countrywide (Ó Gráda 4).[1] As its introductory section indicates, the poem focuses on the famine's effects on a specific rural area, Skibbereen, where the poet has family ties. Described by contemporary commentators Lord Dufferin and G. G. Boyle as "the very nucleus of famine and disease" (par. 2), the area of Skibbereen was perhaps the area hardest hit by the famine. In its investigation of the history of the Irish famine, *that bread should be* embodies, in very literal terms, an especially traumatic sense of intertwined oppression and inarticulacy, which recurs throughout this poet's oeuvre.

The musical score of the folk song "Old Skibbereen" and the saying "that bread should be so dear and human life so cheap" act as starting points and source texts for the poem's exploration of a history involving terrible hardship and displacement. In the ballad "Old Skibbereen," a father passes on to his son the tale of his exile from his beloved homeland. Unable to pay rent and taxes following the loss of crops and livestock, he is evicted from his smallholding by his English landlord and the colonial authorities.[2] Although it is only alluded to by the inclusion of the musical score of the ballad, this story provides a historical frame for O'Sullivan's poem. The folk song points toward a exploitative colonial appropriation of land and resources; as Cormac Ó Gráda's historical account of the famine indicates, the land confiscations of the sixteenth and seventeenth centuries had, by the nineteenth century, "left most Irish land in the hands of a small elite of English origin. In the mid-nineteenth century that elite still owned the bulk of the country's fixed capital" (26). As Marx stated in *Capital*: "Ireland is at present merely an agricultural district of England which happens to be divided by a wide stretch of water from the country for which it provides corn, wool, cattle and industrial and military recruits" (860). The rural working classes, consigned by an oppressive colonial and class system to an impoverished and politically powerless position with no economic resources but their labor, were thus especially vulnerable to the ravages of famine.

The song "Old Skibbereen" and the saying to which the poem's title refers not only mark out a set of specific events and their underlying power relations, they also typify O'Sullivan's sense of history as transmitted orally in song, stories, and everyday speech acts rather than through the written word. This sense of cultural memory is entangled with the specific circumstances of this history and the ways in which it has been passed on to subsequent generations. The largely illiterate agricultural poor families most affected by the famine, such as O'Sullivan's ancestors, left few, if any, written accounts of events; textual records were often produced by those removed from the immediate mortal dangers of this catastrophe such as the Englishmen Dufferin and Boyle, who travelled to Skibbereen to investigate the effects of the famine. For the illiterate poor, and particularly for those who were displaced, this history was primarily passed down via oral and folk forms. This is not to suggest that for O'Sullivan these folk forms transcend processes of suppression and silencing. For example, the ballad "Old Skibbereen" indicates the ways in which the passing on of a cultural heritage is highly gendered, relayed from father to son. For O'Sullivan this folk history is a primary source, providing a way into a history that this poem seeks to "body forth" materially and corporeally. But her poem also sets itself apart from such orally transmitted histories.

The ways in which O'Sullivan's poetry works with the intersections of incorporating and inscribing practices, to hark back to Connerton's terms, is especially evident in its emphasis on various physical qualities of the printed page. One of the most immediately apparent characteristics of this poem as a whole is its consistent bottom-heavy textual layout with the first lines on each page precisely aligned across the opening. Dragging the reading eye immediately downwards, this arrangement iconically presents itself as a landscape; the top lines form a horizon beneath which the series of horizontal lines, long dashes, frequent underlinings, and occasional diagonal lines on each page visually align the poem with the land to which this particular history is so closely tied (see figures 12 and 13). These pages present readers with language as "phenomenological, apprehendable, immanent substance" (*Visible Word* 43), to use Johanna Drucker's pertinent phrasing. Drawing attention to its own status not (or not only) as a vehicle for meaning but as material stuff whose physical dimensions are not subsumable to "the abstract and system-defined elements" (Drucker, *Visible Word* 43) of linguistic functioning, this poetry emphasizes those aspects of inscription that resist assimilation to semantic or cognitive structures.

Robert Sheppard offers a useful further perspective on such a foregrounding of materiality in his notion of a "poetry of saying," which draws on Emmanuel Levinas's distinction between the saying and the said: "Language as *saying* is an ethical openness to the other; as that which is *said*—reduced to a fixed identity or synchronized presence—it is an ontological closure of the other" (qtd. in Sheppard 12). While saying understood as "ethical openness" to the other cannot be entirely separated out from the said, Sheppard measures "successful" poetry by its capacity to keep the saying of the work active in a "dialogic performance" of reading (14). For him, O'Sullivan's work does this most particularly in its "thick devicehood" by which "semantics are held off" (237). Reading becomes an oscillation between a semantic drive that might render the poem's effects as said, and an ethical imperative to acknowledge the otherness of its saying, the resistance of its "thick devicehood," its thingness, to epistemic closure.

For Sheppard, foregrounded materiality in poetry enacts, or instigates, a dynamic *performative* process. Sheppard draws here on notions of performance as kinetic, open-ended, and, crucially, unfolding through dialogue with others; the poem's performance occurs as a collaboration between poem and reader. In so doing, he also brings a sharpened ethical dimension to debates about "open" and "closed" forms ubiquitous in discussions of contemporary experimental poetry. In Sheppard's argument, what the "poetry of saying" performs is a refusal to assimilate otherness to a constrained stasis of the said. By his own admission, Sheppard tends to privilege sonic materiality and sound-based paradigms as exemplary of "saying." Yet the visual performativity of work like O'Sullivan's (especially as entangled with orality and its physical supports) participates equally vigorously in such a saying, a *doing* through performing a *being*. Like the early twentieth-century modernist work that Drucker examines in her study *The Visible Word* by poets such as Mallarmé, Marinetti, and Apollinaire, O'Sullivan's poems insist on "the capacity of the image, the poem, the word, or the mark to *be*, to exist in its own right on an equal stature with the tangible, dimensional objects of the real world" (49). The lines of O'Sullivan's poem present themselves as an ancestral landscape, a terrain with a palpable substance whose thingness, in refusing assimilation to graspable meaning, proposes an ethical openness to the Otherness of this textual topography and its histories.

While the visual arrangement of lines on the page in *that bread should be* embodies a sense of landscape, the verbal material of the poem expands upon the precise nature of this terrain. As the opening depicted in figure 12 indicates, this is a harsh land of "stones" and of unwholesome marshes— "the mucks're / thronging wet ————"—and above all a "ground" infected with "the <u>blight</u> the distemper the ————." The multiple underlinings in this page serve to emphasize certain words or phrases, and the long dashes with which many of the lines end signal a trailing off of speech, an inability to complete an utterance. Such diacritical marks, then, are linked to the oral qualities of the poem, as is clear when O'Sullivan performs the work. Some of the visual elements here can function as a score for a pos-

whole families without a trace my ———

                                dealt ———

it occurs:

the unstory

   – that bread should be –

Song's bleeding wove

       (never more crow – scraping

drawing stones all day on a few ribs to the moon

my guts trail out my eyes & the mucks're

   thronging wet ———

    MAGPIE'S

     black feet slap their brink on the

stems not a ground i tread –

   cavity-sippling –

the blight the distemper the ———

Figure 12. From *that bread should be* by Maggie O'Sullivan, *Etruscan Reader III*. © 1997 etruscan books and Maggie O'Sullivan. Pages 38–9. Reprinted by permission of Etruscan Books and the author.

sible oral performance; capitalized or underlined words, for example, may be spoken loudly or even shouted. While O'Sullivan's soundings rarely go as far as Cobbing's oral renditions of textural pages containing few recognizable words, the visual materiality of her printed language is intimately linked to another kind of materiality: sound.

But O'Sullivan's poem need not be read aloud to perform it acoustically because, as Garrett Stewart has argued, "reading voices." Here, "voices" is to be understood as a verb, as well as a noun. In this way, Stewart's formulation points to ways in which the process of silent reading "proceeds to give voice, or at least to evoke silently such voicing" (1). This notion of how "reading voices" proceeds from the question "[w]here do we read?" And this "where," he suggests, "is none other than the reading body. This somatic locus of soundless reception includes of course the brain but must be said to encompass as well the organs of vocal production, from diaphragm up through throat to tongue and palate. Silent reading locates itself, that is, in the conjoint cerebral activity and suppressed muscular action of a simultaneously summoned and suppressed articulation" (1). Stewart asserts, "[w]hen we read to ourselves, our ears hear nothing. Where we read, however, we listen" (11). This notion of a physical place of reading is important to O'Sullivan's poetry, which insistently brings the "where" of the page into relation with the "somatic locus of . . . reception" and its network of acoustically orientated organs. For example, the capitalization of the word "MAGPIE's" (see figure 12) in O'Sullivan's poem promotes a process of "listening" to the increased, visually indicated "volume" of this signifier. Furthermore, the emphasized "acoustic" qualities of this word induce a subsequent attentiveness to the hard stamping staccato of the monosyllabic series "black feet slap" in the following line. The textual mark is thoroughly intertwined with the sensory dimension of sound. It is not so much that the graphic dimensions of the text function as a score for a sounded performance that takes place off the page. Rather, what Stewart calls "the play between phonic and graphic articulations" (2) functions in this poem to constitute "textuality *as a performance medium*" (11), as a performance on the page, embodied in its sensory dimensions and played out in a dialogue between graphic and phonic dimensions of textuality, between the somatic space of the reading body and the physical, apprehendable, sensory "body" of the text.

Indeed, this notion of performance allows us to extend some of the ideas already encountered in Sheppard's notion of "the poetry of saying" to grasp in somewhat more concrete terms the ways in which O'Sullivan's archaeopoetics functions. If in this work cultural memory is encountered as "amassed, in the body" (Connerton 72) of language forms, then it is through the performative capacities of sounded and inscribed language that these cultural traces gain tangible presence. As in Sheppard's formulation, the paradigm of performance does not solely rely on the presence of the poet's body engaged in the act of reading the work but rather occurs upon the page and in active dialogue with a process of reading. Nor is performance to be understood in solely acoustic terms. As Drucker indicates, "a visual performance of a poetic work on a page or canvas, as a projection or sculpture, installation or score . . . has the qualities of an enactment, of a staged and realized event in which the material means are an integral feature of the work" ("Visual Performance" 131).

This appeal to the somatic processes of reading and the performative dimensions of the textual body are central to O'Sullivan's archaeopoetics in *that bread should be* and its reflection upon the possibilities of an aesthetic engagement with historical events centered on the material conditions of the Irish landscape and the human lives eked out upon it. In this work, the space and substance of the page forges an intimate physical relation with incorporated forms of memory. Romana Huk insightfully remarks upon how O'Sullivan's poetry moves toward "the sensually perceived 'arrival' of what is always already there: the 'living word' in which both past and future are collapsed . . . That word is a living fossil" (51). This notion powerfully suggests how a work such as this claims a sense of physical, bodily proximity to its history, to the nineteenth-century Irish landscape and its inhabitants. Because O'Sullivan's language is "living" and lived-in, this is an encounter not with lifeless and desiccated remains but with animate traces subsisting as incorporated memories enacted through physical arrangements of words and marks.

Such an emphasis on language as embodied and embodying is so crucial in *that bread should be* partly because the history it investigates is intimately entangled with bodies. For example, along the "horizon" of the opening depicted in figure 12, a human body seems to toil, "drawing stones all day . . . ." The poem here alludes to the program of public works set up by the government to provide work for agricultural laborers made destitute by the potato blight. Mostly involving stone breaking and road building, this work was incredibly demanding for famine-wracked bodies and often did not even pay enough to feed a family on starvation rations (Daly 130–31; Ó Gráda 68). Hence the body "drawing stones" does so "on a few ribs to the moon," as a starved skeleton exposed to an expanse of unconcerned sky, which is suggested by the large white space that appears above this line. Dehumanized, made cheap and stripped of agency, the human body of this poem is almost indistinguishable from the disease and decay of the ecological and historical disaster of the famine, tied to the blighted land by processes of production and consumption that render the Irish worker's body and the labor it produces synonymous with the potato and its disease. In the opening of figure 12 the speaker claims "my guts trail out my eyes & the mucks're / thronging wet ——————," "guts" here seeming to "trail out" upon, and to become part of, the "thronging wet" of "the mucks," or marshlands. The "guts," being the body part most immediately affected by the famine, share the land's "blight the distemper." The human "entrails" (*that bread* 32) of the poem are thoroughly entangled and almost synonymous with the land's disease so that the line "their own filthy rots hanging" invokes an image not only of diseased potatoes but of the diseased human body. This image suggests the spectacle of its viscera "hanging," inducing the "screamsticks—white skull over bone—" (*that bread* 31), the horror of decomposition, which also haunts the next line. By such means O'Sullivan's poem not only represents the trauma of this state but also makes it physically tangible. As Isobel Armstrong says of O'Sullivan's poetry, "her language of pain attempts to *be* the 'measure' of pain" (63). By insistently confronting readers with printed and spoken language as "phenomenological, apprehendable, immanent substance" (Drucker, *Visible Word* 43), the poem constitutes itself as a traumatized textual body, foregrounding its own literal materiality as physically proximate to the conditions of the land, people, and animals that form the actualities of history.

Through these performative means, O'Sullivan's poem makes physically manifest a historical trauma rooted in the systemic violence of colonialist and capitalist modes of appropriation and exploitation. This is a violence that is not only inflicted on the human body by the ravages of famine and the power structures that render the laboring classes so vulnerable to its effects, but that also shatters and disperses family, genealogy, and community. *That bread should be* thus investigates the effects of the famine on the passing down of memory and the representation of this history for subsequent generations. The notion that traumatic events resist assimilation to narrative paradigms of cognition, articulated in Freud's work on mourning and melancholia and taken up more recently by trauma theorists in the 1990s, suggests one way to understand the images and effects of O'Sullivan's poetic meditations on memory. As Ulrich Baer puts it, "the phenomenon of trauma presents us with a fundamental enigma, a crisis of representational models that conceive of reference in terms of a direct, unambiguous link between event and comprehension" (10). O'Sullivan's poem points to just such a crisis of the referential claims of language. Its physical disturbances of written and sounded language can be read as an embodiment of the idea that, having resisted comprehension and articulation at the time of its occurrence, the effects of trauma return belatedly. Drawing on a Freudian model of trauma, Dominick LaCapra points out that trauma "does not disappear; it returns in a transformed, at times disfigured and disguised manner" (10).

Think back to Beuys's *Auschwitz Demonstration*, which refers to that central trauma of modernity only obliquely through its enigmatic collection of desiccated and moldering objects connected associatively but not explicitly to the Holocaust. In O'Sullivan's poem, such delayed effects of trauma are registered at the material level of the word as "living fossil" (Huk 51). Repeated failures of articulation, signaled, for example, in the recurrent long dashes that suggest unspoken utterances, or in the breaking apart of individual words, bear belated witness to past events whose effects live on in the material strata of the page. The poem portrays oral forms of representation as especially scarred. In the line "round round as an 0's hoop scouring vowels—" (26), the "round" sound of "an 0's hoop" is represented not by means of the alphabetic character "O" but by the visibly leaner figure for zero. The "round" vowel is depleted as if worn away by a "scouring" force.

A persistent concern with the effects of historical trauma on oral culture shapes O'Sullivan's treatment of memory in this poem, particularly given the crucial role of oral modes of transmission for families most affected by the famine—the descendants of poor, illiterate agricultural workers. In the first lines of the opening of figure 13, an "unbrokenSINGING" is figured as a vital connection to an ancestral homeland, "its Acred Heart's / Umbilicus Chirruping" positing a highly corporeal, umbilical connection between song and land. In addition, the medium of song takes on a viscous material quality: "unbrokenSINGING" forms a "Knee-Deep" layer while the typographic quality of this printed word embodies both physical connection and, by means of capitalization, an increased acoustic volume of "SINGING." Yet this vision of primal song is offered only in a mode of wistful longing, only as something already "s-c-a-t-t-e-r-e-d," as indicated by the dispersed characters further down the page.

This page above all signals a loss of community and of communal memory; "that Shielding Ash of memory bleeding" indicates a hemorrhaging of the symbolic heart of communal life. In Celtic lore this tree is a symbol of protection, of "Shielding"; it was also thought to guard universal truths and form links between inner and outer worlds, the past and present, the dead and the living (Gifford 28–31). The "*ASH*," the previous opening suggests, "it is of an age with the house," possibly "the father's house" (29), the core of a rural Catholic community. The "bleeding" of the ash in O'Sullivan's poem signals disaster, especially for "memory," the ability to pass on communal history to future generations. The "(Bough Siblings," the community who might perform this task, are part of this hemorrhage; the resonance of the phrase "of No Fixed SONG/" with the itinerant label "of No Fixed Abode" indicates a state of homelessness and displacement that alludes to the famine-induced waves of eviction and emigration suffered by communities like Skibbereen.

The "Shielding Ash of memory" of the poem is in the process of being bled dry, transformed into another kind of "Ash," a desiccated, charred residue of memory easily diffused, as the broken-up letters of the word "scattered" indicate, both semantically and visually.

In other words, O'Sullivan's archaeopoetics physically registers the effects of trauma on language. *that bread should be* foregrounds irreparable damage to the means for passing down the history of pre-famine Skibbereen society; the "unbrokenSINGING" that links people and place, past and present, becomes "No Fixed SONG/." Here the forward slash enacts a severing of the itinerant utterance from its roots. Yet in positioning the "SONG/" as a substitute for the inferred word "Abode," O'Sullivan's poem turns the song into a kind of home, a nomadic dwelling for fragments of memory. This diasporic song claims not to recuperate an "unbrokenSINGING" but rather becomes a kind of "UNSINGING" (*that bread* 33) or "COLD PIPING ————," a "half-any-speech ————." The very incompleteness of this utterance indexically tells "the unstory"(*that bread* 39) of a catastrophic history by embodying the echoes of its traumatic effects. Recall the poet's wager in her reflections on "issues of VOICELESSNESS" ("In conversation with Brown" 159) that negatively defined entities might offer some of the most pertinent means of bodying forth states of inarticulacy. We might also note that in this respect, O'Sullivan's "UNSINGING" is not performed entirely in tune with the singer of the ballad "Skibbereen," whose narrative of the famine hovers in the background. The song of *that bread should be* has more in common with the crows, magpies, and ravens referred to throughout its pages. Like these scavenging birds, this poem situates itself among the corporeal leavings of history, articulating its findings not by means of a tuneful and intelligible song but via an abrasive and discordant cry. The work's visual materiality plays a central role in the articulation of this "song"; its pages simultaneously constitute an iconic representation of a spatio-temporal locale, a performance of particular material conditions, a cue for sound and for a reading that "voices," a verbal-visual register of trauma, and an indexical trace of the unsayable, of tales "without a trace" (*that bread* 39). The physical entity that is *that bread should be* makes "unsinging" inarticulacies corporeally apparent as well as the historical forces that contribute to their suppression.

The focus on a specific history in *that bread should be* informs a more diffuse thematics that deals with systematic forms of violence, trauma, and silencing, strands that run through O'Sullivan's wider oeuvre. As in Susan Howe's work, this concern with oppression and trauma buried in the past has as its motivating impulse a concern with violence and voicelessness in the present, although, unlike Howe, O'Sullivan does not seek identifiable historical "causes" for contemporary aggression and intolerance. Rather, for her,

Knee-Deep unbrokenSINGING its Acred Heart's

    Umbilicus Chirruping

that Shielding Ash of memory bleeding

    Sea-Saw fearments

       Eared –

       Eyed –

    (Bough Siblings of No Fixed SONG/

S

  c

    a

      t

        t

          e

            r

              e

                d

anywhere but I –

half-starved-half-clothed-half-eaten-by ——

             half-any-speech ——

                 half-any

rip in the sky's Blue mantling rag for an 0 ——

        dragged

      out of their stares

their own filthy rots hanging

screamsticks – <u>white skull over bone</u> –

)sewing <u>it over</u> –

    LAPWINGS TAKE MY COLD PIPING ——

Figure 13. From *that bread should be* by Maggie O'Sullivan, *Etruscan Reader III.* © 1997 etruscan books and Maggie O'Sullivan. Pages 30–31. Reprinted by permission of Etruscan Books and the author.

the history of the Great Famine functions as a historical event that informs a sense of cultural memory sensitive to broader questions of voicelessness, disempowerment, and marginality. While the particulars of Irish history do not receive such a sustained treatment in any of her other poems, the story of diaspora that shapes her background certainly informs the historical and mythological ground of O'Sullivan's poetic negotiation of wider issues. In a relatively early published work, *A Natural History in 3 Incomplete Parts* (first published in 1985 and reprinted in black-and-white facsimile in *Body of Work* in 2006), references to Ireland and Irishness make up part of a writing of an "incomplete" history. As Peter Manson's article on this poem points out, the middle section "More Incomplete" is headed by an epigraph from Pound's Canto CXVI, "If love not be in the house there is nothing" (O'Sullivan, *Body of Work* 82). The canto's next line, not quoted by O'Sullivan, is "The voice of famine unheard" (Pound, *Cantos* 816). The history of the Irish famine, which is obliquely and silently gestured toward here, echoes "unheard" through the work. Poems such as "(for my mother)" and "(for my dad)" refer to the poet's Irish heritage and explore different gendered forms of marginalization and silencing suffered by the poet's parents. *A Natural History* also alludes to events in recent Irish history and makes links to a broader context of political turbulence and unrest in the mid-1980s, when O'Sullivan was writing. Via collaged juxtapositions of text and image, this work references not only contemporary conflicts in Northern Ireland but also the often violently suppressed Greenham Common anti-nuclear war protests and the miners' strikes occurring at this time. In this way, the poem establishes parallels between the events of Irish history and other contemporary forms of state-sanctioned violence and silencing.

O'Sullivan's sense of a legacy of trauma, marginalization, and inequality rooted in Irish history and class-based forms of oppression informs a further, archaeocritical reflection on the power relations that underpin states of voicelessness and inarticulacy. At the close of a published conversation with Andy Brown, O'Sullivan quotes the words of Tom Leonard: "It's not simply a matter of class register, but the politics of dominant narrative language as would-be encloser of the world, language as coloniser. For this the language has to be presumed 'invisible' to its referent. I like to make it visible in different ways" (160). To "make it visible" is both to simultaneously bring attention to language's complicity in upholding "the dominant narrative" and to attempt an expansion of its capacities beyond the prescribed functions of what O'Sullivan calls "a restrictive culture" ("In conversation with Brown" 160). As we have already seen, such processes of "making visible" often entail for O'Sullivan a literal foregrounding of the physical dimensions of the printed page. Her sense of the political possibilities involved in a focus on visual materiality, in particular, is increasingly evident not only in her own poetry but in her editing of the 1996 anthology *Out of Everywhere*. This anthology opens with one of Howe's dramatically visual pages from *Eikon Basilike* (see Chapter 2, figure 3). Besides Howe's work, the collection also features strikingly visual work by Joan Retallack, Tina Darragh, Diane Ward, and Paula Claire, among others. The inclusion of such conspicuously visual examples of "linguistically innovative poetry" demonstrates the editor's sense of the important role played by visual experimentation in the shared commitment of the work in this collection to "excavating *language* in all its multiple voices and tongues, known and unknown" (O'Sullivan, *Out of Everywhere* 10). Nicky Marsh remarks that the anthology offers "multiple strategies for an enlarged poetic register," complicating "the familiar presence-absence dynamic of critical linguistics by bringing the social procedures of reading and the physical presence of poet, reader, and page into the semantic field" ("Agonal" 81). O'Sullivan's foregrounding of highly material poetries in the anthology proposes an expanded sense of the poetic and the semantic. In her own later poetry this visually orientated mode of "excavating *language*" and "making . . . visible"—both "colonizing" functions and expanded potentials—becomes ever more emphatic.

In recent years, O'Sullivan's engagement with issues of voicelessness and inarticulacy has involved an amplified visual emphasis. Two recent poems, *red shifts* and *murmur*, demonstrate how the poet has increasingly melded her poetic and visual arts practices. In conversation with Dell Olsen in the early 2000s, O'Sullivan explains how she "moved away from making the large colorful expressionistic assemblages/paintings" that she worked on "side by side" with her poetry in the 1980s and '90s toward a practice "where potencies, energy fields, traces of actions/activities move in an open, ongoing dissolving/deformance of the verbal/visual/sculptural into one practice of many heuristic pathings" ("Writing / Conversation" par. 6). This shift is evident in increased use of color, texture, and visual collage in O'Sullivan's later works. Marjorie Perloff convincingly describes *red shifts* as an artist's book, surmising that "bookwork made possible a textual heightening, not available in the traditional production of individual 'contained' poems" ("Saturated" 125). The poem as bookwork is hardly a departure for O'Sullivan, whose practice has often involved literally making her own books, as her printing and publishing work with Cobbing demonstrates. However, Perloff's emphasis on a "textual heightening" and a search for a form that can move beyond the containments of "traditional production" resonates with O'Sullivan's ambitions to enlarge the parameters of her poetic work. Yet even the capacious category of the artist's book seems too restrictive a classification for *red shifts*. Its square-format pages, echoing the archetypal "white cube"

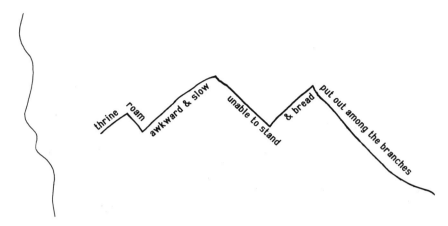

Figure 14. First opening of *red shifts* by Maggie O'Sullivan. Etruscan Books, © 2001 Maggie O'Sullivan. Unpaginated. Original in color. Reprinted by permission of Etruscan Books and the author.

of the contemporary art gallery, wittily position the work as a multi-layered exhibition space and invoke the "sculptural" quality to which the poet refers in her description of recent activities.[3] In so doing, it physically embodies a pursuit of further dimensions and extended capacities, following the expansive impulse evident throughout this poet's oeuvre.

The first pages of *red shifts* offer cues for negotiating O'Sullivan's multi-dimensional poetic terrain (see figure 14). This opening presents itself as a single space, alerting readers to the importance of reading and looking across facing pages. Indeed, in the poem's first pages, this "instruction" for a reading strategy is given almost mimetically by means of two visual "diagrams"— the undulating black line that meanders down the far left-hand side of the opening, imitating the movement of a reading eye, and the red zigzag that moves across the pages and leads, on the far right-hand side, to the rest of the work. In this way, the poem's first pages offer guidance on how to negotiate the work as a series of spaces that require visual navigation and a multi-directional reading practice.

The poem's first opening also sets up a verbal-visual dialogue that is instructive for understanding intermedial relationships in this poem more generally. The visual cues, drawn with marker pens or with a fine brush and ink, differ from the typed dashes and slashes of *that bread should be*; by means of their gestural qualities they claim a direct link with the hand and the body, an immediate genesis in a "body-intensive" ("A Conversation") practice. The heavily pixelated blocky appearance of the verbal matter on this page, however, evinces the mediation of a machine. These contrasting visual qualities suggest different modes of production for verbal and visual material in a way that initially seems to posit a separation between the written and the drawn. Yet at the same time the positioning of words along the contours of the red zigzag integrates word and image; the reading of the printed word/phrase/ line must unavoidably take the movement and contours of the zigzag into account, while the red mark itself is not only a red mark but also a poetic line, a template around which verbal material is shaped. Furthermore, the visible pixels of the printed words highlight the essentially visual quality of all printed words—the pixel being a unit of visual space—and bestow a textural quality upon each rough-edged individual letter. Meanwhile, the red zigzag calls to mind the rising and falling of intonation or sound, its sharp shapes echoing the hard consonants that litter the verbal material on the page. This exchange between optical, textual, oral, and textural dimensions creates a synesthetic space in which, as Dell Olsen puts it, the poem is "moving towards an interchange of senses: hearing seems to become sight and vice-versa" (O'Sullivan, "Writing/Conversation" par. 26). In O'Sullivan's recent work, especially, "[t]he word in the hand is the sound in the eye is the sight in the listening ear" (*Selected* 36), to borrow the words of Robert Duncan.

The phenomenon of synesthesia as neuroscientists have explored it has implications for language which are highly pertinent to O'Sullivan's poetics. Studies conducted by Vilayanur Ramachandran and Edward Hubbard suggest that synesthesia—in which, for example, different musical notes evoke particular colors for some people or certain tactile experiences induce a sensation of taste—are caused by a kind of cross-wiring or "cross activation" (55) between neighboring areas of the brain that deal with sensory experience. Ramachandran and Hubbard suggest that to some extent "we are all closet synesthetes" with the capacity for some level of sensory interchange, and that furthermore, this process may well be central to the development of human thought and language (58). In particular, they argue, "[h]umans have a built-in bias to associate certain sounds with particular visual shapes" (58). For example, a test conducted by psychologist Wolfgang Köhler found that when presented with two shapes, one curvy and the other jagged, and asked to identify which is a "bouba" and which a "kiki," 98 percent of all respondents matched the rounded shape to the name "bouba" and the angular shape to "kiki." Ramachandran and Hubbard make links between such sensory exchange and the development of language: "[t]he brain seems to possess preexisting rules for translating what we see and hear into mouth motions that reflect those inputs" (59), and this provides a basis for the evolution of language involving an intertwining of sight, sound, and gesture. Because this theory of language implies that there is some kind of inherent, physiological relation between word and thing, it seems to be starkly at odds with the Saussurian insistence on the arbitrary nature of the sign, which has become the dominant model of language in much literary theory. Yet while Ramachandran and Hubbard hardly provide a fully worked-out theory of language, their work in this area also allows for the sorts of arbitrary links between signifier, signified, and referent insisted upon by Saussurian linguistics. They suggest that synesthesia could explain a facility for metaphor that relies upon such relationships; "just as synesthesia involves making arbitrary links between seemingly unrelated perceptual entities such as colors and numbers, metaphor involves making links between seemingly unrelated conceptual realms" (57). However speculative these claims, the importance of such neuroscientific theories of synesthesia for O'Sullivan's poetics is that they suggest a model of sensory experience in which different senses become interrelated and even fused. Furthermore, such exchanges become the basis for a conception of language in which sight, sound, touch, and gesture interconnect. Importantly, such notions suggest an understanding of language that acknowledges a corporeality largely disavowed and elided by the biophobic tendencies of structuralist and poststructuralist theory. These ideas about synesthesia are highly consonant with O'Sullivan's archaeopoetic aspirations to stimulate or rejuvenate corporeally rooted linkages between various sensory dimensions and between these sensory dimensions and language.

The first opening of *red shifts* (see figure 14) embodies a multidimensional conception of language that exemplifies O'Sullivan's aspiration toward a "dissolving/deformance of the verbal/visual/sculptural" ("Writing / Conversation" par. 8), a splicing and melding of multiple sensory dimensions. The "dissolving" of distinctions between sound, printed word, and visual mark constitutes the page as a multi-medial *per*formance, as O'Sullivan's coinage "deformance" suggests. But what is it that is being performed in this opening beyond the fusing of textual, visual, tactile, and oral dimensions of experience? O'Sullivan's highly sensory synesthetic pages in *red shifts* heighten the intersections between inscribing and incorporated practices that also appear in *that bread should be*. The hand-drawn marks, patterns, spills, and washes of blood-red ink that occur throughout the pages of *red shifts* emphasize what Connerton refers to as the "irreducible bodily component" (76) of inscription by means of these marks' associations with the body—whether by dint of their correspondence to corporeal elements such as blood or by means of a gestural quality that claims a proximity to the writing or drawing hand. Verbal marks such as dashes and slashes also foreground the presence of print upon the page—writing's own "bodily" presence. The poem thus becomes a somatic entity, a "body" engaged in a process of struggle. A sense of physical debilitation infuses *red shifts* from its first opening, in which the lines "awkward & slow" and "unable to stand" suggest an incapacitated body. The poem's following pages act out a recurrently thwarted corporeal endeavor to perform a speech act. A speaker's whimper "**cant hold by breath/ my breath / sobbing**" (*red shifts* n. pag.), points emphatically to an undertaking hindered by grief and by a silencing violence suggested by "savage / toungesbled" and the repetition of "sh —." This physical striving for speech performs a sense of memory "sedimented, or amassed, in the body" (Connerton 72), an inherited incorporated struggle for voice that informs the poet's "sense of the ancestral self" ("In conversation with Brown" 156). As in *that bread should be*, the poem's task is not just to describe this struggle for speech but also to be or become it.

O'Sullivan's poem gives shape to states of inarticulacy, "bodying forth" an incorporated memory rooted in a history of marginalization, displacement, and silencing. Although *red shifts* is far less explicit about its historical referents than *that bread should be*, fragments of a diasporic Anglo-Irish history are embedded in this later poem's struggle for articulation. Spellings and neologisms regularly suggest Irish pronunciation as in "**windfella**," "**AccurrsZ'd**," or "**Whatter Ye Fukkas**" (*red shifts*) and are often printed in enlarged and/or emboldened fonts that serve to emphasize or "turn up the volume" of these utterances. Narrative fragments of an Irish heritage also surface; "**paddy.took.after.my.grandmother's. / people.**" invokes a story of familial legacy where Irishness is signified by the name "**paddy**." Although this tiny fragment or beginning of a story suggests a sense of generational continuity, the full stop after each word performs a recurrent interruption, pointing to a fracturing of families and links between generations, enacting the ruptures of diaspora. Meanwhile, "**bellowing the roads** used drive them the 10 or 12 miles" (*red shifts*) suggests a rural existence revolving around "bellowing" livestock. The term "used," inferring "used to," suggests nostalgically that this way of life has now vanished into the past. Such references both indicate the roots of an "ancestral self" and, by both linguistic and typographic means, demonstrate a diasporic sense of severance from this familial and cultural past, a "**ruptures crossing**" and "tear of the wind."

As in *that bread should be*, the diasporic "tear" is infused with violence. In particular, the act of speaking is almost always accompanied by an intimation of constantly lurking brutality, as in the lines "hard gutteral / / ~~thread~~ ~~ened~~ ——— threatened to kill." Here, "hard gutteral," suggesting harsh-sounding "guttural" speech, appears to be the subject that threatens "to kill." Yet the source and the target of this murderous threat remain highly ambiguous. The crossing-through of the word "threatened" symbolically declares an intention to eliminate, to "kill" the presence of the word; this typographic move simultaneously suggests a removal of the threat "to kill" and physically demonstrates that the act of killing is no longer merely threatened but actualized. Meanwhile, the word "~~threadened~~" also bears the marks of an attempted erasure, which suggests the violence of the "hard guttural." The replacing of the "d" with a sharper-sounding "t" in this word also embodies this violence in sonic terms. In the process, semantics also shift. For example, the ambiguous neologism "threadened" suggests multiple potential meanings but primarily infers a past act of threading and thus a sense of continuity and succession. However, "threatened," a word with a more sharply defined meaning, closes down the multiplicity and linkages "threadened" embodies. The line that crosses through "threadened" not only marks an erasure but also, because it extends backwards (our usual reading habits tell us) from the beginning of the word, visually suggests a linking thread from a "before" onto which the letters of "threadened" appear to be strung. Furthermore, "threadened" is not only crossed out/threaded but some of its letters are also underlined and emphasized; in this manner "r," "e," and "d" seemingly generate the word "reddened," which makes up the next line. This move is simultaneously a demonstration of the fecundity of even the most uncertain, ambiguous, and incomplete articulations, and at the same time it intimates a kind of "bleeding," a "reddened" stain issuing from the violence previously intimated.

Throughout the process of reading these intricate verbal-visual interactions, the status of the "hard guttural" remains resolutely ambiguous: is this harsh-sounding entity a violent utterance? Is this the source of a murderous threat? Or is it "hard" in the sense of "difficult"? And is the guttural something that issues from the "gutter," from the site of the abject, the expelled, the marginal? And/or is it something that "gutters," that sputters waveringly, inarticulately? O'Sullivan's manipulations of language and the page's visual resources in *red shifts* generate many such open questions. Her poem recurrently weaves together suggestions and enactments of violence, displacement, physical distress, and inarticulacy. While these recurring elements are intimately linked to and informed by an Irish diasporic history, O'Sullivan's poem does not trace any particular historical or social occurrence or referent. Rather, her investigations are leveled at the historically shaped patterns of violence, silencing, and suffering inculcated into language by historical, ideological, and material configurations of power and domination.

This legacy is performed as an inheritance that is "sedimented, or amassed, in the body" (Connerton 72) of the poem. As Huk perceptively argues, O'Sullivan "attend[s] to the often violent *body* of language as both her means of being in the world and as her disease" (39). A foregrounding of the corporeal dimensions of the poetic page induces attention to forms of violence embedded in language but also, crucially, to the possibilities for more open and expansive modes of being and knowing. This multidimensional archaeo-poetics aims to expand the capacities of language, contesting its appropria-tion by and complicity with structures of oppressive power, and aspiring, by putting hitherto untapped resources of written/printed/sounded language into play, to enable it to function as the bearer of an "Unofficial Word," as the title of one of O'Sullivan's other works has it.

Salvaging Materialism

O'Sullivan's work presents itself as "excavation and retrieval of possibilities within oral, aural, visual, and sculptural properties in language, voice and assemblage. Records of search explore dismemberment and reconstitution, divergence and multiplicity in the mattering of material" (*Etruscan Reader III* backmatter). Such an archaeopoetics corresponds no less than Cha's and Howe's to a Benjaminian aspiration to "brush history against the grain" (Ben-jamin, *Illuminations* 248) in pursuit of lost or suppressed aspects of history and culture whose residues might yield hitherto untapped "semantic po-tentials" or "energies" (Habermas 120, 112). For O'Sullivan, the history and culture—both modern and ancient—of the "Celtic fringes" ("Interview") of the British Isles provides a particularly rich terrain for such an "excava-tion and retrieval of possibilities." We have already seen how in *that bread should be* her poetry digs down into the strata of oral and folk traditions of the author's Irish ancestry. O'Sullivan's *red shifts* extends this exhumation and thereby offers opportunities for an examination of the Benjaminian di-mensions of her project and the ways in which her poetics reshapes this his-toricist model.

O'Sullivan's *red shifts* extensively borrows and redeploys motifs and sym-bols from Celtic art and mythology; the zigzags and spirals that recur through-out the poem, for example, are often seen in ancient Celtic art where they are invested with a wealth of symbolic significance. These designs have been found carved into stone at megalithic and Paleolithic sites such as New-grange, Knowth, and Fourknocks in Ireland. Featuring particularly in pas-sage gravesites, these symbolic motifs, especially spirals, are associated with the cycles of organic life and the passage between life, death, and rebirth (Nash 123–43; Kelly 128–85). Archaeologist Richard Bradford proposes that these carvings might have constituted a "prehistoric cosmology" rooted in "a perception of space . . . shaped by mythology as much as topography" (108), a map of the stars in the night sky whose configurations and movements are interwoven with ancient ways of making sense of the material world. These patterns and the lost cultures they reference function in *red shifts* as traces of extinguished ways of life and modes of knowledge whose unfulfilled possibilities the poem seeks to revive.

O'Sullivan's approach to the salvaging and redeployment of such archaic materials owes much to the influence of Joseph Beuys and Kurt Schwitters. Schwitters's "superb use of the UN—the NON and the LESS—THE UN-REGARDED, the found, the cast-offs, the dismembered materials" (O'Sullivan, *Palace* 67) in his Merz works, into which he incorporated scraps of everyday waste matter such as used tickets, food labels, and fragments of newspaper, functions as a model for her own "concern for the retrieval of potentials within material" (67). Whether in the visual assemblages she was making in the 1980s or in her later poetry that melds different aspects of her practice, her weaving of salvaged cultural fragments into multimedia collages similarly aims for a revivifying of the elemental potentialities latent in abject or negatively defined cultural "cast-offs" that possess a transformative capacity hitherto unacknowledged and untapped. This poetics of salvaging is also much informed by her engagement with the work of Beuys. As mentioned earlier, O'Sullivan shares with Beuys an interest in Celtic mythologies and artifacts and a shamanistic veneration for the natural world. Indeed, Beuys also used in his work zigzag and spiral motifs derived from his visits to ancient Irish sites such as Newgrange. For him, these symbols embodied a "sophisticated knowledge of physical and spiritual energies," and they echoed his "Theory of Sculpture," which emphasizes the transformative properties of certain substances (Tisdall, *We Go* 72). O'Sullivan's 1993 work *In the House of the Shaman* uses a quotation from Beuys as an epigraph to its second section, "Kinship with Animals": "To stress the idea of transformation and of substance. This is precisely what the shaman does in order to bring about change and development: his nature is therapeutic" (28). Beuys's work with one of his signature materials—fat—epitomizes this shamanic activity. The ability of fat to change states when heated or cooled, along with its healing properties—Beuys claims that the Tartars who rescued him from his crashed plane treated his burns with fat—embody shamanic principles. O'Sullivan's intimation of the untapped energies of "dismembered materials" echoes Beuys's shamanistic belief in the transformative and "therapeutic" power of particular substances.

The opening from *red shifts* depicted in figure 15, where fragments gleaned from the remains of a lost Celtic culture are collaged together with other verbal and visual elements, exemplifies a poetic "retrieval of possibilities" by means of assemblage, an attention to unacknowledged or "cast-off" cultural remains, and a faith in the transformative energies secreted in such

i have found this red
is breathed
or reply,
water's edge, ~~DECOMPOSITIONS~~
draw ing breath's
broken fanging –
Nion, the Ash, this 3rd
letter of salvages
bridle & gut
aquacity staltic –

pearlful
shoreline paler pelt
amber peep in step in in draping –

Figure 15. From *red shifts* by Maggie O'Sullivan. Etruscan Books © 2001 Maggie O'Sullivan. Unpaginated. Original in color. Reprinted by permission of Etruscan Books and the author.

materials. On the verso page, the zigzags and spirals of Celtic symbolism, drawn and printed in red crayon and black ink, form part of a multimedia collage that also features an enigmatic, partly humanoid form surrounded by rivulets of blood-like ink. Simultaneously fleshy and skeletal, anthropomorphic and animal-like, this figure constitutes a site of intersection between the living and the dead, the mortal and the otherworldly, as well as a fusing of the human and the animal that echoes animistic elements of ancient pagan beliefs and rituals. These visual elements are placed in a dynamic dialogic relation with the text of the facing page. "[T]his red," for example, finds a visual "reply" in the ink and crayon reds on the opposite page, while the red zigzags resonate suggestively with the lines "**draw ing breath's** / broken fanging" forming a "drawing" of ragged breathing. Meanwhile, the humanoid-skeletal form resonates with the crossed-through word "~~DECOMPOSITIONS~~," which linguistically points to processes of corporeal decay intimated by the visual juxtaposition of plump fleshiness and bonelike forms. The Celtic symbolism of the lines "Nion, the Ash, this 3rd / letter of salvages" refers to the "3rd / letter" of the ancient Ogham alphabet named Nion, the Celtic name for the ash tree. This invocation of the potent symbol of "the Ash" (also conspicuous in *that bread should be*) echoes across the opening with a tiny image of a silhouetted house next to a large tree pasted over the red zigzags. In this opening, a process of interplay between various cultural fragments, and between their different materialities, has the effect of invigorating each fragment's significance, sparking off "semantic potentials" (Habermas 120) in a series of dialogues between one reference and another, one kind of materiality and another, one mode of articulation and another.

In a sense, O'Sullivan's pages are concretized Benjaminian "dialectical images" in which disparate indexical fragments of cultures past and present montaged on the surface of the page produce "spark[s] of hope" (Benjamin, *Illuminations* 247) from exhumed remains of the past. Kaleidoscopic collisions and fusions of different materials and physical qualities engender "flashes" of cognition or recognition of latent presences and energies. For example, the miniature image of a house and tree just discernable at the bottom right of the verso side of this opening functions as a found fragment. The diminutive size and blurred indistinct outlines of this tree and house signal its referent's location in an irretrievable and increasingly distant past, while its apparently torn edges materially testify to a process of fragmentation. But as something rescued and revivified in a new context, this scrap also evinces an activity of salvaging that resonates with the line "Nion, the Ash, this 3rd/ letter of salvages" across the page. This designation of Nion as the "letter of salvages" points to the strong associations between the ash tree and the power of the sea in Celtic lore; small pieces of ash wood were (and sometimes still are) used as charms against drowning by those going to sea (Gifford 9, 29). Yet in O'Sullivan's poem, Nion is a "letter of salvages": not exactly a letter equated with safe passage over the sea but one that becomes a sign of shipwreck and rescue. Indeed, it is not only the pagan resonances of "this 3rd / letter of salvages" that have been retrieved here; this opening displays a wider collection of materials, including the tiny image of the house and tree and the spirals and zigzags, which are also "salvages," flotsam and jetsam of lost or forgotten ways of life. O'Sullivan has described the poetic page as "[a] place of damage, savagery, pain, silence," of "broken fanging," of "D̶E̶C̶O̶M̶P̶O̶S̶I̶T̶I̶O̶N̶S̶," of loss and threatened oblivion, but "also a place of salvage, retrieval and recovery" ("Writing / Conversation" par. 8). In the pages of *red shifts*, unrealized potentials for transformative meaning might be glimpsed in the ebb and flow between savagery and recuperation, between the lost and found, or between the skeletal and the fleshly, the jagged and the rounded, the verbal and the visual, the past world of the fragment and the present moment into which it is folded. As in Benjamin's dialectical image, these semantic and material elements are held in a series of perpetually unresolved and potentially productive tensions.

However, O'Sullivan's poetry also performs a reshaping of the dialectical image by proposing a much more dynamic and mobile model of transformative dialectics than Benjamin's image-based "dialectics at a standstill" (*Arcades* 462, N2a, 3). Remarking on the "intimations of the archaic" that infuse O'Sullivan's poems, Charles Bernstein aptly describes her work as "a cross-sectional boring through time, whirling the sedimentary layers into knots. The archaic material pushes up to the surface" ("Foreword" 9). In *red shifts*, the surface of the page quite palpably becomes a site of intersection between the dormant potentials of archaic materials and the present moment of reading/sensory encounter, but relations between such elements are always shifting, as the text's title suggests, or even "whirling," as Bernstein states. The corporeal dimensions of O'Sullivan's poetics play a prominent part in enabling this work to suggest alternatives to Benjamin's arrested dialectical moment, epitomized by the epiphanic "flash" and the fleetingly suspended "constellation" (*Arcades* 462, N2a, 3).

O'Sullivan's embodied archaeopoetics takes as its model the non-teleological flows and transformations of somatic being and the dynamic palimpsestual interplays between intertwined human, vegetal, animal, and textual corporealities, or as she puts it, "Living Earth Kinships on the / vast-lunged Shores of the Multiple Body imbued with / wide-awake slumberings & cavortings" (*Palace* 65). Huk's thought-provoking discussion of O'Sullivan's contribution to a rethinking of metaphysics is helpful here. Huk remarks that "by deploying a poetics of embodiment . . . she enters 'the word's' shifting landscape, a movement that she frequently images as *cutting into* the perceived, the immediate and physical, which 'bleeds' back; she does so 'shamanistically'" (39). This practice enables O'Sullivan's poetry to "signal an alternative to both the vatic pronouncements and the waiting games of western cultural Judeo-Christianity through other kinds of 'metaphysical,' 'interrealmic' . . . *activity*" (39). The collaborative relations with an otherness in language that "'bleeds' back" produces an ongoing and, as Huk emphasizes, *active* process of transformation, imagined and enacted in bodily terms. Crucially, this enables O'Sullivan's work to "pre-empt[ ] the paralysis that comes with waiting for the end-time that might give meaning to the present" (64).

O'Sullivan's shamanistic emphasis on corporeality, ongoing transformative change, and the intertwined relations of "Living Earth Kinships" similarly enable her work to suggest alternatives to a comparable paralysis implicit in the temporality of the fleetingly suspended moments upon which Benjamin's dialectical model relies. The dialogue between entangled materialities in her poetry is crucial to this mobilization of potentials. In the back and forth of reading between the visual and verbal dimensions of a poem, or between a skeletal and a fleshy form, or between the photographic and the hand-drawn, meanings multiply, contradict one another, coexist and change. One of the clearest examples of this is in the multiple incarnations of the color red in *red shifts*. A highly symbolic color, often abstractly associated with anger, violence, danger and alarm, the possible meanings of red become ever more complex in O'Sullivan's poem. In the opening depicted in figure 15, for example, the red of the ink spills form a visual network around the fleshy-skeletal form, suggesting orderly flows of fluids around the body. The watery verbal imagery on the facing page strengthens this inference. The red crayon on the page, however, signifies in different ways—the expressive strokes echoing Celtic designs claim a primal and vital link with past cultures, their gestural quality pointing to a genesis in the drawing hand and the "ancestral self" of the artist. The word "red" printed in black ink on the facing page differs again; it is a "red" that is "found" by an "i" that rarely makes an appearance in O'Sullivan's poetry, a "red" that is "breathed," thus constituting itself as a medium or meditative space in which the breath associated with speaking becomes far less hindered than it is elsewhere in the poem, and a space in which an articulation of selfhood becomes a possibility. Yet the different semantic materialities of these reds are never deterministic; these same spilled, drawn, and printed reds might well be interpreted or experienced differently, as the homonymic overlap between "red" and "read" suggests.

O'Sullivan's red, as the title indicates, constantly "shifts," its semantic and sensory possibilities multiplying, but also sometimes conflicting and contradicting one another. Such indeterminacy and unresolvedness intimates the teeming potentials held within O'Sullivan's pages; the poem's shifting reds manifest the multiplicity of "semantic potentials" embedded in its material strata as well as the expanded range of the "semantic" itself. Indeed, O'Sullivan's work addresses the ways in which an engagement with materiality is itself a "lost" or unacknowledged element of reading practices. Inextricably bound up with the "retrieval of possibilities" in her poetry, then, is a "mattering of material" (*Etruscan Reader III* backmatter), where "mattering" points both to matter and meaningfulness.

O'Sullivan's poetry wants to redeem "sensuous meaningfulness, the kind of nondiscursive meaning that material things have, material meaning" (J. M. Bernstein, *Voluptuous* 47) to recoup some of the lost or disavowed dimensions of language and inscription. Apparent across the body of O'Sullivan's work, this aspiration becomes most evident in the collage techniques of one of her most recent works, *murmur: tasks of mourning*. Comprising a series of highly visual and tactile language and image arrangements, *murmur* continues O'Sullivan's synesthetic practice of "many heuristic pathings" (O'Sullivan, "Writing / Conversation" par. 6) pursued in *red shifts*. Like *red shifts*, this work's "*tasks of mourning*," and its mode of lament, are informed by historical legacies connected to a "familial diasporic" (O'Sullivan, *murmur* n. pag.) referenced at various points in the poem, a heritage carried in the sug-

Figure 16. From *murmur: tasks of mourning* by Maggie O'Sullivan. Veer Press © 2011 Maggie O'Sullivan. Unpaginated. Original in color. Reprinted by permission of the author.

gestion of Irish pronunciation in the word "traipsin'" or in various archaic terms and references. But what is mourned here is less a specific past than a widespread loss of multiplicitous potential in language and culture, which is at least partly linked, in O'Sullivan's thinking, with a delegitimation of sensory modes of meaningfulness in what she refers to as the "restrictive culture" ("In conversation with Brown" 160) of modern rationalized societies.

The example from *murmur* depicted in figure 16 constitutes an embodied archaeocritical reflection on lost potential in language and culture. The literalness and physicality of this collage's components both body forth "sensuous meaningfulness" and evince signs of its disavowal as a legitimate form of cognition. Text printed on fragile tissue paper demonstrates a discord between material surface and semantic coherence, between sensuousness and intelligibility. Creased, wrinkled, and torn, the emphasized materiality of the writing surface results in "Erasures" and the "rupture" of linguistic meaning. Two lines of hand-stitched crosses echo this process of erasure or crossing out and work to highlight the "rupture" that this page embodies even as they suture the torn pieces of tissue-text in a "bruty fissuring," as the very last line of *murmur* has it. The corset-like form of the resulting sutured text, meanwhile, suggests a sense of restriction that is explicitly gendered feminine but which also points to a wider sense of constricted corporeality. These "Erasures," restrictions, and ruptures might be read in the light of a split between discourse-based cognition and sensuous materiality that "silences" the meaning potential of sensuous matter. As J. M. Bernstein indicates, this schism can be traced to Kant's *Critique of Pure Reason* in which "what belongs to the domain of the *intelligible* stands opposed to what belongs to the domain of the *sensible*" (*Voluptuous* 5). According to this Kantian schema, sensory, intuitive experience can only be rendered meaningful insofar as it is subsumable to rational concepts; thus, according to J. M. Bernstein, sensuous meaningfulness has been delegitimized in modernity as a form of knowing or thinking. Furthermore, he argues:

> It is not too much of a stretch to see the abstraction from particularity and sensory givenness as the abstractive device of modern forms of social reproduction: the subsuming of the use values of particular goods beneath the exchange value of monetary worth, or the domination of intersubjective practices by norms of instrumental reason that yield the rationalization or bureaucratization of our dominant institutions. (*Voluptuous* 23)

The "rupture" between the meaningfulness of materials and discourse-based cognition to which O'Sullivan's poem testifies, then, constitutes a reflection on the "restrictive culture" ("In conversation with Brown" 160) of the poet's social world and on its processes of abstracting, instrumentalization, and enclosure. The torn and stitched corset-like text of *murmur* stands as a critique of such processes. Yet at the same time, the flower-like shapes that emerge from the brutalized and sutured corporeal text articulate an aspiration toward recovery and healing, toward a "salvaging" (*murmur* n. pag.) of delegitimized materiality, even as the torn edges of these shapes also carry the enduring physical traces of a process of "savaging" (*murmur*).

In an interview with Charles Bernstein, O'Sullivan says "we're living in such a profoundly materialistic world, that [the] magic and beauty, and joy and power that is in language is not appreciated, or not known" ("Interview"). Her direct, causal connection between the "materialistic world" of late twentieth-century consumer capitalism and a diminishment of the capacities of language echoes some of the early assertions of Language writing. Indeed, O'Sullivan shares much common ground with writers associated with this loose grouping; in particular her dialogues with Bruce Andrews and Charles Bernstein have revolved around numerous shared political and poetic principles. In Ron Silliman's seminal formulation, "[w]hat happens when a language moves toward and passes into a capitalist stage of development is an anesthetic transformation of the perceived tangibility of the word, with corresponding increases in its descriptive and narrative capacities" (125). Under the all-pervasive logic of capitalism, words become part of a transactional process; stripped of their "perceived tangibility," they are made transparent, instrumentalized, and valued only for their referentiality, for the ways in which they can be exchanged for an image of "the World." An attempt to resist this logic of instrumentalization and commodification was a characteristic feature of the early activities and theoretical assertions of Language writers; as Andrews and Charles Bernstein put it in a well-known statement, "[i]t is our sense that the project of poetry does not involve turning language into a commodity for consumption; instead, it involves repossessing the sign through close attention to, and active participation in, its production" (x). For O'Sullivan too, transactional uses of language embody and echo an empty materialism of contemporary existence. Her poetry aims to counter "materialistic" contemporary culture with an alternative kind of materialism: one that acknowledges and employs the physical, visually and acoustically embodied dimensions of language in a production of meaning that critiques logics of instrumentality and consumption.

However, O'Sullivan's particular form of materialism is not only concerned with forming a critique of the commodity forms of contemporary culture; it is also imbued with a shamanistic sense of the unacknowledged "magic and beauty, and joy and power" embedded in the corporeal sensuousness of language. In discussion with Charles Bernstein, she declares a belief "in the transformative, alchemical forces that are inherent in languages," naming not only the aforementioned Beuys but also Jerome Rothenberg as influences on her conception of language's transformative capacities. Rothenberg's work with "primal poetries," she says, provides ample examples of "language constructions designed to bring about change," such as healing chants, for instance, which demonstrate "the magic in language, the potency, transformative potential in language" ("Interview"). This numinous sense of multidimensional language is not quite in tune with the materialist politics that O'Sullivan shares with Language writing. As Hank Lazer indicates, such a "spiritual" sensibility sits uncomfortably with the politics of Language poetics: "While it is common to valorize the importance of such writers as Robert Duncan and Jerome Rothenberg, a closer examination of their poetry and poetics immediately places us within writing traditions that are openly mystical, romantic, and, in the case of Rothenberg, shamanic and magical—all qualities that are disturbing to most innovative contemporary poets, many of whom have developed a poetics more obviously reliant on tenets of cultural materialism and an anti-romantic metaphysics" ("People's

Poetry" par. 19). Indeed, the "shamanic and magical" dimensions of poetries such as Duncan's, Rothenberg's, and O'Sullivan's are on a fundamental level antithetical to the cultural materialist dimensions of Language poetics, which seek to wrest language from the enchantments of the logic of commodity fetishism. Lazer's remark suggests that an attribution of "magical" dimensions and powers to language, no matter how materially embodied, is effectively a re-enchantment of language, albeit one aimed toward offering alternatives to the commodity fetishism of consumer capitalism.

O'Sullivan's melding of a mystical sensibility toward multidimensional language with a materialist understanding not only of contemporary culture but also of the exchange economies of signification in many ways parallels Benjamin's rather fraught combining of messianism and historical materialism. As demonstrated in chapter 1, there are fundamental contradictions in Benjamin's attempt to fuse an antievolutionary messianic view of history with a model of politics that rests on a notion of progress toward political emancipation rooted in materialist struggle. However, as Habermas's "Rescuing Critique" indicates, such contradictions need not negate the value of Benjamin's "semantic materialism" (123). Benjamin's messianism points to a *"further* moment" (Habermas 122) of materialist critique: "besides hunger and oppression, failure; besides prosperity and liberty, happiness" (121), a making-meaningful of the materialist quest for prosperity and liberty. O'Sullivan's re-enchantment of language might be read as performing a comparable move: besides a critique of language's instrumentalization and commodification, her poetry wants to articulate "anger" ("Interview"). Similarly, besides a repossession of the sign "through close attention to, and active participation in, its production" (Andrews and Bernstein x), O'Sullivan's work hopes to rescue "magic and beauty, and joy" (O'Sullivan "Interview"). O'Sullivan's combining of a materialist critique with a mystical sense of language's redemptory potential proposes a *"further* moment" of language politics by articulating a gnosis of the unfulfilled and possibly transformative capacities of language's sensory forms of meaningfulness. For O'Sullivan, the physical, corporeal dimensions of signification form a large part of what is normally "not appreciated, not known" ("Interview") in language. To expand upon the usual modes of writing, saying, and reading and extend the senses used in the processes of reading poetry is to bring about an active engagement not only with the processes of making meaning but also with the numinous, transformative potential of language to expand the parameters of "meaning."

Such a sensibility is perhaps at its most emphatic in O'Sullivan's extensive use in *murmur* of gestural marks, which strongly resemble language but are not recognizable or legible as such. In figure 17, for example, a number of roughly hand-drawn boxes filled in with red crayoned letter-like marks and

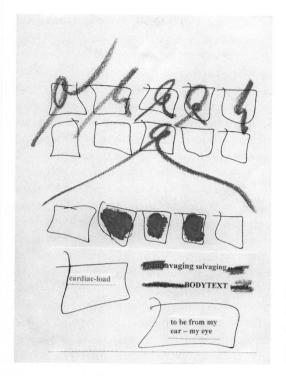

Figure 17. From *murmur* by Maggie O'Sullivan. Veer Press © 2011 Maggie O'Sullivan. Unpaginated. Original in color. Reprinted by permission of the author.

red impasto paint fill the top two-thirds of the page. These boxes recall a bureaucratized world of form-filling. But where the straight, mechanical lines and restrictive options of official forms interpellate the writing subject into a process of self-justification and restrictive categorization, the hand-drawn quality of O'Sullivan's boxes and the non-linguistic nature of the marks that fill them signal alternatives to such imperatives. Such gestural "signs" resist a process of "turning language into a commodity for consumption" (Andrews and Bernstein x); their very illegibility refuses instrumentalization or translation into easily consumed meaning. But as well as critiquing processes of interpellation and the commodity forms of language, *murmur*'s boxes and marks also suggest alternative domains of knowledge and modes of signification. O'Sullivan's visual language forms raise the possibility of an "unofficial world we make by inhabiting" (C. Bernstein, "Foreword" 8) her poetry. This unofficial world is embodied in marks like the glyphs of this page from *murmur*, whose very illegibility and gestural power hint at hitherto unplumbed dimensions of material writing.

Commenting upon the use of "somatic traces" by visual artists such as Mira Shor and Pierre Alechinsky, Johanna Drucker says that the gestural "trace makes itself in the dynamic pleasure of material making and as such, remains a sign which has not yet reached the threshold of meaning" (*Figuring* 65). Indeed, O'Sullivan's marks evince a *jouissance* of making and marking, which induces her illegible signs to ecstatically spill outside of the hand-drawn boxes. Yet this material overflow both suggests that these signs have "not yet reached the threshold of meaning" and at the same time that they exceed it. O'Sullivan's somatic inscriptions, although illegible, are so much like letters that they seem to belong to a secret language or unfamiliar script, a suggestion strengthened by the repetition of certain marks. In this respect, they function as glyphs, which differ from gestural traces in that they implicitly claim to belong to a symbolic system. Drucker remarks that such signs "have meaning not accounted for in linguistic substitution . . . the power of the glyph—whether alchemical, magical, esoteric, or exotic is precisely this resistance to recuperation within the closed system of mere meaning" (*Figuring* 69). O'Sullivan's glyphs embody a dynamic and ongoing process of mark making and deciphering where forms seemingly participate in an esoteric symbolic activity but are never resolvable into an entirely graspable "meaning." As Drucker's phraseology helps to emphasize, the resistance to "mere meaning" embodied in O'Sullivan's somatic inscriptions indicates an aspiration to move beyond linguistically or discursively tied processes of meaning making into a more expansive and multidimensional terrain.

O'Sullivan's corporeal archaeopoetics of salvaging proposes that the lost "magic and beauty, and joy and power that is in language" exist in the sensuous dimensions of language, in a kind of meaningfulness that contributes in unacknowledged ways to processes of meaning making at the same time as resisting subsumption to discursively based forms of cognition. In so doing, her poetic forms call for a "re-cognition" of multidimensional modes of meaningfulness and the traces of "other-than or invisible or dimmed or marginalized or excluded" ("In conversation with Brown" 159) aspects of language, history, and culture. In her work, it is precisely the sensuous dimensions of language and embodied modes of experiencing and "re-cognizing" that are the voiceless aspects of language and culture, and thus they are also domains of the marginalized and excluded. O'Sullivan's excavations of the material page seek to give tangible and meaningful form to "UNofficial" dimensions of the word and the world with which it is intertwined.

5
Isles Full of Noises

KAMAU BRATHWAITE'S ARCHIPELAGIC POETICS

Au bout du petit matin ces pays sans stèle, ces chemins sans
mémoire, ces vents sans tablette.
Qu'importe?
Nous dirions. Chanterions. Hurlerions.

At the brink of dawn these countries with no stela, these roads with
no memory, these winds with no tablet.
What does it matter?
We would speak. Sing. Scream.

Aimé Césaire, *Cahier d'un retour au pays natal/*
Notebook of a Return to My Native Land

As this epigraph indicates, the African Caribbean "poem including history"
faces an array of epistemological challenges: How does a poet access a heritage densely written over by colonial and neo-colonial imperatives? How
does one approach a collective memory fractured by the violent history of
slavery? How can poetry negotiate a landscape rendered culturally unintelligible? Kamau Brathwaite's response to this problematic is (at least) twofold.
His archaeopoetics aspires to excavate submerged traces of African Caribbean history and culture, as they have been creolized in this particular context. However, as the sensibilities of Césaire's lines suggest, this activity also
entails an acknowledgement that the very processes and power dynamics
that render dimensions of Caribbean history so resistant to recuperation are
integral to this history. Brathwaite's archaeopoetics concretizes this recognition as a mode of reflecting upon the capacities of poetry to recover traces
of the violent obfuscated history it negotiates. As Édouard Glissant puts it,
"[a] reality that was long concealed from itself . . . has as much to do with the
problematics of investigation as with a historical organization of things" (*Ca-*
ribbean 65). Therefore, Brathwaite's project is just as much an archaeocritical
reflection upon vexed questions of historical and epistemological inquiry in
a Caribbean context as it is a poetic investigation of Caribbean history itself.

Brathwaite's work investigates a Caribbean nexus of geography, history, and language through material forms that strategically evade lucid comprehension. In the words of Glissant, "the attempt to approach a reality so often hidden from view cannot be organized in terms of a series of clarifications" (*Caribbean* 2). Brathwaite's poetics contests the political valency of a poetics of clarity and accessibility or, as Nathaniel Mackey pithily puts it, "the proscription of such notions, in the name of political urgency, to socially marginalized groups" (*Discrepant* 17). This is a particularly acute issue for Caribbean and African American poetics, where so much politicized emphasis has been placed upon the recovery of silenced voices into readily available cultural forms, although, as was noted in chapter 3, the question of accessibility widely permeates discussions of "minority writing." At times, Brathwaite has been read—or misread—as articulating a fairly straightforward politics of voice, in the sense that his poetry is often thought of as "giving voice" to marginalized vernacular cultural forms. However, his poetics is much more complex. In Brathwaite's work, the impulse to bring suppressed cultural forms into articulation always involves an investigation of the impediments to doing so. Such intractabilities are formally embedded in the work itself.

Brathwaite has often been positioned—and has positioned himself—in contrast to the poetic stance of St. Lucian poet Derek Walcott. The well-worn dichotomy of Brathwaite, cast as the iconoclastic vernacular creole poet, and Walcott, seen as the ironic mimic of traditional literary forms, as the polar opposites of Caribbean poetry has been quite rightly contested by recent criticism (see Pollard, Thieme). Nevertheless, the language politics of these poets are markedly divergent. In a note in his 1987 collection *X/Self* (118), Brathwaite points out that Walcott's poetic aspirations might be aligned with the speaker of his poem "Islands":

> . . . I seek,
> As climate seeks its style, to write
> Verse crisp as sand, clear as sunlight,
> Cold as the curled wave, ordinary
> As a tumbler of island water . . .
> (Walcott, *Collected Poems* 52)

Walcott, in general, addresses his poetics to the task of mastering European cultural traditions and literary forms until they yield a poetic language capable of lucidly articulating Caribbean cultural experience. Brathwaite critiques Walcott's pursuit of a language of "H_2O simplicity," a "pitcher of clear metaphor" (*X/Self* 118, 29) as he somewhat scornfully puts it. Brathwaite also questions the viability of a poetics of clarity by testing the limits of intelligibility and at times literal legibility. His work pursues what Craig Dworkin calls "strategic illegibility" (xxiii), where illegibility does not just block access to meaning but opens up alternative modes of meaningfulness.

It is notable that Brathwaite, in contrasting his poetics with Walcott's, selects an example from the other poet's work that is loaded with geographic metaphors. Brathwaite's own poetics draws explicitly on the historical geographies and physical topographies of the Caribbean archipelago. The archipelagic spatiality of the Caribbean islands, the ebb and flow of the surrounding sea, and the currents of the wider Atlantic constitute a powerful set of imaginative resources for this poet's archaeopoetic engagements with the history of slavery and colonialism in all its materiality as well as with this history's legacies. However, Brathwaite distances himself from Walcott's benignly "crisp . . . sand," gently "curled wave," and domesticated "tumbler of island water." Brathwaite's most well-known statement—"the hurricane does not roar in pentameters" (*History of the Voice* 10)—indicates a quite different sensibility and set of topoi. For him, the hurricane—intimately connected in his geographic imaginary with the *harmattan* winds of Western Africa and the trade winds that brought the slave ships across the Atlantic—represents a distinctive historical and geographical consciousness as well as a contemporary visceral experience for which he seeks appropriate modes of aesthetic articulation.

Above all, the hurricane is noisy; and it is an aesthetics of noise—both sonically and visually invoked in Brathwaite's poetry—which I will investigate in this chapter as the basis for his archaeopoetics. The incorporation and foregrounding of materially emphasized noise constitutes this work's culturally resonant mode of opacity or "strategic illegibility." By incorporating a sense of the submerged, marginalized, and devalued "noises" of Caribbean oral cultures, Brathwaite's work widens the compass of the poetic, materially investigating the possibilities for an articulation of "these countries with no stela, these roads with no memory, these winds with no tablet." Like his precursor Césaire, Brathwaite's work seeks a mode in which to "speak. Sing. Scream" a negated cultural history even as he must acknowledge its forms of negation. The ways in which he does so are often more opaque and discordant than the routes taken by many of his predecessors and contemporaries. "Noise," performed in both oral and visual terms, embodies the twofold impulse to which I pointed at the outset of this chapter: it both reshapes the English language to pursue new kinds of meaningfulness, and investigates the forms of epistemic erasure and marginalization entangled with the normative conventions of Standard English.

It is not only the howling hurricane that features so prominently in Brathwaite's geographically informed archaeopoetics. The submarine currents of the ocean also inform his development of a philosophy of history based on a notion of "tidalectics." Brathwaite's theorization and poetic performance of a tidalectic model of history and culture archaeocritically rethinks materialist dialectical understandings of historical process for a Caribbean context. This move raises provocative questions about the role of geographical imaginaries and material experiences in the constitution of historical understanding.

My consideration of Brathwaite's work engages his theorization of an emphatically oral notion of "nation language," before considering its implications for the development of distinctive modes of visual experimentations in his poetry of the '90s. Discussion of this poetry will primarily revolve around a key work in the evolution of his visual poetics, "Letter Sycorax" from his 1992 collection *Middle Passages*. However, I shall also refer to other works within and beyond this collection.

Caribbeanness and a History of the Voice

In discussion with Leonard Schwartz on an episode of the radio show Cross Cultural Poetics, Brathwaite remarks that "I have never been able to separate my history from my poetry" ("Show 94"). While he is perhaps better known for his many poetry collections spanning more than forty years, Brathwaite has a strong academic background in the discipline of history; his book *The Development of Creole Society in Jamaica 1770–1820* (1971) based on his doctoral research is still much cited and debated by historians of the Caribbean. Indeed, as Brathwaite indicates, the historical and poetic dimensions of his career have always been highly entangled. Furthermore, Brathwaite has never been able to separate either history or poetry from a geographical consciousness specific to his sense of Caribbean cultural identity. Across the body of his work, he has been recurrently concerned with an articulation of a Caribbeanness or what Glissant calls *antillanité*, a poetics that emphasizes a relational sense of Caribbean culture based upon shared histories, with links across languages, social classes, and different island cultures. Brathwaite frequently invokes the cultural and geographical specificities of his home island Barbados in his writing. Yet these islands are not imagined as secure homelands but rather as nodes in a mesh of places and times. Brathwaite's Caribbean cultural identity invariably emphasizes diasporic currents, both historically and in contemporaneity. Even his biography reflects his wider sense that Caribbeanness is always articulated in relation to "elsewhere"; Brathwaite received an extended university education in England in the 1950s and '60s, after which he worked in Ghana and the

University of the West Indies in Kingston, Jamaica; in recent years he has moved between New York and Barbados.

Brathwaite's concern with exploring a common sense of Caribbeanness provided the impetus behind his formation—along with John La Rose and Andrew Salkey—of the Caribbean Artists Movement (CAM) in London, an organization that brought together writers, visual and performing artists, and critics through a series of events and publishing ventures between 1966 and 1972. With clear affinities to the Black Arts Movement, active in the United States at the same time, CAM was concerned with providing space for the articulation of a specifically black aesthetic and sense of unity, although in less openly militant and politically confrontational ways than its American counterpart. For the few years in which it flourished, CAM facilitated links between writers and artists and brought Caribbean arts to the attention of a wider audience through public events such as readings, exhibitions, and conferences, and the publication of a journal, *Savacou*, edited by Brathwaite. Though short-lived in its formal phase, the activities of CAM sparked ongoing dialogues about Caribbean aesthetic and political identity. Many of its members, including poet Linton Kwesi Johnson, painter Aubrey Williams, cultural critics Stuart Hall and Kenneth Ramchand, and Brathwaite himself, subsequently rose to prominence in artistic and academic circles. For Brathwaite, as Anne Walmsley has suggested ("A Sense"), what united Caribbean artists and thinkers was not only a shared history but also a common need to negotiate between a European aesthetic heritage imposed by colonialism and a folk tradition that drew on hitherto denigrated African vestiges of Caribbean culture and society. For a time, CAM functioned as a nexus for a sense of Caribbean cultural community. Despite its gradual dissolution in the 1970s, due in part to the geographical dispersion of its members and in part to a divergence of political agendas, Brathwaite has continued to situate his poetic and critical work in loose relation to an array of other Caribbean artistic and cultural productions.

The question of a Caribbean aesthetic is at the heart of Brathwaite's discussion of "nation language" in his seminal essay *History of the Voice* (1984). In this essay he brings together ideas about poetry, history, and geography that shape his archaeopoetics of noise. The essay relates a long history of cultural "submergence" of African languages and traditions, from the imposition of European languages on African slaves in the Caribbean to the constriction of poetic form to iambic pentameter via an English colonial education. Such imposed languages and cultural forms, argues Brathwaite, cannot provide a "syllabic intelligence" (8) adequate for an articulation of Caribbean culture: "[t]he hurricane does not roar in pentameters. And that's the problem: how do you get a rhythm which approximates the *natural* experience, the *environmental* experience?" (10). As Césaire proclaimed before him, the Caribbean "winds [have] no tablet," no grounding cultural tradition of aesthetic representation. First, note that Brathwaite's reformulation of this observation foregrounds the non-linguistic elements of language, such as rhythm and the notion of "syllabic intelligence," which suggests a mode of understanding embedded in the physical (sonic and tactile) levels of language. The hurricane is a visceral experience and calls for a sensory language. Second, it is important to note that Brathwaite understands the phenomenon of the hurricane not just in terms of a "*natural* experience" that just happens to be specific to the Caribbean region but as a "geo-psychic" (Brathwaite, "Show 94") link to Africa with its genesis in the West African trade wind, the *harmattan*: "It is that same wind that brought Columbus . . . it is that same wind which we call . . . the trade winds . . . which is really, truthfully the slave trade winds; it is that wind which brings the hurricanes every year" ("Show 94"). Thus "the *natural* experience, the *environmental* experience" in the Caribbean is inextricably meshed with *historical* experience. For Brathwaite, "nation language," a vernacular that infuses the imposed language of the dominant culture with the "*submerged*" traces and inflections of other suppressed languages, offers a viable mode of responding to the problem of articulating Caribbean cultural experience (13). His paradigmatic examples of cultural forms that embrace "nation language" include poetry by figures such as John Figueroa, Michael Smith, and Linton Kwesi Johnson, whose work, from the 1960s onwards, variously drew on the rhythms of calypso and reggae and the idioms and diction of everyday vernacular speech: dimensions of folk culture bearing traces of creolized African traditions.

It needs to be acknowledged that, for Brathwaite, the submerged dimensions of Caribbean culture are predominantly *African*. As Denise deCaires Narain puts it, "it is *pan-African* identity that is invoked, rather than an ethnically inclusive one" (91). Brathwaite's poetics pay less attention to the lost traditions of the indigenous peoples of the Caribbean, say, or indentured Asians. He is not unreflective about this; when in an interview Nathaniel Mackey asks him if he has "felt an impulse to go to the Arawak and the Carib mythologies," Brathwaite answers, "Yes. Still, it's for me not comfortable." Brathwaite ascribes fellow Caribbean writer Wilson Harris's ability to draw on such cultures to a somewhat essentialist notion that Harris "has part origins" (20) in an area where these influences have been less thoroughly eradicated. Brathwaite's inattention to a multiplicity of historically submerged presences in the Caribbean leaves his poetics open to charges of exclusivism, to heed Vincent Pecora's cautionary remarks discussed in chapter 2. But it is also the case that "Africa" itself is figured as a multiplicity of cultural traditions, whose forms of creolization are hardly uniform. Furthermore, Brathwaite's privileging of African influences can be seen as a strategic move. Narain argues that in his poetics, "Africa functions as a version of the lost maternal body . . . a kind of *collective imaginary*" (92). This idea of "Africa" stands for something more amorphous and inaccessible than even the enormity of the lost continent. As Brathwaite remarks, "Underground and under the water there are larger forms which have deeper resonance and we haven't yet reached them" ("Interview" with Mackey 21). Like these "larger forms," "Africa" is neither a coherent entity nor entirely recuperable. Rather, it is a way of figuring an array of suppressed cultural forces whose dialectical struggle with dominant European traditions forms the basis for an imagined collectivity, to reverse Narain's phrasing.

Submerged Noises of the Caribbean

Nation language embodies both struggle and intermingling between African and European forms in its very sounds. Says Brathwaite, "It may be in English: but often it is in an English which is like a howl, or a shout or a machine-gun or the wind or a wave . . . sometimes it is English and African at the same time" (*History* 13). He imagines creole English as eluding cultural intelligibility; like "the hurricane," like "a howl, or a shout or a machine-gun or the wind or a wave" it functions above all as *noise*. The *OED* defines noise as:

1. a sound, especially one that is loud or unpleasant or that causes disturbance
2. (technical) irregular fluctuations that accompany a transmitted electrical signal but are not part of it and tend to obscure it
   ORIGIN: from Old French, from Latin *nausea*, "seasickness"

Considered "unpleasant" or undesirable, noise is positioned as "not part" of meaningful processes of signification. It is important to acknowledge that non-European languages have been dismissed as meaningless noise throughout the history and literature of imperialism. Recall, for example, the infamous scene from Conrad's *Heart of Darkness* in which Marlow is confronted with "a mass of naked, breathing quivering bronze bodies" (235) who emit "strings of amazing words that resembled no sounds of human language" (236). Surely, then, to position creole English as "noise" is to risk perpetuating such a denigration? Brathwaite, however, performs a revaluing of noise precisely by unsettling the structure of values within which it operates. To draw on Jacques Attali's influential theorization, noise "does not exist in itself, but only in relation to the system within which it is inscribed" (26). That it functions as unwanted excess, as "disorder, dirt, pollution" (27), is a function of this system, not an essential quality of the sound characterized as noise. In addition, as a material dimension of sound that refuses—or fails—to fit into a particular signifying system, noise disrupts; it is the antagonistic and dangerous other of coherent meaningful sound.

Furthermore, noise contains an affective level of subversive threat. Serendipitously, in the present context, the etymological root of noise, *nausea*, "seasickness," connects it to the particular physical effects of traversing a rough sea. In the case of Brathwaite's poetry and poetics, the noise that infiltrates English in nation language does indeed have intimate links with the particularly turbulent crossings of the Middle Passage. In the noise of nation language is embedded the traces of African cultures carried via the Middle Passage to the Caribbean as well as the violence of this forced displacement. If in normative communication noise is minimized, pushed into the background or to the margins, in Brathwaite's conception of nation language it is a dimension of cultural experience to be acknowledged and brought into the foreground. According to Brathwaite's theory of nation language, the materiality of this language, which is "like a howl, or a shout, or a machine-gun" is all at once a remnant of the Caribbean's displaced cultures, a register of the trauma of enslavement and forced migrancy, and a response to this history's traumatic resonances in the present.

The role of noise in Brathwaite's archaeopoetics, however, is not just to disrupt the meaning structures of the English language, but to create new kinds of meaningfulness. While it may seem that noise, as the disruptive "other" of semantic functioning, is in itself meaningless, Attali argues that "[t]he presence of noise makes sense, makes meaning" (33). Firstly, a disruption by noise "signifies censorship and rarity" (33) in ways that perform a critical commentary on the social strictures of normative modes of communication. Secondly, noise, "by unchannelling auditory sensations, frees the listener's imagination" (33). In so doing, it "makes possible the creation of a new order on another level of organization, of a new code in another network" (33). By resisting subsumption into existing codes, noise stimulates the creation of new codes within which it "makes sense" and new kinds of meaning. Importantly, in Attali's thinking, the simultaneously disruptive and productive capacities of noise have implications that are not only aesthetic but social and political; meaningful sound "simulates the social order and its dissonances express marginalities" (29). For him, noise, in articulating social marginalities, carries within it the potential to create new social structures.

While Attali glosses over the complexity of relations between aesthetic strategies of sonic dissonance and social change, in that one seems too deterministically to entail the other, his theory of noise nevertheless resonates powerfully with Brathwaite's poetics of nation language. Brathwaite says, "[t]he poetry, the culture itself, exists not in a dictionary but in the tradition of the spoken word. It is based as much on sound as it is on song. That is to say, the noise that it makes is part of the meaning, and if you ignore the noise (or what you would *think* of as noise, shall I say) then you lose part of the meaning" (*History* 17). In Brathwaite's thinking, the noises of nation language express the submerged dimensions of African Caribbean culture, those elements hitherto disavowed as "marginalities," as "not part" of colonial culture and its neo-colonial outgrowths. Embedded in the "noise" that Caribbean oral rhythms and idioms bring to the spoken word, then, is a dimension of material meaningfulness that embodies the particular resonances of a cultural history and also the processes of its suppression, a history that is lost if the "noise" is omitted from the utterance or not attended to. Following Attali, such noise has the capacity to unsettle the existing conventions of signification and to create new orders of meaningfulness by which such marginalities might be heard.

When in 1979 Brathwaite initially gave the lecture later published as *History of the Voice*, he imagined an archaeology of nation language's "noise" in narrowly oral terms, asserting "[w]hen it is written, you lose the sound or the noise, and therefore you lose part of the meaning. Which is, again, why I have to have a tape recorder for this presentation. I want you to get the sound of it, rather than the sight of it" (*History* 17). Here, orality and the "sight" of the printed page are positioned as mutually exclusive. Privileging sound, Brathwaite suggests that the printed text inevitably entails a loss, even a silencing, of the sonic and cultural resonances of the spoken word. This implicit distrust of writing has its roots in what Glissant identifies as a "confrontation between the powers of the written word and the impulses of orality" in the processes of creolization (*Poetics* 5n). It is not just that the cultural resonances Brathwaite wants to incorporate into his work come from an oral culture traditionally excluded from the textual domain. It is also important to remember that writing has historically been an instrument of colonial power. "The only thing written on slave ships," Glissant points out, "was the account book listing the exchange value of slaves. Within the ship's space the cry of those deported was stifled, as it would be on the Plantations" (*Poetics* 5n). The inscribed word has functioned integrally as part of the epistemic violence of slavery that reduced Africans to commodities and to numerical values, even more so than imposed forms of spoken European languages. Writing has been one of the very means by which the bodies of deported Africans were violently appropriated and their voices "stifled." It was also a mode of communication that they were widely prohibited from learning.

However, in his poetry of the 1990s, Brathwaite dramatically rethinks his earlier binary understanding of oral and written traditions when he reappraises the resources of the visual page. Indeed, the complicity of the written text in the processes of silencing and suppressing African aspects of Caribbean culture necessitates its appropriation and reshaping. As Stewart Brown perceptively notes, "Brathwaite's most fundamental challenge to the cultural status quo has been to the language of cultural domination itself, and to its most privileged form, as book-bound, grammar-bound script" ("'Writin'" 127). Since the development of what he has dubbed his "Sycorax Video Style" in the early 1990s, Brathwaite's poetry has increasingly connected "the sight of it" and "the sound of it," using foregrounded visual dimensions of the page in an attempt to "unsubmerge" the "noise" of nation language via the resources of the printed page.

Let us turn, then, to a consideration of the visual dimensions of Brathwaite's archaeopoetics and their relations to "noise." In his introduction to *Dreamstories* (viii), Gordon Rohlehr argues that Brathwaite's sensitivity to the visual dimensions of the poetic page can be traced as far back as *Rights of Passage* (1967) and becomes more pronounced by the time of *X/Self* (1987). However, it is in *Middle Passages* (1992), the first of his collections to be printed in "Sycorax video style," that an emphasis on the visual capacities of the printed page becomes most strikingly apparent. Published in the year that marked the 500th anniversary of Columbus's arrival in the Americas in 1492 and the beginning of the transatlantic interconnections and displacements that followed, *Middle Passages* represents an intersection between Brathwaite's focus on the legacies of this key historical moment and his development of a visual poetics. *Middle Passages* is perhaps not one of his most dramatically visual texts; some of his later works, such as *Dreamstories* and *Barabajan Poems* (both from 1994), employ more exaggerated typographical innovations and interrogations of the book form. Furthermore, Brathwaite has expressed deep dissatisfaction with conventional book formats and with a lack of authorial control over the process of typesetting. In conversation with Nathaniel Mackey, he talks about—and subsequently demonstrates in the publication of this discussion—a visual, hieroglyphic language:

which the present concept of the 4 ½" x 7 ½" margin
book with a certain uniform **face,** won't interest and therefo
re can't/won't/won't entertain – hence my struggle with publi
shers and printers over the presentation – the representation –
of all my new 'Sycorax video-style' stuff.
(*ConVERSations* 167–68, typography approximated)

As a fairly conventionally formatted book in terms of its size, shape, and the range of its typographic experimentation, *Middle Passages* hardly represents the epitome of Brathwaite's explorations of the visual page. Nevertheless, it is a key work in the development of his Sycorax video style, which demonstrates how "the presentation"—the look of the page—becomes increasingly central to "the representation" of a Caribbean cultural heritage in his work of the '90s and beyond. Furthermore, it constitutes the site of a "struggle" with the visual conventions of page and book, which forms the basis for later developments in more amplified forms of visual experimentation in works such as *Barabajan Poems*.

As the phrase "Sycorax Video Style" might suggest, Brathwaite's development of a visual poetics from *Middle Passages* onwards is partly a response to new technologies, namely the "video" screen of the personal computer, which makes a range of typographic effects easily accessible, including different page layouts, font sizes, styles and weights, and extra-textual marks and symbols.[1] In Brathwaite's own telling, this move is at least partly attributable to a series of personal traumas, foremost among them the death of his wife, Doris "Zea Mexican" in 1986.[2] It was while learning to use her Apple Mac computer after her death that he developed the Sycorax video style, named after the "forgotten, submerged mother" of Shakespeare's *The Tempest* (Brathwaite, "Interview" with Mackey 18). It is to this mother, and to the "forgotten, submerged" cultural legacies she represents, that one of the most important poems of *Middle Passages*, "Letter Sycorax," addresses itself.

As Lee M. Jenkins has noted, this poem amounts to a "manifesto" (120) for Brathwaite's Sycorax video style. "Letter Sycorax" is an embodied investigation of the possibilities of the material page for an archaeology of submerged African Caribbean history and cultural experience. The poem significantly revises an earlier poem, "X/Self's Xth Letters from the Thirteen Provinces" from *X/Self*, in which the speaker, a modern-day Caliban figure, writes a letter to his mother "pun a computer" (*Middle Passages* 80), reflecting on the possibilities and limitations of the electronic word for producing a mode of articulation "not fe dem/not fe dem" "but fe we" (82–83). In these lines, we might detect the dual aspirations bound up in Brathwaite's emphasis on the "noise" of nation language—on one hand to disrupt the language of domination and create a mode of articulation "not fe dem," and on the other hand to forge new possibilities, a language "fe we." One of the most obvious ways in which these utterances bring "noise" to the printed page is through orthographic and syntactic manipulations, which the poet often refers to as "calibanisms"; these reshaped terms approximate sounds, rhythms, and idioms common to many versions of nation language in the Anglophone Caribbean.[3] Orthographically and grammatically, then, Brathwaite's poem echoes the oral qualities of nation language. But this poem also extends its reshaping of "prospero ling. / uage & // ting" via a computer-aided rethinking of the printed page, as figure 18 demonstrates.

Despite the speaker/writer's professed incompetency at touch-typing, his activity jubilantly "mwangles" the "ling. / uage & / ting" (*Middle Passages* 82) of Prospero, who in Brathwaite's mythopoetics symbolizes and presides over the languages and processes of colonial and neo-colonial power. To "mwangle" multiply suggests to "manage" an articulation through strategies of "wrangling" with the tools of writing, thereby "wangling" a means of expression, but above all "mangling" textual language, mutating and fracturing it in the hope of opening up opportunities for alternative "angles" of representation. The mangling embodied by the word "mwangles" orthographically introduces "noise" into the word, distorting it almost beyond recognition and at the same time engendering a host of possible alternative meanings. Here, Brathwaite makes more than an allusion to Caliban's celebration of the sounds of his island in *The Tempest*:

> the isle is full of noises,
> Sounds and sweet airs, that give delight, and hurt not.
> Sometimes a thousand twangling instruments
> Will hum about mine ears; and sometime voices . . . (3. 2. 131–34)

Whereas Caliban's "noises" become benign "sounds" of "twangling instruments" and disembodied "voices," Brathwaite's more antagonistic noises refuse assimilation into poetic conventions that might domesticate them as mildly exotic, innocuous ornament. Brathwaite answers Caliban's anodyne "twangling" with a far more subversive and physical activity of "mwangling" English and the forms of the poetic page.

This activity occurs not only orthographically but also via the typographic dimensions of the page: its centered layout and differing line lengths, its use of different weights of text, and its frequent use of diacritical marks such as the forward slash and full stop. One way of reading Brathwaite's visual techniques is as a score for the sounds that are so important to the "mwanglings" of "nation language." Indeed, this is how the poet himself often describes the aims of his visual techniques. Gordon Rohlehr remarks that Brathwaite uses different typographical effects "suggesting quietness or loudness in smaller or larger type; or by the use of bold type and italics" (viii). The visual weight of the line "**yu hear/in me mwa?**" for example, certainly suggests an increased volume connected to a desire to be heard. But not all of the visual effects of these lines are linked to sound in such uncomplicated ways. What

yu know me cyaan
neither flat
foot pun de key

boards like
say
charlie chap dance/

in

far
less touch tapp/
in

like bo.
jangles walk/in

doun chauncery lane

yu hear/in me mwa?

but i
mwangles!

Figure 18. From "Letter Sycorax"
in *Middle Passages* by Kamau
Brathwaite. Bloodaxe Books
© 1992 Kamau Brathwaite. Page
80. Reprinted by permission of
Bloodaxe Books, on behalf of
the author.

of the central alignment, uneven line lengths, frequent breaking of words, and insertions of slashes and periods? These dimensions of the page suggest rhythms for a sounded performance off the page—Brathwaite's own readings of his poems are often markedly rhythmic and percussive—but such aspects of typography and layout also function as a performance on the page.

As Johanna Drucker puts it, "The visual IS a performative dimension: it makes the text, makes meaning in its embodiment, as form/expression/ enunciation. Ultimately it's not only that the visual/image/icon/event performs on the stage/theatre arena of the page but that it makes/is made/be's/ becomes [*sic*] through the graphic and visual means" (*Figuring the Word* 108). As in Maggie O'Sullivan's work, heightened material dimensions of the printed page can perform sonically, sculpturally, and gesturally. Indeed, Brathwaite's poem obliquely engages with poetic discourses about the poem as a space of performance or "field of action" (W. C. Williams). In a move that echoes Charles Olson's well-known remarks about the typewriter as a scoring device for the performative poem, the lines of "Letter Sycorax" enact a wrangling with the keyboard and the printed page through typographic means via physical marks, spacings, and alignments. Where Olson praises the "rigidity" (*Selected* 22) of the typewriter, however, it is the flexibility of the electronic word that appeals to Brathwaite. And while Olson's essay makes palpable his sense of mastery over the typewriter, in Brathwaite's poem the speaker's engagement with the computer keyboard, mouse, and screen is much more ambivalent and far less assured. In the example above, the forward slashes that punctuate the verbs with "in" endings physically interrupt the actions in-process, signaling the erratic and stuttering nature of the writer's attempts at "touch tapp/ / in," while uneven line lengths visually signal the writer's jerky and inconsistent rhythms.

These physical interruptions function as "noise" in ways that are typographically analogous to the jazz "dislocations of Bird, Dizzy and Klook" (Charlie "Bird" Parker, Dizzy Gillespie, and Kenny Clarke), which Brathwaite cites as influences in *History of the Voice* (31n). Indeed, as Louis James points out, such "visual patterns of rhythm, dissonance and repetition . . . have clear correlations with the jazz style" (67). The effect here is precisely one of verbal and sonic "dislocation," a tripping, stopping, and starting rhythm with unexpected rests or breaks as in "key / boards" or "dance/ / in," terms which already have especially musical semantic resonances. Above all, the central alignment of the poem recurrently "trips" the eye, whose movements must "dance" across the arrhythmic logics of the variable line lengths. At the same time, though, this central alignment also gives the poem an overall sense of visual coherence, creating symmetrical shapes that, despite the speaker's declarations of clumsiness, evince a tightly controlled process. The poem hangs together on the page, performing its syncopated "dance" around a central visual spine.

To interpret such typographic manipulations as a score for sound or even more loosely as a performative typographic "dance" is to see Brathwaite's "video style" as corresponding to the essentially mimetic impulse articulated in his question "how do you get a rhythm which approximates the *natural* experience, the *environmental* experience?" (*History* 10) Many critics certainly read Brathwaite's visual innovations in this light; for Anne Walmsley, a "video style" poem "sing[s] on every page . . . The varied typefaces and fonts orchestrate the words, signifying here a trombone, there a flute" ("Her Stem" 748–49). Elaine Savory remarks that with his visual effects Brathwaite "has stepped into a space in which orality, the book and the screen combine to project an immediate sense of cultural identity and linguistic freedom" ("Returning" 217). However, such confident assertions of the correspondences between page, orality, and a liberatory politics rather gloss over those aspects of Brathwaite's "video style" that are not easily translatable in terms of sound, semantics, or an approach that seeks a transcendence of language's constraints. Rohlehr acknowledges such intransigence when he points to moments of "arbitrariness in the appearance of the text" (ix): "Brackets, asterisks, abbreviations and various symbols are used sometimes with, sometimes without, clear purpose" (viii). In other words, such "arbitrary" visual effects refuse to make sense either in terms of sound or in terms of linguistic meaning; they function as visual analogies for "pure noise" (Attali 33), inassimilable materiality. For Charles Pollard, this "arbitrariness" is problematic. Disagreeing with Savory, he says there is "too much interpretive work necessary in reading Sycorax video-style to assert such immediacy between this new style and either a collective sense of identity or a free expression of nation language" (128). The video style has "not yet established a system of conventions" by which it can be decoded; for Pollard this weakens the poetry's aspiration to "give voice to the sound of nation language" because "the more Brathwaite strives to represent the particularity of nation language, the more he stretches the conventions of intelligibility and undermines the claim for nation language as common speech" (129).

These accounts miss the tactical value of visual "noise" in Brathwaite's "video style" poems. Such moments of material opacity or undecidability are crucial not so much for the ways in which they conduct a "veiling, or 'opaqueing' [of] the Caribbean through language" that makes "the culture and people of the Caribbean, more obscure, harder for outsiders to grasp easily," as Kelly Baker Josephs argues, but rather for the kinds of material meaningfulness they bring to the work. The resistant materiality of Brathwaite's poems intersects in complex ways with the historical specificities of African Caribbean culture. If traditional poetic forms have not provided the "syllabic intelligence" (Brathwaite, *History* 8) to approximate the hurricane's roar, then a poetry assimilable to established "conventions of intelligibility" is inadequate to articulate the historical and cultural specificities of Caribbean cultures. Indeed, to subsume the particularities of this culture and history too readily to a poetics of intelligibility may be to ignore the historical realities that have kept it "hidden from view" (Glissant, *Caribbean* 2). The Sycorax video style resists the demands of readability and accessibility, which even some of Brathwaite's most sensitive and generous critics apparently demand of this work. Thus, in Brathwaite's words, "The word becomes a pebble stone or bomb and the dub makes sense (or nonsenseness) of politics demanding of it life not death, community not aardvark, new world to make new words and we to overstand how modern ancient is" (*History* 50). This gnomic final statement of *History of the Voice* problematizes the notion of a fairly coherent politics of voice generally ascribed to this celebrated essay and latterly to Brathwaite's visual poetics. With a resistant intransigence of a "pebble stone" or the unstable volatility of a "bomb," Brathwaite's poetry aims for sense as

in sensory, a kind of meaningfulness that risks making nonsense of normative sense-making. Furthermore, Brathwaite's statement of archaeopoetics
emphasizes the task of forging "new words" for a "new world" whose vital
task is to open up fresh modes of encounter with traces of the "ancient" in
the hope of tracing their continuing relevance to contemporaneity.

Nathaniel Mackey has perceptively argued that Brathwaite's articulations
help "impeded speech find its voice" (*Discrepant* 274). By this Mackey does
not mean "speech" that transcends its impediment in a process of coming to
lucid expression. Rather, it is the fact of impediment, and the historical processes of its formation, that "speak" in this work. Brathwaite's abiding concern with impeded speech is apparent in one the poems of *Middle Passages*,
"Noom," in which a speaker who positions himself as an experienced traveler and slave trader offers instruction on how to deal with "certain noble-
men" or "priests" who are influential among the captured Africans:

> stick knives through their tongues
> and when the ship sails for the fair winds of the azores
> strangle them drunk & dunk them overboard
> the dolphins will weep while the sharks rip their watery groves
> (22)

Here, the act of violence is also, importantly, an act of silencing. Those whose
power to influence comes from the fact they "talk too much & mutter &
make zodiac / signs" (*Middle Passages* 22) have their tongues mutilated in
a literal and symbolic act of silencing, as if these ancestral voices might still
speak from "their watery groves." Indeed, in a sense it is precisely such a possibility that Brathwaite's poetry wants to investigate. "Noom" suggests that
it is with this mutilated tongue, maimed symbolically by physical violence,
displacement, and by the enforced dominance of European languages, that
the specificities of African Caribbean historical experience must be spoken.
This is frequently registered in visual as well as verbal terms in *Middle Passages*. In these lines from "Noom," the stumbling reading eye that is forced
to follow a ragged left margin partakes of the condition of the impeded utterance. The misalignments of the left margin put the eye ill at ease, intro-
ducing a kind of visual "noise" as nausea, thus adding a physically palpable
layer of affect to the poem's distressing images of atrocity.

This is not to suggest that the "noise" of Brathwaite's nation language constitutes a speech impediment, but rather that, paradoxically, nation language
cannot be sounded without engaging a history of brutal gagging. According
to Glissant, in order to articulate a poetics of *antillanité*, or Caribbeanness,
"[w]e must return to the point from which we started. Diversion [*detour*] is

not a useful ploy unless it is nourished by reversion [*retour*]: not a return to the longing for origins, to some immutable state of Being, but a return to the point of entanglement, from which we were forcefully turned away; that is where we must ultimately put to work the forces of creolization, or perish" (*Caribbean* 26). So too, for Brathwaite it is not enough to perform a "mwangling" *détournement* upon the English language by physically reshaping it. If this language is to give form to the sounds and textures of submerged African cultural traces, it must also be rooted in—routed through—a return to the historical configurations that inhibit their sounding; "impeded speech" is a "point of entanglement."

To examine this notion further, it is helpful to return to "Letter Sycorax," which constitutes one such *retour* in which the very attempt to render creolized speech as a written form becomes the site of a struggle with historical forces. Battling with the available raw materials of, "prospero ling. / uage & // ting" (82), the speaker of this poem finds himself embroiled in a Sisyphean struggle with "de slope" of the "arch/i/./pell/./a/./go/." The history of colonial oppression reverberates through this language, inhibiting the expressive act (see figure 19). The poem's layout and inclusion of interruptive diacritical marks induces a reading movement that "skips" in an arc down the page. This punctuated curve enacts Brathwaite's mythologized genesis of the Caribbean islands as a stone skimmed across water that "skidded arc'd and bloomed into islands: / Cuba and San Domingo / Jamaica and Puerto Rico / Grenada Guadeloupe Bonaire // curved stone hissed into reef" (*Arrivants* 48). In so doing, the visual shape of the poem also embodies a process of fragmentation that echoes the violent ruptures of slavery, of the history of these islands "ruled by silver sugar cane/ sweat and profit/ cutlass profit" (*Arrivants* 48). The historical and geographical "long curve" of the "arch/i/./pell/./a/./go/." drags the speaker "back / dung" to the oppressions of that history, presided over by the Prospero-like "mahn still mekkin mwe walk up" at the same time as "e push. // in we back dung again."

It might seem that Brathwaite's poem yields to what he elsewhere refers to as a "Sisyphean" treatment of Caribbean culture and history (see, for example, *ConVERSations* 31), which stresses, in V. S. Naipaul's terminology, "West Indian futility." Naipaul infamously asserted that "[h]istory is built around achievement and creation; and nothing was created in the West Indies" (26–27). For Naipaul, the violent fragmentation of the Middle Passage and the oppressions of colonialism render "creation" impossible and Caribbean culture sterile. To return to "where we start/in out start/in out start/in out start/in / out" (*Middle Passages* 83), then, is to risk succumbing to "West Indian futility." But it is significant that Brathwaite's poem performs this return—plotted out both verbally and visually, figuratively and typographically—by

like de mahn still mekkin mwe walk up de slope dat e slide
in black down de whole long curve a de arch

i
.

pell
.

a
.

go
.

some
times smile.
in nice

some
times like e   really laughin   after we & some
times like e   helpin   we up while e push.

in we back
dung
again

Figure 19. From "Letter Sycorax" in *Middle Passages* by Kamau Brathwaite. Bloodaxe Books © 1992 Kamau Brathwaite. Page 84. Reprinted by permission of Bloodaxe Books, on behalf of the author.

means of an emphatic "curve" that (to use Glissant's terminology) constitutes both *retour* and *detour*. The difference between a debilitating Sisyphean process and Glissant's "return to the point of entanglement" is that the Sisyphean movement is passive and involuntary, while a Glissantian movement is an active, energetic mode of political engagement with history, a *retour*, to reverse his formulation, "nourished" by a *detour*, which leads elsewhere as well as back. The historic-geographic curve/slope mapped by Brathwaite's poem constitutes both the fragmenting forces of violence and the conditions of possibility for creolization as the creation of new cultural forms.

"Letter Sycorax" reflects upon how the task of "making it new" so that the printed page of poetry might carry echoes from the "point of entanglement" entails not only an engagement with Caribbean history but also with domi-

what is de bess way to seh so/so it doan sounn like
brigg

flatts or her. vokitz nor de

π.

san cantos nor de souf sea bible

nor like ink. el & yarico & de anglo sa χ on chronicles

Figure 20. From "Letter Sycoraχ" in *Middle Passages* by Kamau Brathwaite.
Bloodaxe Books © 1992 Kamau Brathwaite. Page 83. Reprinted by permission of
Bloodaxe Books, on behalf of the author.

nant Anglophone poetic paradigms. In the lines shown as figure 20, the poem's speaker raises the question of how to differentiate his poem from those other poems "including history" by Basil Bunting and Ezra Pound, or from other literary, historical, and anthropological engagements with African Caribbean culture. These lines materially embody an attempt to both draw on and reshape available literary and historical models. One of the most immediately apparent strategies is the use of the visually iconic enlarged "χ" and "π," which function as verbal-visual references to the Anglo Saxon tradition of the illuminated manuscript and to Pound's notion of the "luminous detail" or ideogram as a node of multitudinous meaning. Commentators on Brathwaite's influences have tended to distance his work from a Poundian tradition, seeing Eliot as a more significant modernist forebear, partly because of Brathwaite's own statements about the bearing Eliot's poetry had on his oral poetics (see Pollard; Jenkins). However, this particular poem evinces an engagement with a Poundian model in the visual strategies that Brathwaite began to adopt in the 1990s even if the speaker is anxious to differentiate his poem from such modernist precedents.

The use of such iconographic signifiers as the "χ" and "π" materially embraces Pound's notion of the ideogram, concretizing the "luminous detail" in an iconic calligraphic form reminiscent of the Chinese ideograms that inspired Pound. The distinctive "χ," which is present in the title of "Letter Sycoraχ" and recurs throughout the poem and Brathwaite's "video style" work more generally, is a particularly significant luminous detail. While in Brathwaite's poetry it often performs the function of the letter "x," its visual distinctiveness marks it as a special kind of signifier in its own right, an ideogram in the Poundian sense, "charged with meaning to the utmost possible degree" (Pound, *ABC* 28). The "χ" functions both linguistically as a component of a recognizable word and extra-linguistically as a visual icon loaded with semantic possibilities. Its presence as part of the name Sycorax in the poem's title and elsewhere, and its materially emphasized status within that word, means that it comes to stand for Sycorax and her story: her repression by Prospero, her continuing but submerged presence, and the "mother tongue" she embodies and which begins to surface—via her son—in Brathwaite's calibanisms. This iconic mark is also representative of the poet's "video style," named after this mother figure. It also stands in for the "x/self" of the poem's earlier title, the creolized subject seeking a language to articulate the specificities of this hybridity. Thus the "χ" embodies a process of crossing, pointing to the cultural intersections of Caribbean culture: the crossing of the Middle Passage and its crossings-out, erasures, and suppressions as well as its processes of intercultural exchange.

"χ" marks a Glissantian "point of entanglement" and visually figures the processes of creolization it puts into play. Indeed, as a cultural ideogram it functions as an icon of a broader creolizing impulse throughout Brathwaite's work. His deployment of and allusion to multiple cultural and aesthetic traditions is strikingly consonant with Pound's ideogrammic method, which was itself intercultural in its impulses. Jahan Ramazani remarks on how European modernists "were the first English-language poets to create a formal vocabulary for the intercultural collisions and juxtapositions, the epistemic instabilities and decenterings, of globalization" (448). The "formal vocabulary" of modernists such as Eliot and Pound instantiates poetic strategies, most particularly collage, or, for Ramazani, bricolage, which "has helped postcolonial poets encode aesthetically the intersections among multiple cultural vectors" (448). Thus the very method of collaging together culturally various materials functions as an embodiment of postcolonial hybridity. Brathwaite's "χ" concretely figures this wider process and brings together the aesthetic strategies of European modernism with the particular cultural resonances of Caribbean culture. At the same time, Brathwaite finds he must reshape such poetic techniques to articulate a cross-cultural poetics more inclusive of submerged and delegitimated dimensions of the Caribbean than earlier modernisms.

Thus while the "χ" can fruitfully be read as a kind of Poundian ideogram and as a figure for an ideogrammic-like method, it also departs from this particular modernist aesthetic strategy in several important respects. One is its intimation of withheld, possibly supernatural, meanings. The "χ" can be read, via the creolized sounds of nation language, as a "hex," perhaps cast by "black Sycorax my mother" (*Ancestors* 47). Intimating a magical significance like "the symbolic chalk designs which are drawn on the ground as part of *vodoun* ritual" (Mackey, "Wringing" 736), part of its meaning is hidden, secret, an embodiment of numinous spiritual forces or energies that do not necessarily lend themselves to semantic decoding. Marjorie Perloff has appositely remarked that Brathwaite's work belongs within a strand of twentieth-century poetry that enacts a kind of "*charging*" that "defies semantic coherence much more fully than do the poems of Eliot and Pound" (*21st Century* 126) and which she aligns with the work of Russian Futurist poets such as Velimir Khlebnikov. This kind of "charging" impedes the normative semantic functioning of language by foregrounding phonic or graphic materiality, "The Word as Such" and even "The Letter as Such," as the manifestos of Khlebnikov and Aleksei Kruchenykh declare. In Viktor Shklovsky's classic formulation of "making strange" or *defamiliarization*, "art exists that one may recover the sensation of life; it exists to make one feel things, to make the stone *stony*. The purpose of art is to impart the sensation of things as they are perceived and not as they are known. The technique of art is to make objects 'unfamiliar,' to make forms difficult, to increase the difficulty and length of perception because the process of perception is an end in itself and must be prolonged" (16). Such an imperative certainly differs from Pound's ideal of the poetic image as "that which presents an intellectual and emotional complex in an instant of time" ("A Few" 95). To prolong the process of perception as "an end in itself" is to resist a drive toward an instantaneously graspable meaning of the "known." It is to open an indefinitely extended aperture within which perceptual effects, and potential modes of meaningfulness, proliferate rather than coagulate. Perhaps by such means the category of the "known" might also be expanded or reshaped. Brathwaite's visually iconic "χ" both carries the charge of an intensified meaningfulness while at the same time marking itself as an "unfamiliar" or "difficult" object that resists, or at least protracts, hermeneutic unpacking. Seemingly paradoxically, its intractability aims to open up, rather than block, interpretive possibilities. To recall the poet's own words, "The word becomes a pebble stone or bomb and the dub makes sense (or nonsenseness)" (*History* 50). Brathwaite's word—or letter—having taken on the concreteness of "a pebble stone," makes an array of sense, nonsenseness, and sensuousness simultaneously possible. It embodies possibilities of fecundity and creation, marking out an aspiration for a "new world to make new words" (*History* 50), for language forms that might register the multiple forces of creolization.

While Brathwaite's "charging" of particular poetic structures, such as his distinctive "χ" has affinities with Russian Futurist poetics, it has its genesis in much less documented traditions. Brathwaite's faith in the highly charged potential of material forms draws on specific African cultural traditions much more avowedly than it does on European modernism, although even in this, he echoes modernist artists' fascination with African art, albeit from a different cultural position. Among the most powerful influences on his visual poetics are traditions of West African sculpture, which the poet himself points to in an interview: "[i]n the African tradition, they use sculpture. Really, what I'm trying to do is create word-sculptures on the page, but word-song for the ear" (qtd. in Rigby 708). This aspiration can be detected in "Letter Sycorax," when the speaker's engagement with the visual materiality of the printed word is described as "chiss. / ellin dark. / ness / writin in light" (87). Rewriting Basil Bunting's "Words! Pens are too light. Take a chisel to write" (63) from a post-diaspora, post-colonial, and "post-modem" (Brathwaite, "Newstead" 653) position, Brathwaite's highly material page pays literal heed to Bunting's directive to engage with the physicality of "Words!" However, it does so by drawing on a markedly different cultural heritage than Bunting's; Brathwaite's highly material word seeks to register the submerged ancestral presences of an African cultural legacy and to tap into its potentially transformative energies.

A key reference point for Brathwaite's conception of his poetry as "word-sculptures on the page" is the work of Jamaican-born British artist Ronald Moody, one of a small group of Caribbean modernist artists who came to relative prominence in Europe in the interwar years and subsequently a core member of CAM in the late 1960s and early '70s. Moody cites a visit to the British Museum in 1928 as the formative moment of his artistic career; at the height of the British Empire's cultural dominance and at the center of its institutionalized display of colonial treasures, he encountered Egyptian and Asian sculptures that acted as the catalyst for his career as a sculptor. His monumental-scale figurative carvings in wood created throughout the 1930s are attempts to give form to a complex heritage and network of affiliations; as Moody put it at a CAM symposium in 1967: "my influences came from Egypt, India and Africa. And gradually an inner fight had to take place, throwing away so much that I had learnt at school . . . and getting down to what I really felt I could do" (qtd. in Walmsley, *Caribbean Artists* 181). Commentators have remarked upon how the stylized facial features of Moody's sculptures might be interpreted as corresponding to Asian, Indian, Egyptian, or even Carib iconographies (Moody 77), revealing an array of ethnic and cultural affiliations. Imagining his practice as an archaeology of his own cross-cultural heritage, Moody attempted through his sculpture to dig beneath imposed colonial aesthetic models to reclaim "the tremendous inner force" (qtd. in Walmsley, *Caribbean Artists* 2) he detected in non-Western art. His phrasing here reveals gnostic leanings; Moody's own sculptures bodied forth a sense of materials animated by spiritual forces. His most famous work, *Johanaan* (1936), carved in elm, employs the pronounced grain of this European wood to emphasize the syncretic facial features of the figure, while an enlarged crack in the wood forms a fissure that runs up the length of the torso, suggesting a fracturing of the self as well as an outpouring of inner energy. Mary Lou Emery remarks upon "an intense and even rigid physical strength, shaped in the warm, heavy matter of wood out of which arises from the visionary head with its gaze directed beyond the material world" (89). The work both proclaims its material presence, then, and intimates an otherworldly elsewhere through which its physicality seems charged with an enigmatic prescience. As Emery suggests, this "elsewhere" might be thought of in conflated spiritual and cultural terms, as an evocation of an array of traditions (89). Alternatively, as Moody put it, "My past is a mixture of African, Asian and European influences and, as I have lived many years in Europe, my present is the result of a friction between Europe and my past" (qtd. in Emery 86). *Johanaan* physically embodies this intercultural sensibility. The animating energy of such a work, then, might be thought of not so much in terms of an infusion of recovered cultural traces but in terms of the *frictional* energies between cultural forces, the past and present, a material here-and-now and a spiritual elsewhere, and a modernist aesthetic and archaic forms of submerged cultural memory.

Moody's sculpture offers an instance, then, of a distinctly transatlantic Caribbean form of modernist charging, which might be seen as an exemplar for Brathwaite's "carving" aesthetic. Brathwaite, however, is more interested in sub-Saharan cultural traditions that have received much less acknowledgement than the ancient Egyptian and Asian forms that Moody found inspiring. In particular, Western African traditions of carving have long held a fascination for Brathwaite, as evinced by the poem "Ogun" from his first trilogy *The Arrivants*.[4] Through a meditation on the very act of carving a sculpture, the poem negotiates a cross-cultural heritage and intimates the presence of animating spiritual energies from "elsewhere" in ways that are strikingly congruent with Moody's work. The poem relates how the poet's uncle Bobby O'Neil, or Bob'ob, when he was not scraping a living from his carpentry, would whittle at a block of wood "until his hands could feel / / how it had swelled and shivered, breathing air . . . its contoured grain still tuned to roots and water" until "a black rigid thunder he had never heard within his hammer / / came stomping up the trunks" (*Arrivants* 243). As in Brathwaite's notion of nation language, noise is figured as the carrier of a submerged cultural tradition, although here the spiritual dimensions of this poetics become much more evident. The otherworldly "thunder" of this poem guides the process of carving: "the wood took shape: dry shuttered / / eyes, slack anciently everted lips, flat / ruined face, eaten by pox, ravaged by rat" (243). The shape that emerges is that of the Yoruba God Ogun of the poem's title, traditionally the god of iron, hunting and warfare but also associated with creation and male potency (Barnes 2). In a later commentary on his uncle's carving in *Barabajan Poems*, Brathwaite identifies this sculpture as a version of *mkissi*, "Bakongo name & concept for powerful sacred often secret objects" (393). Traditional West African *mkissi* were most often small, humanoid woodcarvings that represented "ancestors, great shamanistic healers and, perhaps occasionally, personified earth spirits" and "held charges of active magic" (298), according to anthropologist Allen F. Roberts. However, this tradition was suppressed in Africa by Catholic missionaries and has now virtually vanished.[5] So *mkissi* is a practice that has been all but extinguished by colonial history, not just in the New World but also in Africa.

Furthermore, as Brathwaite describes it in *Barabajan Poems*, Bob'ob's carving is performed "**& 'quietly & seecreetly'**" (155, bold in original). The poet represents Bob'ob's *mkissi* as a manifestation of a cultural legacy that is so submerged that it cannot even be consciously acknowledged by its maker. And crucially, this sculpture is a "**local carving**," (155) not a replication of West African *mkissi* but a Caribbean version influenced by numerous intertwined West Africa traditions—Yoruba, Bakongo, Ashante, for example—but also by the historical experience of the African diaspora. Bob'ob's carving bears the scars of the Middle Passage in its "ruined face, eaten by pox, ravaged by rat / / and woodworm." The carving embodies cultural traditions with roots in West Africa. But at the same time, it physically carries the marks of the Middle Passage that brought West African traditions to the Caribbean and into relation with European imperialism. What takes shape is a creolized deity, an emphatically transatlantic God of the Middle Passage.

In its material forms, Brathwaite's Sycorax video style poetry aspires to the status of such a diasporic tradition of *mkissi*. The visual charging of the Sycorax "χ," for example, endows this iconic mark with both a sculptural quality and a significance that transforms it into something like a "powerful sacred often secret object" in Brathwaite's poetry. The meanings and energies of this "χ" are multiplicitous, constantly shifting, and often associated with the magical potency of Sycorax and the creole folk traditions with which she is associated, such as *vodoun*. Brathwaite's sculpting of line lengths also recalls the *mkissi*, especially in the centrally aligned poems of *Middle Passages*, which at times resemble shape poems. The elegant curving outlines of "Letter Sycorax" (see figure 19, for example) often suggest spectral, ambiguous visual presences that—a little like Ogun "stomping up the trunks" (*Arrivants* 243) in Bob'ob's carving—make themselves physically palpable in the materiality of the page.

In his works since *Middle Passages*, and especially in those in which he has had a major input into the book's typesetting, Brathwaite has increasingly introduced a further sculptural quality into his writing—the visual "noise"

Figure 21. From *Barabajan Poems* by Kamau Brathwaite. Savacou North, 1994. Page 176.

of heavy pixelation. This technique first appears in the New Directions version of *Middle Passages* that was published a year after the initial Bloodaxe edition. In this book, the Sycorax "χ" is given a highly degraded, pixellated appearance that renders it as a very rough-hewn *mkissi*. In some of his more recent collections such as *Ancestors* and *Born to Slow Horses* (2005), whole poems are printed in a heavily pixellated, often hard to read font. At one point in *Barabajan Poems*, this technique's capacity to disrupt legibility is taken to its extreme (see figure 21). Here, Brathwaite follows a revised version of his earlier poem "Folkways" from *The Arrivants* with a very long "word" not included in the earlier poem whose pixels are so large they render it illegible; individual letters become unreadable arrangements of black squares. The visual configuration at the end of the "word" resembles the suffix "less," thus echoing the last lines of the earlier poem that refer to a "poor / land- / less, harbour- / less spade" (*Arrivants* 34) But beyond the suggestion of "less," the complex arrangement of black pixels refuses to cohere into letters that might form a legible word. The "difficulty and length of perception" (Shklovsky 16) becomes extended almost indefinitely. Yet although the semantic drives of reading are almost entirely suspended, the "word" does not lose its charge. It seems rather to hold its meaning(s) in abeyance, just beyond reach, literally just out of focus, a little like the letter-like scrawls in Maggie O'Sullivan's *murmur*, discussed in the last chapter. This unreadable pattern of black-and-white foregrounds the sensuous qualities of the computerized word: words as made up of visual blocks of black ink and white page, words "as they are perceived and not as they are known" (Shklovsky 16).

In his historical study *The Development of Creole Society*, Brathwaite remarks that "[w]ithin the folk tradition, language was (and is) a creative act in itself; the word was held to contain a secret power" (237). For this poet, it is often the sensuous dimensions of language made palpable by various kinds of oral and visual "noise" that possess a "secret power" to harbor presences hitherto suppressed, submerged, or constituted as absence, lack, or "less." From his articulation of nation language to his development of a computer-aided visual poetics, Brathwaite has brought noise into his poetry both to disrupt the conventions of a language that has been instrumental in the epistemic violence of Caribbean history and to register the suppressed African dimensions of this history and culture. Brathwaite's Sycorax video style produces forms of typographic "noise" that work as a score for nation language, a performance on the page, and an impediment to normative sense-making. Brathwaite's foregrounding of intransigent materiality embodies resonances of the Middle Passage to register both its traumas and the intercultural processes of creolization that sustain submerged cultural traditions. Visual materiality becomes a way of infusing printed language with physical indices of this cultural heritage, embodying and reshaping both Euro-American traditions and submerged African ones, such as the carving of *mkissi*. The simultaneously disruptive and productive "noise" of this poetry works to forge new modes of meaningfulness by which these historical and cultural traces might be unearthed or revealed, even if only in glimpses and echoes. Brathwaite's archaeopoetics avowedly runs the risk of incoherence, unintelligibility, and even complete semantic blockage as an integral part of its generation of possibilities for new kinds of meaningfulness: material meaning.

Tidalectics

Brathwaite's returns to "point[s] of entanglement" in Caribbean history and culture might be productively placed in relation to the Benjaminian mode of historicism that I have returned to throughout this book. Like Benjamin's "angel of history," Brathwaite is confronted with the fragmented wreckage of a catastrophic cultural legacy. His poetic investigations sift through this wreckage, seeking unacknowledged and unrealized potentials. By bringing the marginalized "noise" of creolized language forms to the poetic page via "mwangled" printed and sounded language, his poetry strains to revive traces of an African heritage and redeem fragments of a cataclysmic history in ways that allow them to bring new kinds of significance to the present cultural moment. Indeed, in his various statements of poetics, Brathwaite often articulates an explicitly redemptory aspiration "to connect broken islands, cracked, broken words, / worlds, friendships, ancestories" ("Newstead" 653). Above all, his archaeopoetics reflects upon the capacities of the English language and its written forms to body forth the submerged "semantic energies" (Habermas 112) of African Caribbean history, potentials that this language has been complicit in suppressing.

Textual strategies that place emphasis on language's materiality and risk illegibility, even unintelligibility, are central to this endeavor. To foreground the sensory dimensions of the text is, as the Russian Formalists knew, to "increase the difficulty and length of perception because the process of perception is an end in itself and must be prolonged" (Shklovsky 16). For Brathwaite, the "process of perception" is indeed all-important, an "end in itself." But this does not mean a withdrawal from political purposiveness—far from it—because in this work, as in the work of other poets examined in this book, a foregrounding of perceptual encounter performs a sense of history as felt, as physically perceived, rather than as abstractly "known" through rational forms of cognition. Indeed, according to Brathwaite, it is precisely this attention to felt particularities that gives him *privileged* access to histories not acknowledged or acknowledgeable by more discursive rational modes of historicism; poetry's emphasis on sensory perception offers what he refers to as a "prescient knowledge" ("Show 94") of tangible but submerged historical actualities. To bring into the process of perception those material aspects of textuality that are normally not recognized as meaningful is to attune perception to alternative dimensions of experience and understanding and potentially engender new historical perspectives.

In parallel with the mystical Kabbalistic underpinning of Benjamin's philosophy of history, Brathwaite's historicism is infused with a spiritual dimension, in his case influenced by Caribbean practices such as *vodoun*, and a commitment to the palpable presence of ancestral spirits. The poet's use of creolized English, calibanisms, and noisy mutations sculpts and "mwangles" language into sensuously charged material forms that might yield vestiges of what the poet calls the "gods of the Middle Passage" (*Barabajan Poems* 173), the spiritual and cultural traditions of an array of Western African cultures transplanted to a Caribbean context. The ways in which this language discloses such cultural traces can be allied with the notion of spirit possession associated with some of these African Caribbean traditions. As Brathwaite explains in a glossary to his first trilogy *The Arrivants*, "The basic point about African gods and the Caribbean gods that derive from them is that they can 'possess' and be possessed by the ordinary, believing, participating individual worshipper" (272). He goes on to describe ritual dances in which "[t]he celebrant's body acts as a kind of lightning conductor for the god. In the moment of possession, the divine electrical charge becomes *grounded* (so that the earth and the things of the earth assume a special significance)" (271). The highly performative and emphatically material forms of Brathwaite's poetry function something like this celebrant; the physical "body" of his language acts as a medium for the surfacing of the submerged, thwarted potentials of African Caribbean history and culture. Spiritual energy here is imagined as "*grounded*," taking on physical form, so that literal materiality, "the things of the earth," including the physicality of language itself, is revivified as an active mode of meaningfulness. Yet there is always an unresolved dynamic in this work between the pursuit of such regenerative capacities of reshaped language and the need to register language's historically embedded

hindrances to African Caribbean cultural expression, which is made manifest in Brathwaite's often faltering "impeded speech" (Mackey, *Discrepant*
274) and his poetry's recurrent reference to its own struggles with articulation. In Brathwaite's work there is a fraught tension between the regenerative
possibilities of an English reshaped to carry the resonances of its entanglements with multiple cultural traditions in the Caribbean and an awareness
of a history of epistemic violence silted into language that cannot—and ethically should not—be transcended, and which precludes a complete surfacing of hitherto submerged elements. This dialectic between catastrophe and
redemption as well as between repression and awakening echoes Benjamin's
messianic historical vision.

For all that Brathwaite's mode of historical inquiry is broadly Benjaminian, it also archaeocritically recasts aspects of Benjamin's highly influential philosophy of history by reflecting on the material conditions of possibility for historical consciousness in a specifically Caribbean context. The
tensions between salvage and damage, surfacing and submergence, and expression and impediment in this work produce a historical sensibility predicated on a dynamic sense of to and fro rooted in the specificities of Caribbean historical experience and geographical particularity. We may recall how
Benjamin's anti-progressive view of history demands a rethinking of dialectics, resulting in his notion of the "dialectical image" (*Arcades* 475, N10a, 3)
or "dialectics at a standstill" (462, N3, 1). Spatialized and arrested, the process of dialectical "historical awakening" shifts from a temporal to a spatial axis, from linear progress to an arrested moment of epiphanic illumina-
tion comparable to a photographic "flash" (462, N2a, 3). In common with
Benjamin, Brathwaite explicitly articulates a rethinking of dialectics that performs a spatial turn; but where Benjamin's conceptual vocabulary draws on
the modern technologies of his time, Brathwaite's reference points are Caribbean historical-geographical space. In an interview with Mackey he outlines
his idea of "tidalectics" as "dialectics with my difference. In other words, instead of the notion of one-two-three, Hegelian, I am now more interested
in the movement of the water backwards and forwards as a kind of cyclic, I
suppose, motion, rather than linear" (14). The ebb and flow of the Caribbean
Sea and the circular churning of the North Atlantic gyre that, along with its
accompanying trade winds, carried the ships of the triangular trade suggest
a model of history in which time circulates. Events do not pass into the past
but recede and return in an endless recycling. While this spatial conception
of history accords with Benjamin's move away from notions of diachrony and
progress, an oceanic spatio-temporal sensibility has different implications
than Benjamin's notion of the arrest of dialectics in the "image." In common
with the dynamism of the corporeal notion of memory proposed by O'Sulli-

van's poetry, Brathwaite's oceanic imaginary suggests a highly mobile model of historical process. In contrast to the somewhat static notion of the "image" or the "constellation," tidalectics proposes an unceasing process of ebb and flow, displacement and return, modeled both on the "movement of the water" and on the ongoing dislocations of the African diaspora.

The implications of tidalectics are numerous; the geographical metaphors are crucial to Brathwaite's archaeocritical move that routes historical understanding through the concrete particularities of the Caribbean archipelago. Brathwaite is far from unique in foregrounding such a geographical imagination in his negotiation of Caribbean history and aesthetics; his oceanic historical imagination has clear affinities with Paul Gilroy's notion of the black Atlantic as a space of cultural crossings produced by the trade routes of modernity. Brathwaite's approach also shares similarities with Glissant's "poetics of relation," predicated on a geographical conception of the Caribbean as "one of the places in the world where Relation presents itself most visibly [. . .] a place of encounter and connivance" (*Poetics* 33). (I explore further incarnations of such a geographic sensibility in the next chapter.) However, Brathwaite's notion and coinage of tidalectics is a distinctive articulation of a Caribbean nexus of poetics, geography, and history. If archaeocritique scrutinizes the grounds of possibility for historical ways of knowing, then tidalectics brings the question of *grounding*—in a quite literal sense—to attention. Brathwaite's theory is not only an inflection of historical materialism; it is a *geographical* inflection of historical materialism. Its insistence on the physical, topographical—as well as social—conditions of historical knowledge is perhaps more literally materialist in some senses than even Benjamin's historical vision. Indeed, Brathwaite's mode of historical understanding raises questions about the extent to which historical knowledge is intertwined with geographical factors. Considered in this light, Benjamin's messianism can be connected with the geographical imagination of the Jewish diaspora, and with all the associated cultural connotations of dispersal and peregrination. His notion of the dialectical image, meanwhile, forged in the Parisian Arcades, bears the mark of a metropolitan center of modernity, its technologies, and practices of consumption. Brathwaite's notion of tidalectics, however, brings into focus an understanding of historical process engendered by the sensibilities of what cultural critics such as Benita Parry and Harry Harootunian have called "peripheral modernities" (Parry 28, 29). Such peripheral modernities occupy spaces within dynamics of global capitalism but from "a . . . position of structural underdevelopment within an uneven and unequal world system" (Parry 28–29). Brathwaite's geographic historical imagination foregrounds this dynamic of uneven development at the same time as offering a highly concretized sense of how this "world system" is experienced at its peripheries. Rather than suggesting a "natural" illustration of a naturalized configuration of inequality and exploitation, Brathwaite's topographical figures are infused with historical, cultural, and political meanings.

The dynamism of Brathwaite's geographically informed historical consciousness issues not from a sense of place as bounded and contained but from the peculiarities of Caribbean geography—at once a fragmented chain of islands, the coasts of North and South America, and the sea that encompasses the whole—and also from an awareness of the interrelations of this space with a wider topographical, historical, and cultural terrain. The restlessness embodied by the notion of tidalectics also indicates the extent to which, for the African Caribbean poet, relations with this geography are deeply troubled. It is worth contrasting Brathwaite's stance with a figure who looms large in the practice and theorization of intertwined geographical and historical inquiry: Charles Olson. In his study of Melville, *Call Me Ishmael*, Olson notoriously proclaims "I take SPACE to be the central fact to man born in America" (11), a statement that exudes a sense of assurance in the entitlement of "man born in America" to "ride on such space" (12), as Olson sees Melville doing. Olson's geographically specific (and yet expansive) historical investigations in the *Maximus Poems* take up the challenge of American "SPACE" with a comparable forcefulness. For Brathwaite, and for many other African Caribbean writers, however, the process of taking up one's place in geographic space is deeply affected by a historical experience of geographic and linguistic dis-placement, dis-location, and dis-possession. The Tobagoan-Canadian poet M. NourbeSe Philip states that "[s]lavery, servitude, life as a chattel in utter displacement from language, land, culture, religion and even family: these were the events that defined the African's first relationship with the land in the New World" (*Genealogy* 59). For African Caribbean writers, the "first relationship" with the material spaces of the islands is one of "servitude," oppression and "utter displacement" within the space of the plantation, a relationship with the land that has remained powerfully present, both imaginatively and materially. As Brathwaite indicates, the heritage largely bequeathed to subsequent generations is that of the alienated "poor / land / less, harbour / less, spade" (*Arrivants* 34).

The ceaseless to and fro suggested by the notion of tidalectics embodies this uneasy relation with the geographic spaces of the Caribbean islands and their surrounding sea—site of the Middle Passage—a "sea that diffracts" African Caribbean cultural memory (Glissant, *A Poetics* 33). Yet this back-and-forth is also the dynamic between catastrophe and salvage, damage and regeneration that animates all of Brathwaite's work. The physical and imaginary landscape of his archaeopoetics, in common with the spatial nexus occupied by Benjamin's angel, teems with redemptive potential as well as with the palpable marks of violence, oppression, and brutality. In his essay, lecture, and poem *Barabajan Poems*, the poet narrates an "xperience" of attending a prayer meeting in what used to be his uncle's carpentry shop, describing the voices of those around him speaking and singing:

> . . . pebbles & plankton & memories & the shale that is like a low moan now . out out towards a new meaning out there . . .

> with new languages tongues of the water we had not known before or rather had forgotten forgotten till this moment . . .

> I can hear these Bajan Igbo voices the voices of the clamorous re-turning tongues and the doves above them *koh*

> *koh cur cur curu* . . . It's an xperience I say that can describe only as IGBO . . . for it was there all along . but hidden . mau . bosc . maroon cockpit . SUBMERGED like the Igbo they were or have become . rainfall of waters living in and underneath our

> coral

>   **. . . it takes me back and drags me tidalectic into this ta**

> **ngled urgent meaning to & fro . like foam . saltless as from the bottom of the sea.** (182)

The prayer meeting is represented in terms of an immersion in the landscape of Barbados and its surrounding sea; this landscape becomes the material ground for a recovery of the "SUBMERGED" sounds for "clamorous returning tongues" that hold the possibility of "new meaning." The tangible presence of these potentials is rendered through an emphatic materiality pertaining all at once to the physical landscape, its sounds and those of its inhabitants, and the foregrounded sonic and visual presence of language on the page. This long, digressive, fragmented, punctuated, meandering passage evades semantic clarity and instead intimates the not-quite-articulate dimensions of this cultural experience. Its tidalectic sensibility washes to and fro between cultures past and present, Igbo and Bajan, here and elsewhere, the "forgotten" and the "new," the submerged and the surfacing, and the semantic and the material dimensions of the printed page.

    Brathwaite's work suggests that because these are the troubled waters and shifting grounds of possibility for a Caribbean historical consciousness, historiographic and poetic modes of historical encounter must necessarily be reshaped to accommodate the restless currents and inarticulate noises of this particular peripheral modernity. The "SUBMERGED" traces of this history "cannot be organized in terms of a series of clarifications" (Glissant, *Caribbean* 2) or even flashes of Benjaminian illumination if the terrain of writing is itself fraught with a historical freight of epistemic violence. Thus it is "impeded speech" (Mackey) and the tangible, but not always intelligible, charges of sculpted visual language to which Brathwaite's archaeopoetics devotes its energies. In so doing, this poet's language forms and historical sensibilities shift tidalectic between the belated and the not-yet, the not-yet and the belated, the haunting remainders and the embryonic promises of these isles full of noises.

6

Alluvial Siftings

M. NourbeSe Philip's Marine Archaeopoetics

Where are your monuments, your battles, martyrs?
Where is your tribal memory? Sirs,
in that grey vault. The sea. The sea
has locked them up. The sea is History.

Derek Walcott "The Sea is History"

A poetic archaeology of African Caribbean history is necessarily submarine. In common with Kamau Brathwaite, discussed in the previous chapter,
M. NourbeSe Philip negotiates histories so "submerged" that it is as if their
traces are "locked . . . up" in a great, inaccessible "grey vault" from which only
tattered fragments escape, washed up as so much flotsam and jetsam in the
liminal zones of culture. Like Brathwaite, Philip incorporates this dilemma
into poetic forms that resist the imperatives of clarity; for her, to render the
violent history of the Caribbean too readily intelligible might be "to do a second violence. To the experience, the memory—the remembering—hence
the work becomes 'unreadable' in the traditional way" (*Genealogy* 116). As
Philip's emphasis on the "un*readable*" begins to suggest, her archaeopoetics involves a careful scrutiny of the texts and mythologies of Western imperialism, which she examines above all for its omissions and erasures. For
her, exploited African bodies constitute a material foundation of imperialist modernity, and their traces are palpable within its documents, even if
only as the unwritten underside of the text. Such a conviction in some ways
aligns her poetic activities more closely with Susan Howe's textual investigations than Brathwaite's use of oral traditions and tropes. Furthermore,
where Brathwaite's attention to orality gives rise to a simultaneously disruptive and regenerative poetics of noise, Philip's archaeopoetics focuses more
upon the entangled aesthetic and historical potentials of silence. This difference in emphasis is at least partly gendered; as a woman writer acutely aware
of the muffling of women's voices in Caribbean cultures, she directs her attention to the silences, blanks, and missing bodies (Davidson, "Missing") of
Caribbean history, submerged in "that grey vault" of a history which, like
the ocean, contains unknowns.

As any marine archaeologist will confirm, underwater excavation is a particularly challenging process; not only is it constrained by physical limitations and the need for special equipment, but artifacts retrieved from a sea bed will often degrade once brought to the surface. Philip's poetic archaeology faces a parallel set of challenges. The medium through which her excavations must operate both impedes the recovery of submerged historical traces and fundamentally alters the nature of any discoveries. In one of her many provocative considerations of the dilemma she faces, Philip asks:

> What is the word for bringing bodies back from water? From a "liquid grave?" . . . I do an Internet search for a word or phrase for bringing someone back from underwater that has as precise a meaning as the unearthing contained within the word exhume. I find words like resurrect and subaquatic but not "exaqua." Does this mean that unlike being interred, once you're underwater there's no retrieval—that you can never [be] "exhumed" from water? (*Zong!* 201).

Philip's meditation on underwater exhumation here operates on both literal and figurative levels. She is considering the status of those African bodies dumped, often still alive, at sea during the Middle Passage. In so doing, she also highlights the difficulty of recovering traces of histories whose cultural submergence has been carried out by linguistic means. As Philip points out, "Africans in the New World were compelled to enter another consciousness," via a language that "was not only experientially foreign, but also etymologically hostile and expressive of the non-being of the African" (*She Tries* 15). How, then, to engage with traces of these African presences through a language hitherto complicit in their negation? How to render palpable those murmurings muffled by the Middle Passage?

Philip's archaeopoetics investigates silences both as indexical traces of such effaced presences and as vestiges of cultural, legal, and epistemic acts of their disavowal. In order to articulate what Walcott's poem calls "the sound / like a rumour without any echo," Philip, like Brathwaite, finds she must radically remodel the language in which she writes. Increasingly over the course of her career, she has turned to the visual materiality of the poetic page as a means of both investigating cultural and linguistic impediment and enlarging the possibilities for alternative modes of articulation. This chapter will explore how such archaeopoetic strategies engage epistemological questions raised by a history that Philip finds to be highly tangible but also thoroughly suppressed in records of the Middle Passage, and whose fragments are submerged in language and culture as if in the murky sediments of an alluvial terrain.

As these oceanic metaphors signal, this chapter continues the exploration of geographically inflected modes of historical consciousness initiated in chapter 5. The text around which my discussion unfolds lends itself particularly well to such an inquiry; Philip's book-length poem *Zong!* (2008) investigates a key event in the history of the Middle Passage, in which 132 slaves were deliberately cast overboard to drown. It is the deep abysses of the ocean, then, that constitute the primary topological metaphor for the historical consciousness that this text engenders. Thus the archaeocritical dimensions of Philip's writing reflect on the challenges of historical recovery when the silences within language and the deep abysses of the ocean form the conditions of (im)possibility for such a project.

The Sea is History

The spatio-temporal topographies of the Middle Passage, its submerging waves and powerful currents constitute a potent imaginative site for an engagement with Caribbean history. For a number of Caribbean writers, the sea, in particular, often features prominently in attempts to address the collective, historically imposed, cultural amnesia of the African diaspora. In this particular cultural context, "The Sea is History," as the epigraph above indicates (*Collected Poems* 364–67). In Walcott's poem, the history of the Middle Passage is imagined as a terrain peopled by drowned presences, "locked in sea sands," held in "bondage" by "white cowries clustered like manacles" (365) and by "Bone soldered by coral to bone" (364). Both tomb and prison, the sea-as-history is a powerful metaphor (and certainly not *just* a metaphor) for the effects of a regime that not only transformed people into goods (which, like Walcott's drowned slaves, could be jettisoned like cargo) but also systematically suppressed African and indigenous traditions and languages beneath an imposed colonial culture. Thus in Walcott's poem the artifacts held within "that grey vault" fail to constitute a History with a capital "H." Unacknowledged within dominant modes of historical representation, the "tribal memory" sought by the speaker of Walcott's poem is registered only as an absence: "the ocean kept turning blank pages // looking for History" (365). It is only, with the forging of a sense of emerging nationhood at the end of this poem that "the sound / like a rumour without any echo // of History, really beginning" (367) emerges from the shallows.

In Walcott's poem, the notion of the sea-as-history signals an epistemological crisis engendered by the historical fact that, as Fred D'Aguiar's reformulation of Walcott's phrase has it, "the sea is slavery" (3). The act of substitution performed here indicates both that slavery *is* this history and at the same time that slavery displaces the possibility of an African Caribbean history—or, as Walcott's interlocutors demand, History—that can be rendered legible as anything other than "blank pages." The history of slavery demands revised conceptions of history not so much in the sense that those blank pages need to be filled but rather in the sense of proposing alternative ways of encountering the past, both upon and beyond the blank page. Here, too, the oceanic trope performs a crucial function; Elizabeth Deloughrey notes that the geographical metaphor of interaction between land and sea in Caribbean writing provides "an important counter-narrative to discourses of filial rootedness and narrow visions of ethnic nationalism" (Deloughrey 51). As a fluid material geography, the sea suggests a conception of history that is dynamic, unpredictable, contingent, recursive, and spatial as well as temporal. Associated with fluidity, flux, and intersecting currents, the sea offers possibilities for a historical imagination based upon complex, often unknowable genealogies and conflicting, fractured affiliations. In an oceanic historical imaginary, roots are always routes.

Along with fellow Caribbean writers like Walcott, D'Aguiar, and Brathwaite, Philip participates in an oceanic reimagining of Caribbean history. For her, however, the task of retrieving submerged historical traces is rendered much more fraught than in Walcott's poem, where a cautiously hopeful conclusion figures the organic development of new national cultures as a moment of redemptive surfacing and newfound articulacy. Rather than advocate a new beginning that moves away from the irrecoverable history forever anchored in an inaccessible terrain, as Walcott's poem tends to, Philip sees a troubled return to this submerged history as crucial to a renewed articulation of contemporary Caribbean cultural identities.

But most importantly, for Philip, the sea is not only history, and not only slavery, but also language: "the challenge . . . facing the African Caribbean writer who is at all sensitive to language and to the issues that language generates, is to use the language in such a way that the historical realities are not erased or obliterated, so that English is revealed as the tainted tongue it truly is. Only in so doing will English be redeemed" (*She Tries* 19). A "redeemed" English in this understanding is an English that proclaims itself, like the sea, as muddied by the historical freight of slavery and imperialism. Philip's choice of descriptor is noteworthy; etymologically rooted in Middle English, where it means "to convict or prove guilty," deriving from the Latin *tingere*, meaning "to dye, tinge," the term "tainted" signifies both culpability and impurity. In a Caribbean context, this term simultaneously connotes collusion in processes of historical silencing and also ethnic or cultural hybridity. A "redeemed" English is language that orients attention toward both such submerged dimensions of its own embedded, if obscured, "historical realities."

Archaeopoetic Silences

Partly because of Philip's acute sensitivity to the politics of language, and her particular mode of engaging with the "tainted tongue" that is her cultural inheritance, her position in relation to a wider community of Caribbean poets is far from straightforward. Critical discussions of her work often place her alongside other Caribbean women poets, such as Lorna Goodison and Dionne Brand (another Toronto resident), with whom she shares an acute awareness of patriarchal as well as colonial power structures and an impulse to revise the cultural assumptions of an emerging, predominantly male-dominated, poetic tradition in the Caribbean. But her experimentalism distinguishes her from many of her Caribbean contemporaries of both genders. "On the surface at least," she says, "my work does not fit the traditions of Black poetry" because its "'difficult' and 'abstract' or 'innovative'" (*Genealogy* 129) qualities eschew the requisites of accessibility and representativeness so often expected of black poets. Her wariness toward the power dynamics of language, the lyric voice, and notions of authorial control aligns her with certain currents of North American experimentalism, namely Language writing and more especially its outgrowths in the work of African American poets such as Nathaniel Mackey, Harryette Mullen, and Erica Hunt. For Philip, as for these poets, formal tactics such as collage, sampling, multiple voicedness, and an emphasis on the material dimensions of language offer ways of engaging the power dynamics of race, class, and gender entangled in the poetic medium.

Another way of positioning Philip's poetry and poetics is to consider her work in alignment to Brathwaite's, most especially in relation to his strategic eschewal of a poetics of clarity. Like Brathwaite, Philip foregrounds materially embodied opacities in her archaeological poetry as a means by which to reflect upon the possibilities and inherent difficulties of recovering submerged dimensions of Caribbean culture. Her perspectives, however, differ from Brathwaite's in many ways. To begin with, her engagements with language demonstrate an acute awareness of gendered power relationships as well as the suppressions of African dimensions of culture in the Caribbean. Philip's attentiveness to the multiple vectors of language's ideological complicities applies not just to standard English, with its history of colonial imposition, but also to what she prefers to describe as "the demotic" ("Poet of Place" 685) languages of the Caribbean. In an interview with Kristen Mahlis, she says of Brathwaite's nation language, "[w]hile I understand and support what he's doing in that this vernacular or what some call dialect or patois is the language through which people come to assemble themselves as a nation, I can't rest there" because, she points out, "nation is a male discourse"

("Poet of Place" 684). As Anne McClintock and others have argued, while women have often been positioned as allegorical symbols of nationhood and the means by which nations are reproduced both biologically and culturally, national agency is gendered male (see also Yuval-Davis; Chatterjee).

Mindful of the doubly fraught position African Caribbean women occupy in relation to language and identity, then, Philip's relation to Caribbean vernaculars is ambivalent. In an introductory essay to *She Tries Her Tongue, Her Silence Softly Breaks*, she describes Caribbean English as "linguistic rape and forced marriage between African and English tongues," albeit one which has produced a "vital" language "capable of great rhythms and musicality" (23). Her archaeocritique of English thus not only has a gendered dimension but is also routed through an emphasis on connections between language and the subjugated body. For her, the sexual violence at the heart of the colonial Caribbean is embedded in the languages of her poetic medium: "In the New World, the female African body became the site of exploitation and profoundly anti-human demands—forced reproduction along with subsequent forceful abduction and sale of children . . . How then does this affect the making of poetry, the making of words, the making of i-mages if poetry, as I happen to believe, 'begins in the body and ends in the body'?" (*She Tries* 24). Philip's emphatically material language forms aim to render these entanglements between body and word apparent. Her sense of the poetic "i-mage" is articulated around a profoundly problematic "*Dis place*—the space between. The legs," as she puts it in a later essay, the bodily and symbolic site of sexual and reproductive exploitation, which has shaped the historical experience of "the black woman 'dis placed' to and in the New World" ("Dis Place" 290). This recurrently violated, ontologically negated, and silenced "place" necessarily lies at the heart of her notion of the poetic "i-mage."

In contrast to Brathwaite's privileging of orality as a primary mode of engagement with traces of an African heritage in the Caribbean, Philip's domain of inquiry is often, and increasingly, the written text. Although she does address (often difficult) acts of speaking, her negotiations of orality are frequently performed in dialogue with textuality, whether implicitly or explicitly. Whereas Brathwaite for the most part directs his attention toward the task of bringing an orally inflected noise to the printed page, Philip's writing investigates the silences and omissions of historical and cultural documents. As the typographically manipulated terms "i-mage" and "dis place" materially demonstrate, for Philip, as for Susan Howe, "the gaps and silences are where you find yourself" (Howe, *Birth-mark* 158). Indeed, two of Philip's most prominent publications prior to *Zong!*—*She Tries Her Tongue* and *Looking for Livingstone*—are centrally and explicitly concerned with textual silences. In this poet's work, remarks David Marriot, "[t]he question then becomes how one writes and remembers this silence given that it cannot be either easily written or read . . . This task takes on a particular urgency given the traditional historical excision and exclusion of women and blacks from the archive that is writing" (75).

However, Philip's work suggests that this textual elision has not made women and blacks absent in the "archive" of European textual history but rather silently present. In her essay "Dis Place   The Space Between," she describes:

> – a warping and twisting of the filaments of silence between African and body –
> body & text
> body becoming text which she learning to read in a
> newlanguageandshecomingtounderstandhowtosurvivetextbecoming
> bodybodiesdeadbodiesmurderedbodiesimportedbredmutilatedbodies
> soldbodiesboughttheEuropeantrafficinbodiesthattellingsomuchabout
> themandwhichhelpingfueltheindustrialrevolutionsmanytimesoverand
> overandoverandoverthebodies . . . (303)

Because the exploitation of the African body—and especially the female African body—has materially underpinned the processes of European modernity, "helpingfueltheindustrialrevolution," for example, its presence is tangible in the narratives of this modernity. And so "the Body African—dis place—place and s/place of exploitation inscribes itself permanently on the European text. *Not* on the margins. But within the very body of the text where the silence exists" ("Dis Place" 303). As Philip's cramming together of words in the extract above serves to emphasize, the textual bodies of European modernity are materially entangled with the African bodies in whose exploitation modernity is founded. Traces of these bodies, she asserts, are palpable as silences and submerged, negated traces within the "very body" of these texts. Whereas Brathwaite imagines the African presence in the Caribbean as historically excluded from the written text, Philip conceptualizes silence as a trace of African presences always already within the texts of imperialism.

Philip sees it as her poetic task to "learn to read those silences" ("Dis Place" 296). The central dilemma of her project is:

> how to interrupt
>   disrupt
> erupt
>   the body
> of the text
>   to allow
> the silence
>   in erupt
> ("Dis Place" 307–8)

Here, an engagement with the material "body" of the text presents itself as an attempt "to allow / the silence / in," to enable silence to surface or "erupt" into printed language, just as the large white spaces, "the space[s] between" words and lines, physically "interrupt" and "disrupt" the conventions of the page and at the same time constitute themselves as visual "silences" whose presence is made materially evident. Philip performs a range of physical manipulations of the printed page not only in many of her essays but also in her poetic works. A fairly well-known example of this is "Discourse on the Logic of Language" in *She Tries Her Tongue*; this poem comprises a collage of different discourses, printed in different fonts and layouts, which together perform the struggle of speaking as an African Caribbean woman. In her more recent book-length poem, *Zong!* (2008), the poet's engagement with the visual materiality of the text takes on a new intensity.

In similar ways to many of Howe's poems, *Zong!* engages very physically with a specific historical source text, seeking to render its gaps and silences as a palpable presence. Appropriately enough, given that Philip trained and practiced as a lawyer, her poem derives its material from a 1783 transcript of a court decision relating to a massacre carried out on board the slave ship *Zong* as it carried its human "cargo" from the west coast of Africa to Jamaica. In recent years, this particular historical event has captured the imaginations of many other writers and artists of the African diaspora. For example, David Dabydeen's poem "Turner" approaches events through an interrogation of J. M. W. Turner's painting *The Slave Ship* (1840). Fred D'Aguiar's novel *Feeding the Ghosts* (1997) imagines events on board the ship from the perspective of one of the slaves. The African-born British artist Lubaina Himid's painting *Memorial to Zong* (1991) draws attention to the victims' continuing invisibility. The *Zong* episode is registered in more indirect ways through the imagery of drowned slaves deployed in Derek Walcott and Édouard Glissant's writing and in recent work by African American artist Ellen Gallagher, such as her *Watery Ecstatic* series (2002–4) and the large canvas *Bird in Hand* (2006), both of which explore the mythical underwater domain of Drexciya, a Black Atlantis peopled by drowned slaves. As Ian Baucom's critical study *Specters of the Atlantic* (2005) demonstrates, the *Zong* massacre has become a defining event in the cultural memory of the black Atlantic. Philip's poem, then, participates in a contemporary flurry of interest in this historical moment that epitomizes the institutionalized violence of the Middle Passage. One of the characteristics that distinguishes her poetic negotiation of this history from other literary, artistic, and critical accounts is that by drawing all of its material from the two-page document from the *Zong* court case, her poem "is not *about* the event but *of* it, in a material sense" (172), to borrow Lee M. Jenkins's perceptive remark.

Historian James Walvin has described the *Zong* case as "the most grotesquely bizarre of all slave cases heard in an English court," and one that "takes us right to the heart of the slave system" (14). On September 6, 1781, the slave ship *Zong*, owned by a group of Liverpool merchants and captained by a Luke Collingwood, set sail from the coast of Africa with its cargo of 440 slaves.[1] Twelve weeks later, lost in the Caribbean Sea (normally the journey took 6 to 8 weeks), the *Zong* had not reached Jamaica. By this time more than 60 Africans and seven crew members had died due to lack of provisions and particularly "for want of water." Collingwood decided to throw 132 sick and dying slaves overboard, as he claimed "for preservation of the rest" (qtd. in "Gregson v. Gilbert," included as an appendix in *Zong!*).[2] He also allegedly told his men "if the slaves died a natural death, it would be the loss of the owners of the ship; but if they were *thrown alive into the sea, it would be the loss of the underwriters*" (qtd. in Walvin 15, emphasis in Walvin). When the ship's owners tried to claim insurance for the drowned slaves, however, the underwriter, Thomas Gilbert, refused to pay. The case went to court not as a murder trial but as a dispute over insurance monies. The abolitionist Granville Sharp did attempt to bring murder charges but failed to do so, so the case remained, as Walvin puts it, "a simple matter of maritime insurance" (14).

In its engagement with these events via the *Gregson v. Gilbert* decision, Philip's poem seeks to recuperate that which is submerged in this document, to "exaqua" traces of "a story that cannot be told" (*Zong!* 190), to find "echoes . . . of what it must have been like for those Africans aboard the Zong" (198), and, above all, to restore some element of humanity to those consigned to a watery grave as jettisoned "cargo." Yet Philip insists that the tale of what happened on that ship remains a story that cannot be told. She questions the capacity of such an event to be fully knowable, especially when its only remains are documents complicit with a system that permitted the massacre on the Zong and then refused to recognize it as murder because the enslaved Africans did not function within this discourse as human individuals. As Baucom starkly points out, "no names survive . . . We know almost nothing of them . . . Not as individuals. As 'types' they are least partially knowable, or imaginable. Indeed, what we know of the trans-Atlantic slave trade is that among the other violences it inflicted on millions of human beings was the violence of becoming a 'type': a type of person, or, terribly, not even that, a type of nonperson, a type of property, a type of commodity, a type of money" (11). The log book for the *Zong* has not survived. Even if it had, the slaves on board would have been listed as numbers rather than names, as was common practice. Indeed, in the transcript of the decision from the *Gregson v. Gilbert* court case, one of the only surviving records of their lives, the victims are recorded only as "slaves" or as "150 . . . negroes" (*Zong!* 210). Not only are they reduced to undifferentiated and objectified "types," the rounded numbers also suggest a process of approximation that fails even to recognize these persons as individual numbers. Furthermore, as Baucom suggests, and as the very existence of the court case confirms, these numbers translate into money, £30 per head, to be a little more precise (see, for example, Webster 291).

The epistemological challenges that Philip's inquiry faces are thus enormous, given her source text's complicity in producing and reproducing the literal and epistemic forms of violence perpetrated on the massacred slaves. Legal historian Jane Webster's study of the case suggests that the enslaved Africans' status as insurable property may even have helped provoke the massacre because insurance law led captains like Collingwood to believe that "jettison was their *best* option in terms of a successful insurance claim" (293). However, she also contends that the *Zong* case "exposed *for the first time* the problems that human 'cargoes' posed for insurers" because it revealed the extent to which slaves "occupied a problematic, liminal position in maritime law—a position somewhere between personhood and property" (296). Indeed, Philip's source text tacitly acknowledges this difficulty. When the plaintiff's solicitors, for example, declare that "[i]t has been decided, whether wisely or unwisely is not now the question, that a portion of our fellow-creatures may become the subject of property" (*Zong!* 211), the document highlights the problematic status of "fellow-creatures" as "property" even as it attempts to abdicate responsibility for this state of affairs and to put the debate about its ethics aside. Moments such as this destabilize the excision of the slaves' humanity from the text's legal discourse. As Webster puts it, "Slave ship insurance cases forced to the surface the issue of the humanity and agency of slaves. Every time counsel mentioned murder in the *Zong* case, for example; every time it was acknowledged that human "cargoes" could attempt to seize control of a ship . . . personhood was implied in court, undermining the legal status of slaves as cargo" (297). It is precisely such moments of instability, evasion, and implicit acknowledgement of personhood that Philip's poem attempts to lever open. Philip insists that neither the individual identities of the Zong slaves nor their stories can be recovered from the *Gregson v. Gilbert* court document. To attempt to transpose the elisions, silences, and disavowals of the Zong case into a coherent narrative might be "to do a second violence. To the experience, the memory—the remembering" (*Genealogy* 116). Instead, this is a story which, Philip maintains, must function "through its un-telling" (*Zong!* 207). As Evie Shockley has remarked in an article on *Zong!* Philip's poetic engagement with this historical event "does not attempt to fill the 'hole' in the record but rather to remember the absences, the silences and to remember that they are evidence of an irrecoverable 'w/hole'" (806). Philip seeks the spectral presences of the story that cannot be told in what the historical text cannot say but nevertheless cannot help hinting at. *Zong!* operates around a "belief that the story of these

African men, women, and children thrown overboard in an attempt to collect insurance monies . . . is locked in this text. In the many silences within the Silence of the text" (*Zong!* 191). Philip understands silence not just as a homogenous emptiness or lack, waiting to be filled with words, but as a potentially fecund trace of that which the source text cannot say.

This principle leads Philip to posit two kinds of silence: silence(s) and Silence. She explains that in her earlier book *Looking for Livingstone*, she "explored [silence] as one would a land, becoming aware that Silence was its own language that one could read, interpret, and even speak" (*Zong!* 195). In this text, a woman traveler journeys through the "silence(s)" of the colonized, seeking, and eventually attaining, a different kind of silence, "a Silence that arises from a rooting in tradition and a knowing of what the colonial script was all about" (*Zong!* 196), a silence of potential agency. To approach a text looking for Silence with a capital "S" is to conduct a critique of the "colonial script" and thereby establish a "rooting in tradition." This Silence is a mode of archaeopoetics that reflects on processes of silencing as necessarily constitutive of the tradition in which Philip writes. This conception of Silence also asks how silences might be aesthetically rendered as something other than straightforward negation, as the generative basis for a "rooting" and a "knowing." As Denise deCaires Narain remarks of *Looking for Livingstone*, "[b]y the end of this 'odyssey of silence,' the reader is given a set of indulgently imaginative images and vocabularies with which to imagine silence" (209). Silence thus holds the potential for a transformation from lack and erasure into a proliferation of possibilities:

in the beginning was

                        not

word
    but Silence
    and a future rampant
                  with possibility

and Word
(*Looking* 40)

Here, Philip rewrites St. John's gospel to posit not the "word" but "Silence" as the ground of "beginning." As performed by the large white space that appears to engender "and Word," Silence is represented not just as privation but as an opening fecund with potential.

Philip's notion of Silence as the ground of language (and perhaps even of existence as such) is strikingly consonant with Pierre Macherey's theory that silence is the "prior condition" (87) of all speech, a *certain absence, without which it would not exist*" (85). But this silence "is not a lack to be remedied . . . a temporary silence that could finally be abolished," insists Macherey, "the work cannot speak of the more or less complex opposition which structures it; though it is its expression and embodiment. In its every particle, the work *manifests*, uncovers, what it cannot say" (84). The silence of the text cannot be made to speak but rather is made "*manifest*" in the text in its very structure; its "every particle" brings into perception that which functions as unacknowledged predicate. A manifest is also the document listing a ship's cargo. For Philip, in the imperial texts of the transatlantic trade the silence of the text is bound up with the silenced presence of the African, and for her, as for Macherey, this silence cannot simply be brought to voice; it cannot be "remedied" but must be detected *as silence*. As a further parallel, recall Spivak's deployment of Macherey in her famous essay on subaltern speech, where she uses his theory to suggest a process of "measuring silences" ("Subaltern" 81). Such an activity, she intimates, might reveal the workings of epistemic violence in the texts of imperialism and yield traces of presences suppressed by such elisions and disavowals.

It is just such a sense of Silence that Philip seeks to make tangible in the pages of *Zong!* The six sections of this book-length poem—forming three distinct phases—chart a process of sifting through the *Gregson v. Gilbert* decision in pursuit of its submerged "story." These three stages do not constitute a recovery of this story but rather the process of searching for it. The first phase, comprising the first section entitled "Os" (Latin for bone), is made up of 26 poems and a "Dicta" of six unnumbered poems, all of which are constructed from words and phrases lifted directly from the court record. The poem's second phase comprises the next four sections, also with Latin titles. "Sal" (salt), "Ventus" (wind), "Ratio" (reason), and "Ferrum" (iron) are a series of fractured long poems that draw more loosely on the *Gregson v. Gilbert* document, fragmenting and recombining words. The short final phase of *Zong!* consists of a section entitled "Ẹbọra" (a Yoruba word for underwater spirits) made up of seven pages of overlaid textual fragments printed in a ghostly grey type. Taken as a whole, *Zong!* embodies a process that begins with the material of its source document and moves increasingly toward fragmentation and finally literal illegibility.

It is worth comparing Philip's manner of confining her composition to the material of her source text to the cut-up experiments of artists and writers such as Brion Gysin and William Burroughs as well as the procedural techniques of John Cage and Jackson Mac Low. The compositional processes in *Zong!* are neither as arbitrary as Gysin and Burroughs's nor as governed by self-imposed conditions as Cage and Mac Low's writings-through. Furthermore, Philip's manner of repeatedly revisiting the text, rather than working through it in any particular "direction," constitutes her source text as an obsessively worked-over site of trauma in ways that are very different from the more controlled methods of these precedents. Yet her more intentional and intuitive processes share with such prior experiments a desire to reveal alternative articulations, or latent potentials. For example, Mac Low's diastic writing-through of Pound's *Cantos, Words nd Ends from Ez*, refashions the authoritarian posturing of *The Cantos* as ludic play and transforms its totalitarian aspirations into dislocated fragments. The process performs a reading "against the grain," bringing to light things which the source text attempts to control or suppress. Perhaps most interestingly, because there were no more letter *z*'s in *The Cantos* to fulfill the procedure's requirements based on the letters of the poet's name, *Words nd Ends* concludes with a blank page, which Mac Low describes as "a silence" ("Discussing" par. 24). This poem's final statement, says Charles Bernstein, forms "a resonating comment on Pound's final years of relative silence and on all the unspeakable grandness and horror that hovers over his epic poem" ("Pound" 165). Mac Low's method thus leads his poem toward an articulation of what the source text could not say. So too, Philip's poem mines its source text's unspeakability for the Silence at its core.

Physical manipulations of textual material are crucial to a parallel archaeopoetics in *Zong!* Many of the fairly sparse and minimalist poems of the first section, "Os," visually echo the "meagre" (Philip, *Zong!* 194) quality of the two-page court document from which Philip works. The expanses of white space in these poems embody the less visible gaps and silences in the poem's source text. In the piece entitled "Zong! #24," for example, the interplay of text and white space, and of verbal and visual effects, demonstrates Philip's sense of Silence (see figure 22). What is most visually striking here is the dense black column on the right, juxtaposed against a vast white space that takes up the majority of the page. This column exhibits a sense of ontological assurance, reinforced by the rigid right alignment of the verb "is" and the dense appearance of the single-spaced lines. As the poem states, "africa / is/ the ground" upon which this assertive column is constructed and "the ground/ is/ negroes." The repetition of "negroes" at bottom right positions this word as the possible culmination of every statement in the column—so

is
justice

africa

is
the ground
is
negroes

evidence is
sustenance is
support is
the law is
the ship is
the captain is
the crew is
perils is
the trial is
the rains is
the seas is
currents is
jamaica is
tobago is
islands is
the case is
murder is
justice is
the ground is
africa is

negroes

was

Figure 22. M. NourbeSe Philip. From *Zong!* by M. NourbeSe Philip © 2011
M. NourbeSe Philip. Page 42. Reprinted by permission of Wesleyan University
Press.

the column can read "sustenance is / negroes," "support is / negroes" and so on. This repetition creates a circularity in which everything begins with, is made up by, and comes back to those exploited bodies. The poem's last lines, meanwhile, state that "negroes / was," the past participle simultaneously pointing to a sense of lost or expired being and, in its singular rather than plural form, treating "negroes" as an unindividuated mass stripped of specificity. The large white space around which these articulations take place embodies this status of "non-being" and acts as an (in)visible presence upon which the columnar imperialist script on the right seems to materially depend for its contrasting sense of robustness.

The poems of "Os" body forth a Silence that makes palpable the epistemic violence of imperialist domination and exploitation. But Philip's Silence also functions to critique and resist the ontological negation of the *Zong*'s Africans. The only words in the poems of "Os" not lifted directly from the source text are the African names listed at the bottom of every page. Their positioning as footnotes, sunk beneath a horizontal black line that visually echoes the surface of the sea, points to their submerged status within the historical document. Not only does the *Gregson v. Gilbert* decision fail to acknowledge them as individual human lives, it assigns these lives the status of *obiter dicta*, factors incidental to the core of a legal case where the judicial decision revolves around a *ratio decidendi* or central principle concerned with the question of insurance. As Philip puts it, this "is what the Africans on board the Zong become—*dicta*, footnotes, related to, but not, the *ratio*" (*Zong!* 199). The discourse of center and periphery that structures both imperial ideologies and their supporting legal edifices is demonstrated here in very concrete terms. But even though as "footnotes" the drowned Africans remain marginal, Philip's lists of names also attempt to bestow upon these drowned Africans a sense of specificity and humanity denied to them by the imperial text.

If the first section of *Zong!* functions as the bones or skeletal remains of the *Zong* tragedy, as the title "Os" suggests, then the sections that follow attempt to flesh out these remnants to retrieve a tangible sense of the drowned and unheard voices on the *Zong*. The four sections "Sal," "Ventus," "Ratio," and "Ferrum" that make up the second phase of *Zong!* conduct this process, paradoxically, by fragmenting the source text's individual words. This mode of composition (or *de*composition) follows an impulse, as Philip puts it in a letter, "to explode the words to see what other words they may contain" (*Zong!* 200). Philip also describes this as a process of carving, with analogies in visual arts practices and especially sculpture: "I use the text of the legal report almost as a painter uses paint or a sculptor stone—the material with which I work being preselected and limited. Henry Moore observed that his manner of working was to remove all extraneous material to allow the figure that was 'locked' in the stone to reveal itself" (*Zong!* 198). The parallel with Brathwaite's "sculpting" practice is striking; the analogy with the practices of painting and sculpture emphasizes a sensuous physicality of the poetic medium. There are also significant differences. Where Brathwaite invokes a West African tradition, Philip's point of reference in the visual arts is one of the most canonical figures of European modernist sculpture. This difference is instructive. Brathwaite sees his sculpting process as a remaking of language and the poetic page by turning to traditions positioned as peripheral, while Philip looks to the dominant narrative of modern sculpture for instruction on how to give tangible form to presences already "'locked' in" one's materials. One presence already "'locked' in" to the very forms of a sculpture practice such as Moore's was non-Western art. By referencing his ideas about art as a parallel to her own practice, Philip highlights the tangibility of African presences not outside but at the very heart of canonical modernism, just as for her the bodies of Africans are detectable not at the margins but as the very underpinnings of imperial texts. In common with numerous modernists before him, such as Jacob Epstein and Gaudier-Brzeska, whose work he admired, Moore was highly influenced by "an inexhaustible wealth and variety of sculptural achievement (Negro, Oceanic Islands, North and South America)" (Moore 104). Like that lesser-known sculptor of the same generation mentioned in chapter 5, Ronald Moody, Moore cites encounters with non-Western art in the galleries of the British Museum as the formative moment of his career as an artist. His subsequent famous pronouncements on "direct carving" and "truth to material," as well as the forms that his own work took, are predicated in part on the lessons he learned from the array of sculptural examples he found there (104).

It is these well-known statements of Moore's of which Philip is thinking when she cites him; their pertinence for her archaeopoetics in *Zong!* is worth unpacking. Although Moore was only one of a large number of British, American and French artists promoting ideas of "direct carving" and "truth to material" drawn from encounters with non-Western art in the first part of the twentieth century, he has certainly become an emblematic figure for this discourse. In an essay on "Primitive Art" published in *The Listener* in 1941, Moore praised the varied examples of "direct carving" he came across in the British Museum galleries for their "truth to material; the artist shows an instinctive understanding of his material, its right use and possibilities" (*Henry Moore* 104). His attribution of the "instinctive," along with notions of this art's "simplicity," "direct and strong feeling," and a "concern with the elemental" (103) echoes problematic notions of non-Western peoples as primal, "closer to nature," and, as Moore himself puts it, as capable of "direct and immediate response to life" (103). Direct carving, then, is associated in Moore's thinking with notions of a lost "primitive" authenticity that his work wanted to recapture. At the same time, Moore was wary of the term "primitive"; he argued strenuously against any notion of non-Western art as unsophisticated and instead admired and wanted to emulate its rendering of an intimate tangible knowledge of materials that enabled their intrinsic characteristics to be expressed in the form of the work.

It is this aspiration to reveal the latent but physical and empirically present qualities of the material that Philip finds so appealing. She is far from alone in affiliating her practice with this aspect of Moore's practice. British artist Susan Hiller has also remarked on Moore's influence for her work. Although she much more explicitly articulates an ambivalence toward his primitivism, his work has suggested to her ways of "making visible suppressed or repressed meanings, hidden or unacknowledged aspects of what can be discovered through looking hard at what already exists in the world of cultural objects" (72).

A further dimension of Moore's practice that corresponds in interesting ways with Philip's archaeopoetics is his inclusion of holes as integral elements of many of his sculptures. In an article of 1937, Moore asserted that "[a] hole can have as much shape-meaning as a solid mass" and that "[s]culpture in air is possible, where the stone contains only the hole, which is the intended and considered form" (196). This insistence on the meaningfulness of holes, and the notion that a sculpture's primary purpose might be to *contain* a hole, resonates interestingly with Philip's focus upon silences in the imperial text, which, through an act of imaginative carving, might be transformed into potent Silences.

For Philip, then, as for Moore, the process of sculpting aims to render tangible something that is already present, "'locked' in" the materials, even, or perhaps especially, if this "presence" takes the form of a hole or silence. This activity entails a hands-on process of "carving." In parallel with the sculptor's physical struggle with highly resistant materials such as stone, Philip treats the text of *Gregson v. Gilbert* as resistant material in a very literal sense. In the sections that follow "Os" she begins physically "carving words out of other words" (*Zong!* 198) and recombining them. In so doing, she discovers latent presences and voices within her source text. From the first, this "carving" yields words in multiple languages, African as well as European, for which Philip provides a glossary, describing her "found" material as "words and phrases overheard on board the *Zong*" (183). This attempt to imaginatively occupy the space of the *Zong* as it made its 1781 journey resonates with Paul Gilroy's notion of "getting on board," which he proposes in *The Black Atlantic*. Ships, he says, "need to be thought of as cultural and political units rather than abstract embodiments of the triangular trade. They were some-thing more—a means to conduct political dissent and possibly a distinct mode of cultural production" (16–17). For Philip, as for Gilroy, the imagina-tive space of the ship represents not just the atrocity of the triangular trade but also an opportunity to trace a series of concrete interactions in which multiple languages, traditions, and enunciations clash and intertwine. From the first lines of the section entitled "Sal," Philip's "carving" activity yields such possibilities with the lines "water parts / the *oba* sobs" (59). *Oba*, a word found within the name of the poet's home island "Tobago," mentioned in her source text, is Yoruba for "king" or "leader," and it is his repeated "sob" that opens and concludes the second, four-part phase of the poem. The sob is a lament, both for the losses incurred through the slave trade in general and for the massacre of the *Zong* slaves, as the "water parts" to receive their jetti-soned bodies. However, the sob is also an utterance, although not an entirely articulate one, which symbolically breaks the silence of the *Zong*'s Africans.

Just as she carves out the *oba*'s sobs from the *Gregson v. Gilbert* docu-ment, Philip finds numerous other "voices" within the text; narratives form from their disjointed utterances. One voice tells a tale of capture, in fractured and entangled English, French, and Spanish: "*de men   dem cam fo mi* / for me for / *yo* for *je pour moi & para* / *mi* flee / the fields   *gun bam   bam* / it was   oh oh / a falling" (66, spaces shortened). The disjointed, multilin-gual phrases that constitute this narrative fragment embody a series of spa-tial and linguistic displacements that formally echo the displacements ex-perienced by those captured and sold into slavery. Elsewhere, another voice relates how "the *oba* smiles / he has *owó* / guineas / *cedis* too   i have / guinea   negroes / they / shed / tears" (82, spaces shortened); the references to three different currencies, to "negroes," and to their "tears" create a scene of slave trading, in which both the speaker and the (this time smiling) *oba* are complicit. Thus the source text's silences erupt into a multiplicity of com-peting voices and "stories," fractured and disjointed as they are.

One of the most prominent voices in the poem is that of "someone who appears to be white, male, and European" (*Zong!* 204), as Philip herself notes. Through this voice, which functions both as perpetrator and witness, a tale of gluttony, gambling, lust, violence, and rape emerges. Often addressing a "ruth," as if in a letter or diary entry, the voice increasingly confesses to "sin" (158 and elsewhere). While one speaker in "Sal" authoritatively justifies the drowning of the slaves by claiming "our aim   to rid the good ship of dying & death" (74), other narratives emerge that present the drownings not as a rational act "for preservation of the rest" ("Gregson v. Gilbert," *Zong!* 210), or even as a cold-blooded and calculated move to collect the insurance, but rather as an attempt to "des troy the evi / dence" of multiple crimes, including bloody violence ("*le / sang* runs"), sexually transmitted disease ("now he / s got the c lap"), and rape and murder ("my l / ust rode her / then s he was go ne was no / more"). In moments such as these, Philip's "carving" exposes the "disorder, illogic and irrationality . . . masquerading as order, logic and rationality" (*Zong!* 197) within the *Gregson v. Gilbert* report. Philip's process reveals what this source text not only cannot say but also refuses to acknowledge as present in its own discursive mode: the unreason within its *ratio*.

This carving-out of counter-narratives is also a dissection and mutilation of the source text that treats it *as* a corporeal entity in quite a literal sense. Philip explicitly acknowledges this process and imagines it in highly visceral terms: "I murder the text, literally cut it to pieces . . . create semantic mayhem, until my hands bloodied, from so much killing and cutting, read into the stinking, eviscerated innards, and like some seer, sangoma, or prophet who, having sacrificed an animal for signs and portents of a new life, or simply life, reads the untold story" (*Zong!* 193–94). The poet's understanding of her process of composition as analogous to the rituals of traditional African shamanic figures is significant, for such activities often aim to bring about a process of healing by means of a sacrifice that opens up channels of communication with ancestors. Philip's route to the ancestral spirits is through the "stinking, eviscerated innards" of her source text, whose mutilation she imagines in terms of a ritual sacrifice, as a "murder" that, however paradoxically, seeks signs of "a new life" in the dismembered remains of its victim. Thus, just as Philip imagines silence as potentially fecund, she also figures textual violence as potentially generative of a mystically inflected productive power: "This is the axis on which the text of *Zong!* turns: censor and magician" (199).

The metaphor of sacrifice and regeneration reveals a spiritual dimension in Philip's process. Although she references an African cultural tradition here, there is also an echo of Romantic notions of the poet as medium. Indeed, *Zong!* presents itself as a book "told to the author by Setaey Adamu Boateng," and in her narrative of the poem's composition Philip describes permission-seeking journeys to Ghana and Liverpool to offer libations to the ancestors and uncanny happenings that guide her writing process. As she puts it at one point, "The spirit in the text and of the text is at work" (204). Importantly, Philip sees her mutilation of the source text as a process over which she has minimal control. Not only does she work within the constraints of her source material, she acknowledges and even actively capitulates to an agency located within language itself. Rachel Blau DuPlessis describes a parallel sensibility: "The blank page (or screen), the open silent space, and the words well up, as from a conduit. What writes?" (162) Like

DuPlessis, Philip understands this "what" that writes partly to consist in a subject positioning that gives and withholds certain kinds of permission. But in attributing a hauntological spirituality to this other agency of writing she also intimates the potential for alterity to "well up, as from a conduit." The question "What writes?" is an opening, and Phillip actively yields to this other agent or "spirit." In particular, she compels herself to abstain from imposing coherence on her materials: "*my urge to make sense must be resisted*" (193).

What is sacrificed along with the literal textual "body" of the *Gregson v. Gilbert* report, then, is linguistic coherence or "the story," as Philip might put it. While Philip's mutilated text affords glimpses of alternative narratives of events on the *Zong*, there is also an inexorable drift toward "semantic mayhem," toward a not-telling that rebuffs the processes of linguistic sense-making. This process is largely performed through increasing linguistic and visual fragmentation as *Zong!* progresses. The visual disruption of syntax plays an important role here. As the page discussed above indicates, Philip's process of carving up the text increasingly opens such large gaps in lines and words that syntactic and semantic coherence becomes radically unstable. While the activity of reading methodically from top left to bottom right does undoubtedly yield recognizable words and phrases, the large white spaces in the text (often so large that I have been unable to quote them) frequently send the reading eye elsewhere than on a march from left to right, top to bottom. The pages of "Ventus," for example, are all visually laid out as drifts or eddies of words and phrases, recalling Eugen Gomringer's 1953 concrete poem in which the letters w-i-n-d are arranged in intersecting diagonal lines to create an overall visual effect of letters caught in a gust of wind. In Philip's poem, as in Gomringer's, these layouts create visual shapes that mimetically echo the wind of the title, and the "contrary winds and currents" (*Zong!* 210) referenced in the *Gregson v. Gilbert* text. They also divert the reading eye from the usual process of top-left-to-bottom-right reading. Physical relationships between words, clusters of words, and word fragments become equally—if not more—significant than linguistic relations. In the example shown as figure 23, the cluster of fractured words near the center of the page forms a downward-sloping arrangement that might, for example, be read "were / ward / ed / for / d / own / do / wn / n / water / drag s." Such a reading process sidesteps linguistic coherence in favor of an engagement with the material relations between word fragments that enact the downward movement of a drowning body. The drift of the words "against / the grain / air / in / vain" creates a series of eye rhymes, some of which are also auditory rhymes, pulling the words together in an image cluster. This collection of words signals both resistance and futility, its "air" repeated at the very bottom of the page, forming a contrary bubble amid a wealth of terms relating to watery death.

Such word clusters constitute constellations, to borrow Eugen Gomringer's term, by which "something is brought into the world. It is a reality in itself and not a poem about something or other. The constellation is an invitation" ("From Line" 67). Indeed, as my readings demonstrate, Philip's constellations are a literal "invitation" to find alternative modes of textual negotiation and by extension to produce ways of reading events of the *Zong* "against / the grain," as Philip's poem reflexively puts it. Philip's constellations undoubtedly exhibit a higher degree of verbal and visual complexity than Gomringer's. They are far less "functional object[s]" (Gomringer, "Poem as Functional Object" 69) in which semantic and visual effects coincide than unstable entities where concrete arrangements and linguistic meanings are likely to follow "contrary winds and currents" (*Zong!* 210). Nevertheless, through the mutilation of the "body" of the historical document, "something is brought into the world." Philip's intimation of "portents of a new life, or simply life" is notably contiguous to Gomringer's rhetoric of birth and renewal. By creating the possibility of new textual meanings, the text performs an attempt to revive the murdered and silenced potentials with which the *Gregson v. Gilbert* text is entangled. If the legal text was able to largely deny the *Zong* slaves' ontological status, then its eviscerated and rearranged remains bring other possibilities into being.

Philip's archaeological constellations "drag the se   a s for bo / ne for sou   nd for b / one song &   sound of bon / e as if   from the de / ep" (Z 158, spaces shortened) in the manner of a marine archaeologist sifting the sea bed for material traces of the past. In this example, the visual relations of these fragments means that they might equally be read as "gut drag the se / yes shut with cat / a s for bo / nd for b / one song & / from the de / sound of bon," or indeed in any number of other permutations. Such arrangements lead to new potentials, then, enabling fragments to signify on their own, as in the shift from "the" to the demotic "de," or in the possibility that the truncated "bon" might be read as the French *bon*. Or fragments might combine to make new combinations, as in the happy accident of "bond," for example, which seems reflexively to comment on its own embodiment of a fortuitous coincidence of semantics and material relations, among other possibilities. But such constellations also enact radically disjointed forms of syntax and sense that point to the impossibility—and for Philip the undesirability—of piecing together a coherent "story" from these textual debris. Instead, what the poem offers is a tangible sense of what a "b / one song & / sound of bon / e as if from the deep" might sound like, its phonemes truncated, scattered, muffled, and intermingled.

Figure 23. From *Zong!* by M. NourbeSe Philip © 2011 M. NourbeSe Philip. Page 91. Reprinted by permission of Wesleyan University Press.

The second phase of *Zong!*, comprising the long poems "Sal," "Ventus," "Ratio," and "Ferrum," moves progressively toward literal illegibility as well as unintelligibility, so that by the last pages of "Ferrum," almost every other word is physically broken and scattered. It is in the poem's final, short phase, entitled "Ębọra," that the work achieves its highest degree of illegibility. Comprising seven pages of overlaid type printed in a spectral light grey, this section resonates in material ways with the underwater spirits of the section's title. Philip tells of how, having completed drafts of "Sal," "Ventus," "Ratio," and "Ferrum," "the laser printer for no apparent reason prints the first two or three pages [of each section of *Zong!*] superimposed on each other" (*Zong!* 206). Presumably, the pages that make up "Ębọra" are derived from these palimpsestual printouts, and so they contain elements of each of the earlier sections. In their visual qualities they reenact, in condensed form, the poem's increasing fragmentation, compression, and opacity. Because of the increased illegibility brought about by overprinting and the non-standard faded grey type, which renders the individual visual dots of the lithographic process visible, the physicality of this printed language becomes ever more evident. In the densely crowded final page of the poem (see figure 24), words and phrases collide and become entangled, forming all but unintelligible sequences, while in places nodes of overprinted text are so dense that their component letters, sounds, or words cannot be discerned at all. In moments such as these, readable text gives way almost entirely to the materiality of its printed medium, becoming a thicket of halftone dots.

These final pages most fully resist the sense-making urge that Philip wants to avoid (*Zong!* 193). Moments of visual opacity and jumbled and entangled strings of letters, words, and phrases ensure that the material of these pages often blocks even the most elementary processes of linguistic signification, let alone narrative sense or "story." Yet this does not mean that these pages are utter nonsense. As Craig Dworkin's insightful study of illegibility reminds us, "while the physical opacity of a text prevents communication from ever being perfect, meaning is always being conveyed by that very materiality" (75). Even where it is impossible to make out a word or even a single letter, the increasingly opaque text of the poem's final section communicates a palimpsestual "babble." Of a comparable palimpsestual text, Charles Bernstein's 1987 poem *Veil*, Dworkin writes, "the writing *peeks a boo* to *let a hidden essay emerge* in a constantly switching dialectic of revelation and concealment. Those glimpses work to *excite the curious EYE level scrutiny wch makes the lines CRISS CROSS* until the reader once again *cant make out the typing* laid over and *over the same material in a variety of* ways to form *overprint with a density* so great that language *itself is tangible and one feels* the physicality of type" (51).

found   a negroes to was   gin my us   in afric?
y/our ear   a ropiggott airy are   rum   my faith negroes
the godere aster/s oh oh   o migto em cam fo m found africa the mast must be teak men
state at the deed under who can cure me   supine sapta from ain
eclat &   wat captain ver   for yo the cur   that that proved
    justi long the se from   danger on de for je ifa that hat
the vent   the lawmy lieg award   deep   pour nifai life cut the cards
    days   para rime *   of dig hig &nder from ifa i   I won the throw
weeks   my plea is negli going the field her   sos sos f shit as so fig luce
fa   monfate   from us   i say   of which absleme doge
comes far commo   for o mortality fall high motwo.aces   she smiles
cut her open   in li will be grounds justice stars do be   b smile
the noise mber cordera the sui kinds I   in lives & am   a disch ge
i die at de ni art as th is   oveam save tuo ching   throw falling
le p'tit m re crew t nigh you fode ble en fe ley   Ruth   throw them
                of salt of mortality in rations murder st d e is fate crusts
but why Ru the noise sum   am   tone & f ince She see there is creed
    the bones she do the stars   app gn sig nig if shine there isunder   if only
        & f lls inmin der mif de us   & yog where by smy aide   oh oh
her sha faifaifa   salve our souls th fo ha sods again
with m peanf lbing   if only ifa   nag int ob tense   ifa ifa ifa i
serve   round b bon soub   is all wrong port   the the oba sobs again
and fit mctee men   rum rai night   over here was piss cum
seas   more rum   & mil f hilge corm gin Ruth
f pea ve s   th uilt sh ramsom ora   salve the slave   they sang &
    with s f ntan om and and my de t de s   sang he w nsed t with sin we map
    uncommon rues le p b o salve   ora pro you s jal u igh ra water/s leak   time
    vid she negro deo   with me a se mch ble al g g   put ashe s he r the bith
to market this is ble t ve ground   tim t p sang   av cord   such
th b t p l i pis g her i say groan ve   a rose i pen th t b ny g r sky l r d er f ther
p po b rth coat for Rut fat nig dugs here ther tea th de se ra th ver seen l faut
fl rget go th m c sity thhere v rd   lot ds of t ai m all lord   payment
nah God no we were write   for tru th to yo fi gg o you a lace cap for my what for
yh C dst hear m f can ill s nim i lity s   of f rc on lif rt th p dpse trp ly the negroes with
            toys o l ph lebt dben th a   do you hear the lute
for ding lady a gold f kould cut the cord of this story sound to ra se oba sobs
take every th g ls y f onl p w n   on   from i st my case
cum gran of h lf icen   a song v rson head is pport   sow   in negligence
with a grain of salt dire vision t vesper sch hear t pt ll /smy p le ig t night s water parts
    the bel ing o ght evid nze   the h igo l p l ky r on jsoch ds h s necessity
th ne Rut reed then   vedic   mund ki mi   negr us   ave t d you
th rim sde org gs gr st sur uth   a rose prom ight o you   to ile ife
told cold   at de fiki o w ar su groes   sow the sea   np r k r my lord
ky h t nf ling my lieg ord um se di vld se n ding
him hi ng rsu ra sh sos   de wide y o Ruth   os   w ys de ks &
Kib too us   I d ml she f d ratio   Ben   reason

Figure 24. From *Zong!* by M. NourbeSe Philip © 2011 M. NourbeSe Philip. Page 182. Reprinted by permission of Wesleyan University Press.

Like reading the tangled text of Bernstein's *Veil*, picking a way through the final pages of Philip's long poem induces awareness of the physical presence of printed language. Perhaps especially in the movement between the poem's densest undecipherable overprintings and its moments of legibility (although never, for long, intelligibility), this poem, like *Veil*, concretely embodies the play between the absorptive and antiabsorptive discussed by Bernstein in "Artifice of Absorption":

> The antiabsorptive does not so much prevent
> absorption as shift its plane
> of engagement–forcing
> a shift in attentional focus.
> (*A Poetics* 76)

It is precisely this "shift in attentional focus," generated in this case by a highly resistant visual materiality, that is so crucial to the archaeopoetics of *Zong!* Resistant forms and materials do not prevent understanding but rather transform the "plane/ of engagement." Philip's final pages reorient the processes of making sense to such a degree that from the silences of the *Gregson v. Gilbert* text, the poem disinters a visually apprehendable sense, as in sensory. Perhaps especially in physical tangles of undecipherable words, the text embodies a Silence that bodies forth, a "b / one song & / sound of bon / e as if from the deep" from the corporeality of ink and paper. Ghostly presences are born from the matrix of lithographic dots that simultaneously silence linguistic signification and ululate a Silence of the submerged.

Abyssal Archaeocritique

Philip's archaeopoetic process in *Zong!* scours the imperial text in pursuit of the suppressed presences that teem within its silences. The poem very literally "brush[es] history against the grain" (Benjamin, *Illuminations* 248), physically dismantling its source text in order that it might yield palpable traces of those whose histories and voices have not been recorded but are, the poet feels, nevertheless entangled with written records that represent them only as blanks and elisions. Through poetic strategies that foreground the physicality of textual material, Philip's writing re-orients perception toward those dimensions of the written word normally subjugated to the semantic drives of reading. Language presented not as transparent signification but as a muddied medium has potential to induce "a shift in attentional focus" (C. Bernstein, *Poetics* 76) to its own processes of functioning and to its own complicities, denials and, above all, silences. By such means, Philip seeks a "redeemed" English, "revealed as the tainted tongue it truly is" (Philip, *She Tries* 19). To reveal language's taint is potentially to make visible hidden presences, "as in biochemistry, the stain allowing you to identify otherwise invisible substances" (C. Bernstein, "An Interview" 31). For Philip, the English language, in its historical entanglement with the bodies of enslaved Africans through the discourses of imperialism, carries hints of such presences emphatically "*Not* on the margins. But within the very body of the text where the silence exists" ("Dis Place" 303). To redeem English is for her to open up the textual "body" to reveal and explore these stained silences that both function as an index for African presences and register the powerful processes of their suppression. In a language enduringly "tainted" by its complicity with imperial ideology these presences cannot be rescued and brought to voice but must, rather, remain muffled articulations.

In common with other writers examined in this book, Philip's approach to historical inquiry can be aligned with a Benjaminian mode of conducting, and also reflecting upon, historiography and historical process. Her engagement with the texts of colonial history in the Caribbean amply and viscerally demonstrates that "[t]here is no document of civilization which is not at the same time a document of barbarism" and most especially that "just as such a document is not free of barbarism, barbarism taints also the manner in which it was transmitted" (Benjamin, *Illuminations* 248). For her, to reveal this "taint" inherent in the "document of civilization" might also be to detect traces of those elided by this very barbarism. Like Brathwaite, though, Philip's work archaeocritically reconsiders the Benjaminian paradigm in relation to the specificities of Caribbean historical and geographical conditions that form the grounds of possibility for her historical consciousness. Recall how Brathwaite's tidalectics echo and also reshape Benjamin's own archaeocritique of dialectics. As we have seen, Benjamin's mode of historical awareness based "not [on] progression but image, suddenly emergent" (*Arcades* 462, N2a, 3) shifts dialectical thinking from a linear temporal model to a spatial one. Brathwaite's tidalectics, however, draws on a geographical-historical imaginary of the Caribbean region to propose a model of historical process grounded in the ceaseless ebb and flow or displacement and return of the Caribbean Sea, the wider Atlantic, and the histories of diaspora so intimately imbricated with these tidal dynamics. In this understanding the sea is indeed history and the "grounds" of historical knowledge are oceanic.

Philip's thinking runs parallel with Brathwaite's notion of tidalectics when she says, "Our entrance to the past is through memory—either oral or written. And water. In this case salt water. Sea water. And, as the ocean appears to be the same yet is constantly in motion, affected by tidal movements, so too this memory appears stationary yet is shifting always. Repetition drives the event and the memory simultaneously, becoming a haunting" (*Zong!* 201). Whereas Benjamin's "dialectical image" conceptualizes significant historical configurations as encapsulated in epiphanic moments of arrest, the fluid space of the ocean suggests a conception of history as constantly flowing and transforming. The previous chapter explored some of the implications of this shift in relation to Brathwaite's tidalectics; Philip shares Brathwaite's understanding of history as a highly dynamic and unceasing process of displacement and return modeled on the geographic and historical particularities of the Caribbean. Indeed, in a recent essay exploring her sense of the sea-as-history, Philip outlines a Caribbean reshaping of historicist poetics that "is restless is kinetic add kinopoesis to pound's ordering of language phanopoesis melopoesis logopoesis" (Wor[l]ds). She even refers to this sensibility as explicitly "Brathwaitian" (Wor[l]ds). But Philip's articulation of this historical modality also brings further dimensions of an oceanic historical imaginary into focus. In this recent essay, she proposes a notion of Caribbean history as a "kari basin," a vast "liquid archive [Chambers 26] that holds the secret of History in subterranean spaces" (Wor[l]ds). Here she explicitly draws on cultural theorist Iain Chambers's notion of the "liquid archive," which suggests that "[d]eposited in the sea are histories and cultures held in indeterminate suspension, connected, rather than simply divided by, water; they suggest other histories, other ways of narrating both a local and a planetary modernity" (2). The sea is imagined as a crucible of modernity, holding traces of its intercultural mixings as well as its violent schisms, its unspoken dimensions, and hegemonic imperatives. Thus the sea is a site of potential for reimagining the past and the ways it might be possible to know it. The notion of the liquid archive not only chimes with Philip's interest in the historical text as material artifact, it also brings into focus a subtly different oceanic imaginary than Brathwaite's. To put this in topographical terms, where Brathwaite's historical imagination is attentive to the ocean's dynamic relations with land masses, archipelagoes, and shores, Philip is also interested in its deep abysses where historical traces amass. Philip sees the sea as a space of dynamic, shifting, and cyclical currents that represents a material and imaginative *repository* for traces of the past silted into vast alluvial terrains, many of which lie beyond reach.

This dimension of her thinking bears comparison to the arguments of literary theorist Ian Baucom, whose book *Specters of the Atlantic* builds a convincing case that writers such as Paul Gilroy, Walcott, Glissant, and Philip herself collectively rearticulate a Benjaminian model of history to produce "a diasporic philosophy of history" (34) in which "[t]ime does not pass, it accumulates, and as it accumulates it deposits an ever greater freight of material within the cargo holds of [the] present" (325). According to Baucom, for whom the *Zong* massacre and its attendant image of the drowned slave becomes a paradigmatic hauntological event, this history is not history because it is not over and done with. Its violence continues to haunt a contemporaneity in which the "protocols which are that atrocity's conditions of possibility have not waned but intensified" (23–24). Here Baucom is referring to the workings of finance capitalism, whose roots lie in slave-trade-era systems of credit and which constitute practices and ways of conceptualizing the world predicated on the abstraction of Africans as objects of exchange and thus as capital. Because finance capitalism in its "intensified" forms has come to define and indeed determine our present, the "specters of the Atlantic" continue to haunt a contemporaneity in which this past is not past but rather a present in which the specters of the past are piled up like cargo in a ship's hold. Or, to bring Philip's oceanic model back into focus, as debris silted in to the shifting alluvial sediments of the Atlantic.

Baucom's wide-ranging analysis identifies a key shift between Benjamin's notion of the dialectical image, in which history is accumulated but whose meaningfulness emerges instantaneously within a "now of particular recognizability" (*Arcades* 463, N3, 2), and a black Atlantic philosophy of history in which an amassed history is endured in an ongoing, unending process. As Philip's *Zong!* puts it, "this is / not was" (7). This sensibility is also highly apparent in Glissant's thought, upon which Baucom draws extensively. In *Caribbean Discourse*, Glissant declares that "the poetics of the American continent, which I characterize as being a search for temporal duration, is opposed in particular to European poetics, which are characterized by the inspiration or the sudden burst of a single moment" (144). In *Poetics of Relation*, this idea receives a fuller articulation: "We no longer reveal totality within ourselves by lightning flashes. We approach it through the accumulation of sediments. The poetics of duration . . . reappears to take up the relay from the poetics of the moment. Lightning flashes are the shivers of one who desires or dreams of a totality that is impossible or yet to come; duration urges on those who attempt to live this totality, when dawn shows through the linked histories of peoples" (33). The allusions to Benjamin are only too apparent. Whereas for Benjamin "what has been comes together in a flash with the now" (*Arcades* 462, N3, 1), Glissant proposes a historical imagination based on an "accumulation of sediments." Rather than "a poetics of the moment," he argues for a "poetics of duration," in which is embedded a sense of the lived effects of an accumulated history. As Baucom's discussion of this passage points out, the modernist lightning flash—contingent in its moment of occurrence but universalist in its ambition—directs itself toward a dreamed moment of futurity. On the other hand, Glissant's rhetoric of accumulated sediments—global in its outward reach but specific in its historical grounding—constitutes an ontology of modernity as it is endured and lived in the now as an amassed historical experience (see Baucom 319–20). For writers of the black Atlantic, history is a great "grey vault" (Walcott 364) holding a vast alluvial freight of a past that endures, a past that continually washes up in the present.

It is important to keep the oceanic topographical metaphors deployed by Philip and Glissant in mind. They help to bring to the fore something which Baucom's analysis, for all its rhetorical flair and theoretical sophistication, is in danger of sidestepping: the epistemological *challenges* posed by this particular history. Accumulated sediments are not only a piling up of historical traces, they are also, in this particular context, submerged and incredibly murky. In positing a contemporary moment in which the freight of history is amassed, Baucom infers that this history, by being now, is fairly readily available, even if only spectrally.[3] Indeed, his wide-ranging analysis of the variety of documents and artifacts accumulated around his topic treats the eighteenth-century *Zong* atrocity as an event witnessed in a fairly direct way by this mass of materials whose paradigms constitute our present moment. Baucom's analysis proceeds on the basis that the significance of these amassed materials can thus be grasped in a "now of particular recognizability" (Benjamin, *Arcades* 463, N3, 2). It makes a difference that his theory of history is more interested in tracing the dominant discourses and prominent counter-discourses that have come to produce a hegemonic contemporaneity than in seeking those nameless, unwritten, invisible, and inaudible presences of a peripheral modernity, which function here only as "specters."

By articulating a desire to flesh out the submerged, spectral dimensions of the history of the Caribbean, Philip's archaeopoetic mode suggests a philosophy of history in which the past is not only accumulated freight but also submarine sediment. As the lines by Derek Walcott that form my epigraph indicate, many of the traces of Caribbean history are "locked . . . up" (364), all but inaccessible except as fragments scattered as if across a submarine terrain. Glissant reminds us, time and again, of "[t]he loss of collective memory," the sea-like "careful erasing of the past . . . and so time keeps turning around in us" (*Caribbean* 161). Above all, Philip's work calls attention to *language* as the roiling, erasing seascape that is so much part of this history, simultaneously an agent of its submersion and necessarily the primary medium of attempts at recovery. As the subtitle of her recent essay emphasizes, this is the key challenge involved in excavating "The *Un*history of the Kari Basin" (Wor[l]ds, my emphasis).

A poetics of accumulated sediments that is lived in language, through language, and its entanglement with the histories of the African diaspora recognizes that these (un)histories cannot quite be "seized" in a Benjaminian poetics of the epiphanic moment but might instead be perceived in the mobile alluvia of language forms that tilt attention toward the unwritten, unnoticed, and unheard. The material strata of words is usually that which goes unacknowledged in the normative drive for intelligible, transcendent meaning; Philip often turns to these submerged dimensions and their dynamic interaction with linguistic meaning to explore the possibilities of encountering the muffled presences of Caribbean history. The poetic page becomes an alluvial textual terrain peopled by an accumulation of silences that might be made palpable, "present," by means of its material dimensions. Philip's poetry physically reshapes language in an attempt to orient attention toward historical dimensions that are tangible but resistant to subsumption by the dominant structures of English and its legacies of epistemological violence. This move constitutes a project aimed at generating a genuine diversity of the word, for, to borrow from Glissant once more, "[t]he landscape of your word is the world's landscape. But its frontier is open" (*Poetics* 33).

Afterword

ARCHAEOPOETIC AFTERLIVES

The writing examined in *Archaeopoetics* is part of a significant historicist orientation in recent poetry that seeks to refashion the modernist "poem including history" in a range of contemporary contexts that pose particular challenges to the task of historical investigation. Digging through the concrete specifics of the textual history of the English regicide, or the seemingly unpromising and inadequate traces of Korea's troubled past, or the embodied memories of the Irish famine, or the illegible noises and silences of the Caribbean enables this poetry to provoke wider epistemological questions. Throughout *Archaeopoetics*, I examine a tension between the irretrievability of silenced, effaced, and elided historical evidence, and the claim that poetry might indeed body forth such unrecoverable traces. This tension, I have suggested, is productive, activating a form of aesthetically enacted epistemological inquiry. I have explored how and why poets have turned emphatically to the sensuous materiality of texts, to the flesh of the word, and most especially to the visual manifestations of this physicality to propose alternative modes of historical encounter. In this poetry, the concreteness of the visual word or image as well as the spatial modes of thinking embodied by the constellation or field suggest compelling alternatives to narrative or discursive models of historical knowledge. Activities of writing and reading become akin to fieldwork. The concrete particularities of encountered objects generate semantic energies that cannot be folded into a coherent discourse, though they can impart tangible forms of knowledge. By enlarging the field of the poetic, and by prompting a reconsideration of what the activity of reading might entail, such work pushes at the limits of what counts as meaning and what counts as knowledge.

The powerful historicist strand I scrutinize in contemporary poetry is a corrective to dominant critical narratives of "innovation" and present-oriented politics. In closing, I want to offer a glimpse of how the impulse to critique specific aspects of contemporary modernity by excavating and reinvigorating specific historical materials remains strong in a proliferation of new work; poets such as Jena Osman, Mark Nowak, Craig Santos Perez, Harriet Tarlo, Caroline Bergvall, Evelyn Reilly, Jennifer Scappettone, Frances Presley, and others are currently producing work in this mode. Such writers reflect critically on specific dimensions of their present moment by conducting poetic investigations of highly pertinent historical phenomena.

Consider, for example, Jena Osman's 2010 *The Network*. This book-length serial poem continues the archaeological tradition of writers such as Howe, Brathwaite, and Cha (whom Osman has explicitly acknowledged as influences [see *The Rumpus* interview]) as well as extending a longer trajectory reaching back through Olson, Pound, and others. Osman's poem digs down into historical sources, geography, and language to investigate histories of the politics of race, financial crisis, and ecological damage intertwined with the poem's own contemporary moment. Through research involving historical records, etymologies, and specific geographical foci and phenomena such as the Mummers Parade on the streets of Philadelphia, Sir John Franklin's failed 1845 Arctic expedition, and the histories of street names and trade in New York's Financial District, Osman's series picks away at the entangled roots of language, slavery, finance capitalism, and colonial engagements with the American landscape.

From the outset, Osman's poem declares that "[r]ather than invent a world, I want a different means to understand this one" (3). Let us consider a specific example of this activity, from the fourth section, "Financial District," a site-specific poem conducting interlinked inquiries into the physical geography of Lower Manhattan, its histories of colonialism and trade, and the genealogies of financial terms. The section is made up of a series of tripartite clusters, comprising a poem focusing on a particular street, a second presenting an etymological diagram of a word associated with finance, and a third that combines the titles of the first two and generates connections between them. In the triad "WALL," "DEPRESSION," and "WALL+DEPRESSION," we learn that Wall Street has its beginnings in an actual wall, built in 1653 under the direction of Peter Stuyvesant, the Dutch Governor of New Amsterdam at the time. Its purpose was initially to keep livestock in, but eventually functioned as a means to keep the British and Native Americans out. The poem's prose section states: "With word of each new possible enemy, Stuyvesant orders the **wall** to be re-fortified, and this is done with slave labor" (52). Thus Wall Street, the heart of global finance, has as its foundations a mode of spatial appropriation that relies on divisionary logic—a logic of exclusion—of insiders and outsiders, which mirrors the workings of contemporary finance capital and its local and global effects of uneven development. Furthermore, the poem foregrounds how this demarcation of space and privilege is built—quite literally—through the exploitation of commodified bodies. Slave labor,

DEPRESSION

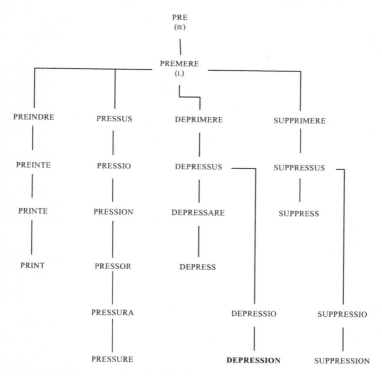

Figure 25. Jena Osman. "Depression." *The Network*. Fence Books © 2010 Jena Osman. Page 53. Reprinted by permission of Fence Books and the author.

Osman's poem reminds us, was one of the earliest commodities traded in the financial district. New York was in its early years "a slave trading port" (52) and Wall Street the site of "a whipping post, pillory and stocks . . . public lashings of slaves up and down the block beyond the market established for their purchase" (55).

The second poem of the triad, "DEPRESSION," consists of an etymological diagram unearthing the word's roots (see figure 25). "Depression," a term "synonymous with high finance," (55) has close relations with "suppression," "pressure," and, interestingly, with "print," the very medium of the poem and its sources, not to mention paper money. All of these terms, the chart demonstrates, are rooted in the Latin "premere," from the Indo-European root "pre," variously defined in the following prose section as "literally and figuratively, to squeeze" (54), "to press out" (55), and most suggestively "to press or under (hence to put down), to press under foot, hence to cause to disappear, to subjugate" (56). The triad "WALL," "DEPRESSION," and "WALL + DEPRESSION" reveal—through spatial mapping and the material juxtapositions of different discourses and modes of representation—some of the dimensions of finance capital that have been "cause[d] to disappear," "suppressed," and "press[ed] out" from contemporary representations. Not only do the poems exhume the roots of slavery, appropriation, violence, and subjugation from which contemporary capitalism has grown, but they also emphasize, through numerous physically tangible poetic means, the material bases of a financial system whose contemporary forms of self-representation are increasingly and bewilderingly abstract and dematerialized. The "depression" that has emanated from this world center from time to time, meanwhile, is recast in the poem as a physical force acting in highly material ways.

Osman was writing in the immediate wake of the global financial crisis of 2007–2008. Commentators have often compared this crisis with the Great Depression of the 1930s, although they rarely apply the word "depression" to this most recent manifestation of capitalism's patterns of boom and bust. Instead, economic discourse has posited a "recession" proceeding from a "financial crisis" caused by factors such as the bursting of the "credit bubble," a "liquidity crisis," and "capital flight." Such abstract terminology relies on metaphors of water and air, substances with a fluidity and amorphousness that suggest escape from more weighty forms of earthbound materiality. Osman's archaeology of the language of finance works against such dematerializing impulses by revealing a long history of finance capital and its material roots in physical commodities, geography, and social and ethnic inequalities. Importantly, she avoids positing a linear narrative in which financial markets once had a material basis but have now transcended the physical world into more abstract forms. Her poetic mode of investigation utilizes physical juxtapositions, invokes spatial relationships, and uses the figure of the network to render a much more complex dynamic between the histories and contemporary forms of capital.

Osman's mode of engagement with the intertwined geographies, histories, and language of finance capital puts her in conversation with a body of experimental site-specific post-war poetry and visual art that Lytle Shaw recently dubbed "fieldworks" in his compelling book of that name. The work he examines by writers such as Olson, Creeley, and Snyder, and artists like Smithson, he contends, "has almost always operated as an alternative mode of historiography" (22), drawing on models of fieldwork from anthropology, ethnography, and geography to develop a spatialized poetics that "challenged *narrative itself* as the unstranscendable frame for historical understanding" (48). Osman's site-specific poetic archaeology can be seen as a contemporary development of this poetics of fieldwork. Seeking "a different means to understand" its contemporary world and its historical formation, the poem operates as a kind of field that traces not cause-and-effect narratives but a network of forces and connections. As an early section of the series puts it, Osman's poem concretizes a dynamic that is "not causal but a knot. of derivations and kinships. an attempted unraveling" (7).

This sensibility is quite tangibly concretized and condensed in Osman's etymological diagram poems, such as in the one that traces the "derivations and kinships" of the word "DEPRESSION" (see figure 25). The chart is a spatial mapping of the word's genealogy, its "kinships," and also its movements across cultures. It physically embodies a non-narrative mode of understanding connections and relationships, where lateral associations and spatial relations produce meanings not entirely translatable into narrative or discursive paradigms but palpably meaningful nonetheless. Furthermore, in common with the poetry that Shaw examines and with the work I have explored in *Archaeopoetics*, this poetic mode strikes up a dialogue with correlating practices in the visual arts. Osman is keen to attribute her etymological excavations to the influence of Cecilia Vicuña's "instruction . . . 'to enter words in order to see'" (3). Indeed, the practice of this visual artist, poet, and political activist has been an important touchstone for Osman, who has written about Vicuña's *Precarios*, a long-running series of small-scale works engaging with social and ecological themes and constructed from found, often discarded, materials. Osman says that these pieces "ask the viewer or reader to become aware of the rich interior of the ambient, to shift attentions, to read seemingly insignificant objects in a different way, with the idea that a more connective reading that joins past to present and the monumental to the ephemeral might lead to different acts in the future" ("Is Poetry the News" par. 25). Something similar might be said of Osman's own etymological investigations. In addition, she draws stimulus from Vicuña's practice of working with the tangible materiality of found objects whose potentials have hitherto been ignored.

Osman's etymological inquiries delve into the hidden strata of words to "shift attentions" to unnoticed or "ambient" phenomena. The form of these archaeological excavations on the page draws attention to literal materiality, both in terms of its own physicality and that of the semantic field it investigates. One occurrence—or reoccurrence—that is thereby brought to attention in the etymological chart for "depression" is the abiding physical presence of the root "pre" within its descendants, mutated to "pri" in "print." The "pre" of physically pressing and squeezing out, as if wringing value from the material world, the diagram reveals, is still very much present in "depression" and its etymological cousins. What this poem makes palpable is that despite finance capital's idealized imaginaries of forms that transcend the material, its sources and effects remain troublingly, if often indirectly, connected to material levels of exploitation and subjugation. Wall Street may no longer trade in slaves but such forms of exploitation have mutated and moved elsewhere, often out of plain sight, surfacing only when a factory collapse in Bangladesh kills more than a thousand sweatshop workers or when the explosion of an oil rig in the Gulf of Mexico causes a catastrophic spill of hitherto unprecedented ecological and social consequence.

Osman's poem does not "discover" new facts about such contemporary issues and their pasts but rather proposes an alternative way of perceiving. Through forms that reach beyond the conventionally poetic, *The Network* performs shifts of focus that bring the background into the forefront of attention and trigger unexpected connections between historical and contemporary phenomena "wherein what has been comes together in a flash with the now to form a constellation" (Benjamin, *Arcades* 462, N2a, 3). In so doing, it enacts an inquiry into the ways in which we know the past and the present, and whether we might know them otherwise.

Osman's poem demonstrates that the archaeopoetic impulse is thriving. My book seeks to provoke an attentional shift of its own, by bringing the historiographical dimensions of contemporary experimental writing into sharp focus and indicating some of the wide-ranging questions it raises. But if, as I believe, poetry can act as a mode of historical and philosophical inquiry, it is also my conviction that this activity occurs most powerfully and convincingly in the poetry itself. The best demonstration of my argument lies ultimately in the intricate workings of the poetries themselves and in their epistemological activities, for which we still lack adequate vocabularies. Or, to borrow a line from Philip's *Zong!*

the be̶l̶ing o̶u̶ught e̶v̶i̶d̶e̶n̶c̶e̶ the̶t̶h̶i̶n̶g̶s̶h̶o̶u̶l̶d̶wrong̶s̶u̶c̶h̶d̶e̶a̶t̶h̶necessity

Notes

Chapter 1

1. See especially the "Against Theory" polemic of Steven Knapp and Walter Benn Michaels, and Michaels's subsequent *The Shape of the Signifier*, which presents arguments that entirely depend on the distinction between language and mark-making, sign and material mark.

2. There are of course exceptions; the most notable is Paul Naylor's book-length project *Poetic Investigations*, although Brian McHale's *Obligation Toward the Difficult Whole* and Peter Middleton and Tim Woods's *Literatures of Memory* contain important chapters on contemporary poetry and history. In addition, there are a number of historically oriented articles on some of the individual poets I discuss: see especially Ma, Montgomery, Nicholls, and Perloff on Howe; Davidson and Lowe on Cha; Mackey and Pollard on Brathwaite; and Marriot and Shockley on Philip.

3. This separation of verbal and visual spheres of artistic activity has been tested by hybrid modernist and postmodernist practices themselves as well as by critics who position themselves within an alternative tradition of thought that stresses similarities and parallels between the arts as in Horace's ancient maxim "*ut pictura poesis*" ("in poetry as in painting"). However, for all its critique of the verbal/visual dualism and its binary logic, this mode of criticism actually implicitly retains many of the assumptions of those discourses that posit a separation between verbal and visual forms along lines that make distinctions between a temporal, immaterial, and ideational verbal domain and a spatial, material, and sensory visual domain. For example, critics such as Norman Bryson and Mieke Bal have proposed ways of approaching verbal and visual media not as separate sign systems but as different *modes* of representation which participate in comparable processes of making meaning. However, as W. J. T. Mitchell rightly notes, Bal and Bryson fail to appreciate the extent to which semiotics privileges linguistic frameworks of meaning: "Far from avoiding 'the bias of privileging language,' semiotics continually reinstates that bias" (*Picture* 99n). Indeed, this partiality can be detected in the terms that Bal and Bryson use. In a coauthored article, they offer a theory of the sign understood "*not as a thing but as an event*" (194), as a process rather than a static object. They propose "a view of image-seeing that is dynamic and positioned in time" (191). By treat-

ing the sign "*as an event*" with a dynamism that invokes the qualities of the verbal sign and most emphatically "*not as a thing*" with a brute materiality associated with the visual sign, this method recurrently falls back on the binary structures it aims to circumvent. Moreover, the privileged term is always one rooted in a linguistic model. This approach retains a key assumption of discourses that posit a divide between the verbal and visual arts: the notion that meaning is essentially language-based and that visuality is effectively "mute" until it is transposed into a language-based system of interpretation. In so doing, it illustrates and, to a great extent, unwittingly perpetuates distinctions between verbal and visual modes of signification. Other valuable contributions have come from Charles Bernstein, Michael Davidson, Marjorie Perloff (especially *Radical Artifice* and *Unoriginal Genius*), Jerome McGann, Eleanor Berry, Willard Bohn, and Richard Bradford.

Chapter 2

1. I refer to *Eikon Basilike* and *Thorow* in italics because both poems were previously published as works in their own right, though my references are to the more widely available versions published in *The Nonconformist's Memorial* and *Singularities*.

2. Some of Howe's early works are held in the Mandeville Special Collection at the University of California, San Diego.

3. When in the aforementioned interview Foster asks Howe, "[t]hen you do feel history is an actuality?" Howe replies simply, "Yes" (*Birth-mark* 158). The relations in Howe's work between this sense of history as "an actuality" and textual history have been addressed at length elsewhere. See especially Ming-Qian Ma, "Poetry as History Revised."

4. This line can be found in the "genetic text" of Melville, *Billy Budd*, 412.

5. Will Montgomery's meticulous research presented in his article "Appropriating primal indeterminacy: language, landscape and postmodern poetics in Susan Howe's *Thorow*," later revised as a section of *The Poetry of Susan Howe*, gives an excellent account of Howe's engagement with these sources.

6. Many of the isolated words here come from various places in Thoreau's works. The unusual words "drisk" (meaning light drizzle) and "cusk," for example, can be found in "Allegash & East Branch" in *The Main Woods*.

Chapter 3

1. There are ten vowel graphemes in Hangul. Interestingly, Cha omits the grapheme that is sounded "yu."

2. This is one of Cha's pieces exhibited from time to time in the Berkeley Art Museum and elsewhere. I saw it at an exhibition in Los Angeles called *WACK! Art and the Feminist Revolution* in June 2007.

Chapter 4

1. This introductory part of the poem is omitted in the version reprinted in *WATERFALLS* (2009).

2. The song "Skibbereen," derived from an oral tradition, has numerous differ-

ent versions, many of which continue to be disseminated via websites as well as (less commonly now) in books of Irish folk songs.

3. Indeed, Etruscan Books, the publisher, names this object as an "exhibition" on its cover and backmatter.

Chapter 5

1. For an early account of the role of new computer technologies in Brathwaite's shift to a more visually attuned mode of writing, see the poet's interview with Stewart Brown, "Interview with Kamau Brathwaite" 86–87.

2. Brathwaite gives several accounts of the traumas he suffered in the late 1980s and early 1990s—his wife's death in 1986; the devastation of his home and archives at Irish Town, Kingston in 1988; and in 1990 his near death at the hands of armed burglars in his flat in Kingston. See, for example, Brathwaite, *ConVERSations with Nathaniel Mackey* and "Newstead to Neustadt."

3. It is important to remember that there are many different versions of Caribbean nation language, utilising different sounds and rhythms, even among English-speaking islands. In this poem, Brathwaite's speaker adopts sounds common across the Caribbean rather than highlight that which is distinct to, say, Bajan (Barbadian) speech, as he does in some of his other, more recent works.

4. The poet gives an account of his uncle and prints a Sycorax video revision of this poem in *Barabajan Poems* 156–58.

5. Roberts has studied this tradition among the Tabwa and neighbouring peoples of southeastern Zaire, northeastern Zambia and southwestern Tanzania. He says that most *mkissi* that survive are held in Western museums.

Chapter 6

1. Philip, following James Walvin, puts the number of slaves on board at 470. I follow the figures given in Ian Baucom's *Specters of the Atlantic*, which he takes from the letter abolitionist Granville Sharp sent to the Lords Commissioners of the Admiralty, and accompanying court transcriptions, held in the National Maritime Museum, Greenwich, catalogued as REC/19.

2. Again, I follow Baucom's claim that 132 slaves were thrown overboard. Philip and the version of the court transcript she supplies as an Appendix to *Zong!* give the number drowned as 150. Walvin gives the figure as 131 but explains that one of the slaves thrown overboard managed to catch hold of a rope and climb aboard again.

3. Iain Chambers's article, cited by Philip and mentioned earlier, is also at risk of this inference.

Works Cited

Adorno, Theodor. *Aesthetic Theory*. Trans. Robert Hullot-Kentor. London: Athlone, 1997.

———. "Introduction to Benjamin's *Schriften*." *On Walter Benjamin*. Ed. Gary Smith. Cambridge, MA and London, England: MIT P, 1998. 2–17.

Alberro, Alexander. "Reconsidering Conceptual Art." *Conceptual Art: A Critical Anthology*. Cambridge, MA and London, England: MIT P, 1999. xvi–xxxvii.

Almack, Edward. *A Bibliography of the King's Book; or, Eikon Basilike*. London: Blades, East and Blades, 1896.

Andrews, Bruce. "Writing Social Work and Political Practice." *The L=A=N=G=U=A=G=E Book*. Carbondale and Edwardsville: Southern Illinois UP, 1984. 133–36.

Andrews, Bruce and Charles Bernstein, eds. *The L=A=N=G=U=A=G=E Book*. Carbondale and Edwardsville: Southern Illinois UP, 1984.

Andrews, Bruce and Maggie O'Sullivan. *eXcLa*. London: Writers Forum, 1993.

Antin, Eleanor. *Carving: A Traditional Sculpture*. 1972. Black-and-white photographs. Art Institute of Chicago.

Armstrong, Isobel. "Maggie O'Sullivan: The Lyrical Language of the Parallel Tradition." *Women: a cultural review* 15.1 (2004): 57–66.

Attali, Jacques. *Noise: The political economy of music*. Manchester: Manchester UP, 1985.

Back, Rachel Tzvia. *Led by Language: The Poetry and Poetics of Susan Howe*. Tuscaloosa: U of Alabama P, 2002.

Baer, Ulrich. *Spectral Evidence: The Photography of Trauma*. Cambridge, MA and London, England: MIT P, 2005.

Bal, Mieke. "Reading Art?" *A Mieke Bal Reader*. London and Chicago: U of Chicago P, 2006. 289–312.

Bal, Mieke and Norman Bryson. "Semiotics and Art History." *The Art Bulletin* 73.2 (1991): 175–208.

Barnes, Sandra T. "The Many Faces of Ogun: Introduction to the First Edition." *Africa's Ogun: Old World and New*. Ed. Barnes. 2nd ed. Indiana UP, 1997.

Barry, Peter. *Poetry Wars: British Poetry of the 1970s and the Battle of Earls Court*. Cambridge: Salt, 2006.

Barry, Peter and Robert Hampson. "Introduction: The Scope of the Possible." *New*

British poetries: The scope of the possible. Ed. Hampson and Barry. Manchester: Manchester UP, 1993. 1–11.

Barthes, Roland. *Camera Lucida.* London: Vintage, 1993.

Baucom, Ian. *Specters of the Atlantic: Finance Capital, Slavery, and the Philosophy of History.* Durham and London: Duke UP, 2005.

Beach, Christopher. *ABC of Influence: Ezra Pound and the Remaking of American Poetic Tradition.* Berkeley, California: U of California P, 1992.

Benjamin, Walter. *The Arcades Project.* Tran. Howard Eiland and Kevin McLaughlin. Cambridge, Massachusettes, and London, England: Belknap Press of Harvard UP, 1999.

——. "Excavation and Memory." *Selected Writings.* Vol 2: 1927–1939. Ed. Michael W. Jennings. Cambridge, MA and London, England: Belknap Press of Harvard UP, 1999. 576.

——. *Illuminations.* Trans. Harry Zorn. London: Pimlico, 1999.

——. "A Small History of Photography." *One Way Street.* London: Verso, 1979. 240–257.

Bernstein, Charles. "Charles Bernstein Interview." With Eric Denut. *The Argotist Online.* Accessed on web July 2011. <http://www.argotistonline.co.uk/Bernstein%20interview.htm>

——. *Content's dream: essays 1975–1984.* Los Angeles: Sun and Moon, 1986.

——. "Foreword: O'Sullivan's Medleyed Verse." *Body of Work.* By Maggie O'Sullivan. Hastings: Reality Street Editions, 2006. 7–9.

——. *A Poetics.* Cambridge: Harvard UP, 1992.

——. "Pound and the Poetry of Today." *My Way: speeches and poems.* By Bernstein. Chicago: U of Chicago P, 1999. 155–165.

Bernstein, J. M. *Against Voluptuous Bodies: Late Modernism and the Meaning of Painting.* Stanford, CA: Stanford UP, 2006.

——. *Recovering Ethical Life: Jürgen Habermas and the future of critical theory.* London: Routledge, 1995.

Berry, Eleanor. "The Emergence of Charles Olson's Prosody of the Page Space." *Journal of English Linguistics* 30.1 (2002): 51–72.

Bersani, Leo. *The Culture of Redemption.* Cambridge, MA and London, England: Harvard UP, 1990.

Bertin, Jacques. *Semiology of Graphics.* Trans. William J. Berg. Madison, WI: U of Wisconsin P, 1983.

Biro, Matthew. "Representation and Event: Anselm Kiefer, Joseph Beuys, and the Memory of the Holocaust." *The Yale Journal of Criticism* 16.1 (2003): 113–146.

Bradford, Richard. *The Look of It: A Theory of Visual Form in English Poetry.* Cork: Cork UP, 1993.

Brathwaite, Edward. *The Arrivants: A New World Trilogy: Rights of Passage, Islands, Masks.* Oxford: OUP, 1973.

——. *The Development of Creole Society in Jamaica 1770–1820.* London: OUP, 1971.

Brathwaite, Edward Kamau. *History of the Voice.* London: New Beacon, 1984.

——. "Interview with Edward Kamau Brathwaite." With Stewart Brown. *Kyk-over-al* 40 (1989): 84–93.

Brathwaite, Kamau. *Ancestors: A Reinvention of Mother Poem, Sun Poem, and X/Self.* New York: New Directions, 2001.

——. *Barabajan Poems*. New York: Savacou North, 1994.

——. *Born to Slow Horses*. Middletown, CT: Wesleyan UP, 2005.

——. "Caliban's Guarden." *Wasafiri* 8.16 (1992): 2–6.

——. "The Caribbean Artists Movement (1968)." *Writing Black Britain, 1949–1998: An Interdisciplinary Anthology*. Ed. James Procter. Manchester: Manchester UP, 200. 167–170.

——. *ConVERSations with Nathaniel Mackey*. New York and Minneapolis: We Press and Xcp: Cross-Cultural Poetics, 1999.

——. *DreamStories*. Harlow, Essex: Longman, 1994.

——. "An Interview with Kamau Brathwaite." With Nathaniel Mackey. *The Art of Kamau Brathwaite*. Ed. Stewart Brown. Bridgend, Wales: Poetry Wales, 1995. 13–32.

——. *Magical Realism*. New York and Kingston, Jamaica: Savacou North, 2002.

——. *Middle Passages*. Newcastle upon Tyne: Bloodaxe, 1992.

——. "Newstead to Neustadt." *World Literature Today* 68.4 (1994): 653–660.

——. "Show number 94." Cross Cultural Poetics Radio Show. Host. by Leonard Shwartz. KAOS-FM, Olympia, Washington, 2005. Penn Sound Centre for Programs in Contemporary Writing. U of Pennsylvania. Sound file. Accessed on web Feb. 2014. <http://writing.upenn.edu/pennsound/x/Brathwaite.php>

——. *X/Self*. Oxford: OUP, 1987.

Brodhead, John Romeyn. *History of the State of New York*. New York: Harper and Brothers, 1853.

Brown, Stewart. "'Writin' in Light': Orality-thru-typography, Kamau Brathwaite's Sycorax Video Style." *The Pressures of the Text: Orality, Texts, and the Telling of Tales*. Ed. Brown. Birmingham: Centre of African Studies, 1995. 125–13.

Buck-Morss, Susan. *The Dialectics of Seeing: Walter Benjamin and the Arcades Project*. Cambridge, MA and London, England: MIT P, 1989.

Buell, Lawrence. *The Environmental Imagination: Thoreau, Nature Writing, and the Formation of American Culture*. Cambridge: Belknap Press of Harvard UP, 1995.

Bunting, Basil. *Complete Poems*. Newcastle upon Tyne: Bloodaxe, 2000.

Butterick, George F. *A Guide to the Maximus Poems of Charles Olson*. Berkeley: U of California P 1990.

Césaire, Aimé. *Cahier d'un retour au pays natal/ Notebook of a Return to My Native Land*. Trans. Mireille Rosello with Annie Pritchard. Newcastle Upon Tyne: Bloodaxe, 1995.

Cha, Theresa Hak Kyung, ed. *Apparatus: Cinematographic Apparatus: Selected Writings*. New York: Tanam, 1980.

——. *DICTEE*. Berkeley: U of California P, 2001.

——. *DICTEE*. New York: Tanam, 1982.

——. *EXILÉE*. 1980. Video. Theresa Hak Kyung Cha Collection, Berkeley Art Museum/Pacific Film Archive, (BAM/PFA) Accession No: 1992.4.111.

——. "EXILÉE / TEMPS MORT." *Hotel*. New York: Tanam, 1980. 133–189.

——. "*Mouth to Mouth* Documentation." Preparation materials. Theresa Hak Kyung Cha Collection, BAM/PFA, Accession No: 1992.4.534.

——. *Mouth to Mouth / Vide o eme / Re disappearing*. Video. 1987. Theresa Hak Kyung Cha Collection, BAM/PFA, Accession No: 1992.4.198.

———. *Other Things Seen Other Things Heard.* 1978. Installation/Performance. San Francisco Museum of Modern Art and Western Front, Vancouver.

———. *Passages Paysages.* 1978. Video. Theresa Hak Kyung Cha Collection, BAM/PFA, Accession Number: 1992.4.208.

———. "Pause Still (80 Langton Street, SF, CA)." Theresa Hak Kyung Cha Collection, BAM/PFA, Online Archive, Accession No: 1992.4.182. Accessed on web July 2015. <http://www.bampfa.berkeley.edu/images/collection/1992.4.182/1992.4.182.jpg >

———. "Preparation materials for *Passages Paysages.*" Theresa Hak Kyung Cha Collection, BAM/PFA, Accession Nos. 1992.4.162 and 1992.4.44.

Chambers, Iain. "Maritime Criticism and Lessons from the Sea." *Insights: Institute of Advanced Study* 3.9 (2010): 2–11.

Chatterjee, Partha. *The Nation and its Fragments.* Princeton, NJ: Princeton UP, 1995.

Cheng, Anne Anlin. "Memory and Anti-Documentary Desire in Theresa Hak Kyung Cha's *DICTÉE.*" *MELUS*, 23.4 (1998): 119–133.

Cobbing, Bob. *Shrieks and Hisses.* Buckfastleigh, Devon: Etruscan, 1999.

———. "W OW R OM WRO RMM." [1966] *An Anthology of Concrete Poetry.* Ed. Emmett Williams. New York: Something Else, 1967. Unpaginated.

Cobbing, Bob and Lawrence Upton, eds. *Word Score Utterance Choreography in verbal and visual poetry.* London: Writers Forum, 1998.

Colby, Sasha. "'Man came here by an intolerable way': Charles Olson's Archaeology of Resistance." *Arizona Quarterly* 65.4 (2009): 93–111.

Collis, Stephen. *Through Words of Others: Susan Howe and Anarcho-Scholasticism.* Victoria, BC: English Literary Studies Editions, 2006.

Connerton, Paul. *How Societies Remember.* Cambridge: Cambridge UP, 1989.

Conrad, Joseph. *Heart of Darkness and Other Stories.* Oxford World's Classics. Oxford: Oxford UP, 1998.

D'Aguiar, Fred. *Feeding the Ghosts.* London: Vintage, 1998.

Daly, Mary E. "The Operations of Famine Relief, 1845–47." *The Great Irish Famine.* Ed. Cathal Póirtéir. Dublin: Mercier, 1995. 123–134.

Davidson, Michael. *Ghostlier Demarcations: Modern Poetry and the Material Word.* Berkeley: U of California P, 1997.

———. "Hunting Among Stones: Poetry, Pedagogy, and the Pacific Rim." *Guys Like Us: Citing Masculinity in Cold War Poetics.* Chicago and London: U of Chicago P, 2004. 196–219.

———. "Missing Bodies: Disappearances in the Aesthetic." Seminar paper given at the U of Southampton, UK. November 27 2013.

———. "Palimtexts: Postmodern Poetry and the Material Text." *Postmodern Genres.* Ed. Marjorie Perloff. Norman and London: U of Oklahoma P, 1988. 75–95.

DeCaires Narain, Denise. *Contemporary Caribbean Women's Poetry: Making Style.* London: Routledge, 2002.

Deloughrey, Elizabeth M. *Routes and Roots: Navigating Caribbean and Pacific Island Literatures.* U of Hawi'i P, 2007.

Derrida, Jacques. *Of Grammatology.* Trans. Gayatri Chakravorty Spivak. Baltimore and London: John Hopkins UP, 1974.

Descartes, Rene. *Mediations and Other Metaphysical Writings 1642–49.* London: Penguin, 1998.

Drucker, Johanna. *Figuring the Word: Essays on Books, Writing and Visual Poetics*. New York: Granary, 1998.

———. *The Visible Word: Experimental Typography and Modern Art, 1909–23*. Chicago and London: U of Chicago P, 1994.

———. "Visual Performance of the Poetic Text." *Close Listening: poetry and the performed word*. Ed. Charles Bernstein. Oxford: Oxford UP, 1998. 131–161.

Dufferin and Boyle, G. G. *A Narrative of a Journey from Oxford to Skibbereen During the Year of the Irish Famine*. Oxford: John Henry Parker, 1847.

Duncan, Robert. *Selected Poems, Revised and Enlarged*. Ed. Robert J. Bertholf. New York: New Directions, 1997.

DuPlessis, Rachel Blau. *The Pink Guitar: writing as feminist practice*. New York and London: Routledge, 1990.

Dworkin, Craig. *Reading the Illegible*. Evanston, IL: Northwestern UP, 2003.

Eikon Basilike, The Portraicture of His Sacred Majestie in His Solitudes and Sufferings. Ed. Edward Almack. London: De La More, 1904.

Eisenstein, Sergei. "The Cinematographic Principle and the Ideogram" and "A Dialectic Approach to Film Form." *Film Theory and Criticism: Introductory Readings*. 4th Ed. Ed. Gerald Mast, Marshall Cohen and Leo Braudy. New York and Oxford: Oxford UP, 1992. 127–154.

Fenollosa, Ernest. "The Chinese Written Character as a Medium for Poetry: An Ars Poetica." [1919]. *The Chinese Written Character as a Medium for Poetry: A critical edition*. Ed. Haun Saussy, Jonathan Stalling and Lucas Klein. New York: Fordham UP, 2008. 41–74.

Flint, F. S. "Imagisme." [1912]. *Modernism: An Anthology*. Ed. Lawrence S. Rainey. Oxford: Blackwell, 2005. 94–5.

Foucault, Michel. "Nietzsche, Genealogy, History." *Language, Counter-Memory, Practice: Selected Essays and Interviews*. Trans. Donald F. Bouchard and Sherry Simon. Oxford: Blackwell, 1977. 139–163.

———. *This is not a Pipe*. Ed. and trans. James Harkness. Berkeley: U of California P, 1983.

Fraser, Kathleen. "Translating the unspeakable: Visual poetics, as projected through Olson's 'field' into current female writing practice." *Translating the Unspeakable: Poetry and the Innovative Necessity*. Tuscaloosa and London: U of Alabama P, 2000. 174–200.

Freud, Sigmund. "Mourning and Melancholia." *Collected Papers*. Vol 4. London: Hogarth, 1950. 152–170.

———. "Remembering, Repeating, and Working-Through." *The Standard Edition of the Complete Psychological Works*. Trans. James Strachey. Vol 12. London: Hogarth, 1958. 147–156.

Fried, Michael. "Almayer's Face: On 'Impressionism' in Conrad, Crane, and Norris." *Critical Inquiry* 17.1 (Autumn, 1990): 193–236.

Frost, Elisabeth Ann. "Unsettling America: Susan Howe and Antinomian Tradition." *The Feminist Avant-Garde in American Poetry*. Iowa City: U of Iowa P, 2003. 105–135.

Gallagher, Ellen. *Bird In Hand*. Painting/collage. 2006. Tate Collection.

Gates, Henry Louis, Jr. "Writing, 'Race,' and the Difference It Makes." *Loose Canons: Notes on the Culture Wars*. Oxford: Oxford UP. 43–69.

Gifford, Jane. *The Celtic Wisdom of Trees: Mysteries, Magic and Medicine*. London: Godsfield, 2006.

Gilroy, Paul. *The Black Atlantic: Modernity and Double Consciousness*. London: Verso, 1993.

Glissant, Édouard. *Caribbean Discourse: Selected Essays*. Trans. Michael Dash. Charlottesville: UP of Virginia, 1992.

——. *Poetics of Relation*. Trans. Betsy Wing. Ann Arbor: U of Michigan P, 1997.

Golding, Alan. "'Drawings with Words': Susan Howe's Visual Poetics." *We Who Love to Be Astonished: Experimental Women's Writing and Performance Poetics*. Ed. Laura Hinton and Cynthia Hogue. Tuscaloosa: U of Alabama P, 2002. 152–164.

Gomringer, Eugen, "From Line to Constellation." [1954]. *Concrete Poetry: A World View*. Ed. Mary Ellen Solt. Bloomington: Indiana UP, 1970. 67.

——. "The Poem as Functional Object." [1960]. *Concrete Poetry: A World View*. Ed. Mary Ellen Solt. Bloomington: Indiana UP, 1970. 69.

——. "wind." [1953]. *Concrete Poetry: A World View*. Ed. Mary Ellen Solt. Bloomington: Indiana UP, 1970. 93.

Greenberg, Clement. "Towards a Newer Laocoon." *Clement Greenberg: The Collected Essays and Criticism*. Ed. John O'Brian. Vol 1. Chicago and London: U of Chicago P, 1986. 23–38.

Habermas, Jürgen. "Walter Benjamin: Consciousness-Raising or Rescuing Critique." *On Walter Benjamin*. Ed. Gary Smith. Cambridge, MA and London, England: MIT P, 1998. 90–128.

Harris, Kaplan P. "Susan Howe's Art and Poetry." *Contemporary Literature* 47.3 (2006): 440–471.

Hejinian, Lyn. "The Rejection of Closure." *The Language of Inquiry*. Berkeley: U of California P, 2000. 40–58.

Himid, Lubaina. *Memorial to Zong*. Painting. 1991. Artist's Collection.

Homer. *The Odyssey*. London: Penguin, 2003.

Hoover, Paul. *Postmodern American Poetry*. New York: Norton, 1994.

Howe, Susan. *A Bibliography of the King's Book, or, Eikon Basilike*. Providence: Paradigm, 1989.

——. *The Birth-mark: Unsettling the Wilderness in American Literary History*. Middletown, CT: Wesleyan UP, 1993.

——. "The Difficulties Interview." *The Difficulties* 3.2 (1987): 17–27.

——. "The End of Art." *Archives of American Art* 14.4 (1974): 2–7.

——. *The Europe of Trusts*. New York: New Directions, 2002.

——. *Frame Structures: Early Poems 1974–1979*. New York: New Directions, 1996.

——. "An Interview with Susan Howe." With Lynn Keller. *Contemporary Literature* 36.1 (1995): 1–34.

——. *The Midnight*. New York: New Directions, 2003.

——. *My Emily Dickinson*. Berkeley: North Atlantic, 1985.

——. *The Nonconformist's Memorial*. New York: New Directions, 1993.

——. *Secret History of the Dividing Line*. New York: Telephone, 1978.

——. "Since a Dialogue We Are." *Acts* 10 (1989): 166–173.

——. *Singularities*. Middletown, CT: Wesleyan UP, 1990.

——. *Souls of the Labadie Tract*. New York: New Directions, 2003.

———. "Speaking with Susan Howe." With Janet Ruth Falon. *The Difficulties* 3.2 (1987): 28–42.

Huk, Romana. "Maggie O'Sullivan and the Story of Metaphysics." *The Salt Companion to Maggie O'Sullivan*. Cambridge: Salt, 2011. 36–79.

Jabès, Edmond. *From the Book to the Book: An Edmond Jabès Reader*. Trans. Rosmarie Waldrop. Hanover, NH: Wesleyan U P, 1991.

James, Louis. "Brathwaite and Jazz." *The Art of Kamau Brathwaite*. Ed. Stewart Brown. Bridgend, Wales: Poetry Wales, 1995. 62–74.

Jameson, Frederic. *Postmodernism, or the cultural logic of late capitalism*. London: Verso, 1991.

Jenkins, Lee M. *The Language of Caribbean Poetry*. Gainsville: UP of Florida, 2004.

Jeon, Joseph Jonghyun. *Radical Things, Radical Forms: Objecthood in Avant-Garde Asian American Poetry*. Iowa City: U of Iowa P, 2012.

Jonas, Joan. *Vertical Roll*. Video. 1972. Museum of Modern Art, New York.

Josephs, Kelly Baker. "Versions of X/Self: Kamau Brathwaite's Caribbean Discourse." *Anthurium: A Caribbean Studies Journal* 1.1. (2003). Accessed on web July 2009. <http://anthurium.miami.edu/volume_1/issue_1/josephs-versions.htm>

Kang, L.Hyun Yi. "The 'Liberatory Voice' of Theresa Hak Kyung Cha's *Dictée*." *Writing Self, Writing Nation: Essays on Theresa Hak Kyung Cha's DICTEE*. Ed. Elaine Kim and Norma Alarcón. Berkeley: Third Woman, 1994. 73–99.

Kant, Immanuel. *Critique of Pure Reason*. Trans. and ed. Paul Guyer and Allen W. Wood. Cambridge: Cambridge UP, 1998.

Kelly, Michael J. *Newgrange: Archaeology, art and legend*. London: Thames and Hudson, 1982.

Khlebnikov, Velimir and Aleksei Kruchenykh. "The Word as Such" and "The Letter as Such" *Words in Revolution: Russian Futurist Manifestos 1912–1928*. Ed. Anna Lawton. [1988]. Washington: New Academia Publishing, 2005. 57–62 and 63–4.

Kibbey, Ann. *The Interpretation of Material Shapes in Puritanism: A study of rhetoric, prejudice, and violence*. Cambridge: Cambridge UP, 1986.

Kim, Elaine. "Interstitial Subjects—Asian American Visual Art as a Site for New Cultural Conversations." *Fresh Talk / Daring Glances: Conversations on Asian American Art*. Ed. Kim. Berkeley: U of California P, 2003. 1–50.

Kim, Elaine and Norma Alarcón, eds. *Writing Self, Writing Nation: Essays on Theresa Hak Kyung Cha's DICTEE*. Berkeley: Third Woman, 1994.

Kosuth, Joseph. "Art After Philosophy." *Conceptual Art: A Critical Anthology*. Alexander Alberro and Blake Stimson, eds. Cambridge, MA and London, England: MIT P, 1999. 158–177.

Krauss, Rosalind E. *The Optical Unconscious*. Cambridge, MA and London, England: MIT P, 1993.

Kruchenykh, Aleksei. "Declaration of the Word as Such." *Words in Revolution: Russian Futurist Manifestos 1912–1928*. Ed. Anna Lawton [1988]. Washington: New Academia, 2005. 67–68.

LaCapra, Dominick. *History and Memory After Auschwitz*. Ithaca and London: Cornell UP, 1998.

Lacy, Andrew. *The Cult of King Charles the Martyr*. Woodbridge, England and Rochester, NY: Boydell, 2003.

Lazer, Hank, "The People's Poetry." *The Boston Review.* (2004). Accessed on web July 2015. <http://bostonreview.net/archives/BR29.2/lazer.html>

———. "Returns: Innovative Poetry and Questions of 'Spirit'." *Facture* 2 (2001). Accessed on web Sep. 2008. <http://epc.buffalo.edu/authors/lazer/writing/Spirit%20essay%20in%20Facture.pdf>

Lessing, Gotthold Ephraim. *Laocoön: An Essay on the Limits of Painting and Poetry.* Baltimore and London: John Hopkins UP, 1962.

Lewallen, Constance M., ed. *The Dream of the Audience.* Berkeley: U of California P, 2001.

Lippard, Lucy, ed. *Six Years: the Dematerialization of the Art Object from 1966 to 1972.* [1973]. Berkeley: U of California P, 1997.

Lowe, Lisa. "Unfaithful to the Original: The subject of *Dictée*." *Writing Self, Writing Nation.* Ed. Elaine Kim and Norma Alarcón. Berkeley: Third Woman, 1994. 35–69.

Ma, Ming-Qian, "Articulating the Inarticulate: Singularities and the Counter-Method in Susan Howe." *Contemporary Literature* 36.3 (1995): 446–489.

———. "Poetry as History Revised: Susan Howe's 'Scattering as Behavior Toward Risk'." *American Literary History* 6.4 (1994): 716–737.

Mac Low, Jackson. "Discussing Pound." An email posted to POETICS@UBVM.CC.BUFFALO.EDU and posted on epc. Accessed on web May 2010. <http://epc.buffalo.edu/authors/maclow/pound.html>

———. *Words nd Ends from Ez.* Bolinas, CA: Avenue B, 1989.

Macherey, Pierre. *A Theory of Literary Production.* Trans. Geoffrey Wall. London: Routledge, 1978.

Mackey, Nathaniel. *Discrepant Engagement: Dissonance, Cross-Culturality, and Experimental Writing.* Cambridge: Cambridge UP, 1993.

———. "Wringing the Word," *World Literature Today* 68.4 (1994): 733–740.

Mallarmé, Stéphane. *Un Coup de dés jamais n'abolira le hazard.* Paris, 1914.

Manson, Peter. "Maggie O'Sullivan: Palace of Reptiles." Accessed on web July 2015. <https://petermanson.wordpress.com/prose/maggie-osullivan-palace-of-reptiles/>

———. "A Natural History in 3 Incomplete Parts (London: Magenta Press, 1985)." *How 2* 3.1 (2007). Accessed on web Jun. 2008. <http://www.asu.edu/pipercwcenter/how2journal/vol_3_no_1/cambridge/manson.html>

Marriot, David. "Figures of Silence and Orality in the Poetry of M. NourbeSe Philip." *Framing the Word: Gender and Genre in Caribbean Women's Writing.* Ed. Joan Anim-Addo. London: Whiting and Birch, 1996. 72–85.

Marsh, Nicky. "Agonal States: Maggie O'Sullivan and a feminist politics of visual poetics." *The Salt Companion to Maggie O'Sullivan.* Cambridge: Salt, 2011. 80–96.

———. "'Out of My Texts I Am Not What I Play': Politics and self in the Poetry of Susan Howe." *College Literature* 24.3 (1997): 124–137.

Marx, Karl. *Capital: A Critique of Political Economy.* Trans. Ben Fowkes. [1897]. Vol. 1. London: Penguin, 1990.

Marx, Karl and Friedrich Engels. *The Communist Manifesto.* [1848]. London: Penguin, 2002.

McCaffery, Steve. *North of Intention: Critical Writings 1973–1986.* New York and Toronto: Roof, Nightwood Editions, 1986.

McClintock, Anne. *Imperial Leather: Race, Gender and Sexuality in the Colonial Contest*. London: Routledge, 1995.

McGann, Jerome. *Black Riders: The Visible Language of Modernism*. Princeton, NJ: Princeton UP, 1993.

——. *The Textual Condition*. Princeton, NJ: Princeton UP, 1991.

McHale, Brian. "Archaeologies of Knowledge: Hill's Middens, Heaney's Bogs, Schwerner's Tablets." *New Literary History* 30 (Winter 1999): 239–262.

——. *The Obligation toward the Difficult Whole: Postmodernist Long Poems*. Tuscaloosa and London: U of Alabama P, 2004.

Melville, Herman. *Billy Budd, Sailor (An Inside Narrative): Reading and Genetic Text*. Ed. Harrison Hayford and Merton M. Sealts. Chicago and London: U of Chicago P, 1962.

Merrill, Thomas F. "'The Kingfishers': Charles Olson's 'Marvelous Maneuver.'" *Contemporary Literature* 17.4 (1976): 506–528.

Mesch, Claudia and Viola Michely, eds. *Joseph Beuys: The Reader*. London and New York: I. B. Tauris, 2007.

Middleton, Peter. "On Ice: Julia Kristeva, Susan Howe and avant-garde poetics." *Contemporary Poetry Meets Modern Theory*. Ed. Antony Easthope and John O. Thompson. London: Harvester Wheatsheaf, 1991. 81–95.

——. "Poetry After 1970." *The Cambridge History of Twentieth-Century English Literature*. Ed. Laura Marcus and Peter Nicholls. Cambridge: Cambridge UP 2004. 768–786.

Middleton, Peter and Tim Woods. *Literatures of Memory: History, time and space in postwar writing*. Manchester: Manchester UP, 2000.

Mitchell, W. J. T. *Iconology: Image, Text, Ideology*. Chicago: The U of Chicago P, 1986.

——. *Picture Theory: essays on verbal and visual representation*. Chicago and London: U of Chicago P, 1994.

Montgomery, Will. "Appropriating primal indeterminacy: language, landscape and postmodern poetics in Susan Howe's *Thorow*." *Textual Practice* 20.4 (2006). 739–757.

——. *The Poetry of Susan Howe: History, Theology, Authority*. New York: Palgrave Macmillan, 2010.

Montrose, Louis A. "Professing the Renaissance: The Poetics and Politics of Culture." *The New Historicism*. Ed. Harold Veeser. New York and London: Routledge, 1986. 15–36.

Morris, Robert. "Size Matters." *Critical Inquiry* 26 (2000): 474–487.

Mottram, Eric. "The British Poetry Revival, 1960–75." *New British poetries: The scope of the possible*. Ed. Robert Hampson and Peter Barry. Manchester: Manchester UP, 1993. 15–50.

Mulvey, Laura. "Visual Pleasure and Narrative Cinema." [1975] *Film Theory and Criticism: Introductory Readings*. 4th ed. Ed. Gerald Mast, Marshall Cohen, and Leo Braudy. New York and Oxford: Oxford UP, 1992. 746–757.

Nahm, Andrew C. *Introduction to Korean History and Culture*. Seoul, Korea: Hollym, 1996.

Naipaul, V. S. *The Middle Passage*. London: Andre Deutsche, 1962.

Nash, George. "Light at the End of the Tunnel: the way megalithic art was viewed and experienced." *Art As Metaphor*. Ed. Aron Mazel, George Nash, and Clive Waddington. Oxford: Archaeopress, 2007. 123–143.

Naylor, Paul. *Poetic Investigations: Singing the Holes in History*. Evanston, IL: Northwestern UP, 1999.

Nicholls, Peter. "Beyond the Cantos: Pound and American Poetry." *The Cambridge Companion to Ezra Pound*. Ed. Ira Bruce Nadel. Cambridge: Cambridge UP, 1999. 139–160.

———. "Difference Spreading: From Gertrude Stein to L=A=N=G=U=A=G=E poetry." *Contemporary Poetry Meets Modern Theory*. Ed. Anthony Easthope and John O. Thompson. New York: Harvester Wheatsheaf, 1991. 116–127.

———. "Unsettling the Wilderness: Susan Howe and American History." *Contemporary Literature* 37. 4 (1996): 586–601.

Ó Gráda, Cormac. *Black '47 and Beyond: The great Irish famine in history, economy, and memory*. Princeton, NJ: Princeton UP, 1999.

Olson, Charles. *Additional Prose: A Bibliography on America, Proprioception and Other Notes and Essays*. Ed. George F. Butterick. Bolinas: Four Seasons Foundation, 1974.

———. *Call Me Ishmael*. San Fransisco: City Lights, 1947.

———. *The Collected Poems of Charles Olson*. Ed. George Butterick. Berkeley: U of California P, 1997.

———. *The Maximus Poems*. Ed. George Butterick. Berkeley: U of California P, 1983.

———. *Selected Writings*. Ed. Robert Creeley. [1950]. New York: New Directions, 1966

Osman, Jena. *The Network*. Albany, NY: Fence, 2010.

———. "The Rumpus Book Club Interviews Jena Osman." December 12, 2010. Accessed on web Nov. 2014. <http://therumpus.net/2010/12/the-rumpus-poetry-book-club-interview-with-jena-osman/>

O'Sullivan, Maggie. *Body of Work*. Hastings: Reality Street Editions, 2006.

———. "A conversation with Maggie O'Sullivan." *Close Listening Studio 111*. Hosted by Charles Bernstein. October 11, 2007. Penn Sound Centre for Programs in Contemporary Writing. U of Pennsylvania. Sound recording. Accessed on the web Aug. 2008. <http://writing.upenn.edu/pennsound/x/OSullivan.html>

———. "In conversation with Andy Brown." *Binary Myths 1and2: Conversations with Poets and Poet-Editors*. Ed. Brown. Exeter: Stride, 2004. 155–160.

———. *In the House of the Shaman*. London: Reality Street, 1993.

———. "Interview by Charles Bernstein (1993)." Penn Sound Centre for Programs in Contemporary Writing. U of Pennsylvania. Sound recording. Accessed on web Aug. 2008. <http://writing.upenn.edu/pennsound/x/OSullivan.php>

———. *Maggie O'Sullivan.co.uk*. Accessed on web Jul. 2013. <http://www.maggieosullivan.co.uk/>

———. *murmur: tasks of mourning*. 2004. Maggie O'Sullivan website. Accessed on web Jun. 2008. <http://www.maggieosullivan.co.uk/murmur.html>

———. *murmur: tasks of mourning*. London: Veer, 2011.

———, ed. *Out of Everywhere: Linguistically Innovative Poetry by Women in North America and the UK*. London: Reality Street, 1996.

———. *Palace of Reptiles*. Willowdale, Ontario: Gig, 2003.

———. *red shifts*. Buckfastleigh: Etruscan, 2001.

———. *Unofficial Word*. Newcastle upon Tyne: Galloping Dog, 1988.

———. *WATERFALLS*. Exbourne, Devon: Etruscan, 2009.

———. "Winter Ceremony" and *that bread should be. Etruscan Reader III*. Buckfast-leigh: Etruscan, 1997. 8–42.

———. "Writing / Conversation: an interview by mail November–December, 2003." With Dell Olsen. *How2* 2.2 (2004). Accessed on web Nov. 2007. <http://www.asu.edu/pipercwcenter/how2journal//archive/online_archive/v2_2_2004/current/workbook/writing.htm>

Ovid. *Metamorphoses*. Trans. A. D. Melville. Oxford: Oxford UP, 1986.

Owens, Craig. "Earthwords." *October* 10 (1979): 120–130.

Park, Josephine Nock-Hee. "'What of the Partition': Dictee's Boundaries and the American Epic." *Contemporary Literature* 46.2 (2005): 213–242.

Parry, Benita. "Aspects of Peripheral Modernisms." *Ariel: A Review of English International Literature* 40.1 (2009): 27–55.

Pecora, Vincent. "Benjamin, Kracauer, and Redemptive History." *Secularization and Cultural Criticism: Religion, Nation, and Modernity*. Chicago and London: U of Chicago P, 2006. 67–100.

Peirce, Charles Sanders. *Collected Papers*. Vol. 2. Cambridge: Harvard UP, 1932.

Perloff, Marjorie. "'Collision or Collusion with History': The Narrative Lyric of Susan Howe." *Contemporary Literature* 30.4 (1989): 518–533.

———. *Radical Artifice: Writing Poetry in the Age of Media*. Chicago and London: U of Chicago P, 1991.

———. "'The Saturated Language of Red': Maggie O'Sullivan and the Artist's Book." *The Salt Companion to Maggie O'Sullivan*. Cambridge: Salt, 2011. 123–135.

———. *21st Century Modernism: The "New" Poetics*. Malden, MA and Oxford: Blackwell, 2002.

———. *Unoriginal Genius*. Chicago: Chicago UP, 2010.

Philip, M. NourbeSe. "Dis Place The Space Between." *Feminist Measures: Soundings in Poetry and Theory*. Ed. Lynn Keller and Cristanne Miller. Ann Arbor: U of Michigan P, 1994. 287–316.

———. *A Genealogy of Resistance and other essays*. Toronto: Mercury, 1997.

———. *Looking for Livingstone: An Odyssey of Silence*. [1997]. Toronto: Mercury, 2006.

———. "A Poet of Place: An interview with M. NourbeSe Philip." With Kristen Mahlis. *Callaloo* 27.3 (2004): 682–697.

———. *She Tries Her Tongue, Her Silence Softly Breaks*. Charlottetown, PEI, Canada: Ragweed, 1989.

———. "Wor(l)ds Interrupted: The Unhistory of the Kari Basin." *Jacket2* (2014). Accessed on web Apr. 2014. <http://jacket2.org/article/worlds-interrupted#5>

———. *Zong!* Middletown, CT: Wesleyan UP, 2008.

Phu, Thy. "Decapitated Forms: Theresa Hak Kyung Cha's Visual Text and the Politics of Visibility." *Mosaic: A Journal for the Interdisciplinary Study of Literature* 38.1 (2005): 17–36.

Plutarch. *Plutarch's Lives*. Trans. John and William Langhorne. Vol. 1. London: Sharpe and Son, 1819.

Pollard, Charles W. *New World Modernisms: T. S. Eliot, Derek Walcott, and Kamau Brathwaite*. Charlottesville and London: U of Virginia P, 2004.

Pound, Ezra. *ABC of Reading*. [1934]. London: Faber and Faber, 1991.

———. *The Cantos of Ezra Pound*. New York: New Directions, 1996.

———. "A Few Don'ts by an Imagiste." [1912]. *Modernism: An Anthology*. Ed. Lawrence Rainey. Oxford: Blackwell, 2005. 95–97.

———. *Selected Prose 1909–1965*. London: Faber and Faber, 1973. 19–44.

———. "Vortex." [1914] *Modernism: An Anthology*. Ed. Lawrence Rainey. Oxford: Blackwell, 2005. 97–99.

———. "Vorticism." *Gaudier-Brzeska: A Memoir*. New York: New Directions, 1970. 81–94.

Quartermain, Peter. "And the Without: An Interpretive Essay on Susan Howe." *Disjunctive Poetics: From Gertrude Stein and Louis Zukofsky to Susan Howe*. Cambridge: Cambridge UP, 1992. 182–194.

Raczymow, Henri. "Memory Shot Through With Holes." *Yale French Studies* 85 (1994): 98–105.

Rainbird, Sean. *Joseph Beuys and the Celtic World*. London: Tate, 2005.

Ramachandran, Vilayanur S., and Edward M. Hubbard. "Hearing Colors, Tasting Shapes." *Scientific American* 288.5 (May 2003): 42–49.

Ramazani, Jahan. "Modernist Bricolage, Postcolonial Hybridity." *Modernism/Modernity* 13.3 (2006): 445–462.

Reed, Brian. "'Eden or Ebb of the Sea': Susan Howe's Word Squares and Postlinear Poetics." *Postmodern Culture* 14.2 (2004). Accessed on web Jan. 2007. <http://muse.jhu.edu/journals/pmc/v014/14.2reed.html>

Retallack, Joan. *The Poethical Wager*. Berkeley, U of California P, 2003.

Rigby, Graeme. "Publishing Brathwaite: Adventures in the Video Style." *World Literature Today* 68.4 (1994): 708–714.

Roberts, Allen F. Exhibition entry. *Africa: The Art of a Continent*. Ed. Tom Phillips. London: Royal Academy of Arts, 1996. 298.

Rogoff, Irit. "The Aesthetics of Post-History: A German Perspective." *Joseph Beuys: The Reader*. Ed. Claudia Mensch and Viola Michely. London: I. B. Tauris, 2007. 270–283.

Rohlehr, Gordon. "Dream Journeys" *DreamStories*. By Kamau Brathwaite. Harlow, Essex: Longman, 1994. iii–xvi.

Rosler, Martha. *Hot House, or Harem*. 1972. Photomontage.

———. "In, around, and afterthoughts (on documentary photography)." *The Contest of Meaning: Critical histories of photography*. Ed. Richard Bolton. Cambridge: MIT Press, 1992. 303–342.

Rothenberg, Jerome and Pierre Joris, eds. *Poems for the Millennium*, 2 vols. Berkeley: U of California P, 1995–98.

Ruthven, K. K. *A Guide to Ezra Pound's* Personae (1926). Berkeley: U of California P, 1969.

The Salt Companion to Maggie O'Sullivan. Cambridge: Salt, 2011.

Sartre, Jean-Paul. *What is Literature?* London and New York: Routledge, 2001.

Savory, Elaine. "Returning to Sycorax/ Prospero's response." *The Art of Kamau Brathwaite*. Ed. Stuart Brown. Bridgend, Wales: Poetry Wales, 1995. 208–230.

Schneemann, Carolee. *Fuses*. Film. 1965. Museum of Modern Art, New York.

———. *Interior Scroll*. 1975. Performance. East Hampton, NY and elsewhere.

Scholem, Gershom G. *Major Trends in Jewish Mysticism*. Jerusalem: Schocken, 1941.

Shakespeare, William. *The Tempest*. Ed. Burton William Raffel and Harold Bloom. New Haven, CT: Yale UP, 2006.

Shapiro, Gary. *Earthwards: Robert Smithson and Art after Babel*. Berkeley: U of California P, 1995.

Shaw, Lytle. *Fieldworks: From Place to Site in Postwar Poetics*. Tuscaloosa: U of Alabama P, 2013.

Sheppard, Robert. *The Poetry of Saying: British Poetry and Its Discontents, 1950–2000*. Liverpool: Liverpool UP, 2005.

Shih, Shu-Mei. "Nationalism and Korean American Women's Writing: Theresa Hak Kyung Cha's *Dictée*." *Speaking the Other Self: American Women Writers*. Ed. Jeanne Campbell Reesman. Athens and London: U of Georgia P, 1997.

Shklovsky, Viktor. "Art as Technique." *Literary Theory: An Anthology*. Ed. Julie Rivkin and Michael Ryan. 2nd ed. Malden, MA, and Oxford: Blackwell, 2004. 15–21.

Shockley, Evie. "Going Overboard: African American Poetic Innovation and the Middle Passage." *Contemporary Literature* 52.4 (2011): 781–817.

Sieburth, Richard. "Benjamin the Scrivener." Assemblage 6 (1988): 6–23.

Silliman, Ron. "Disappearance of the Word/ Appearance of the World." *The L=A=N=G=U=A=G=E Book*. Ed. Bruce Andrews and Charles Bernstein. Carbondale and Edwardsville: Southern Illinois UP, 1984. 121–132.

——— , ed. *In the American Tree*. Orono: U Maine P, 1986.

Silverman, Kaja. *The Subject of Semiotics*. New York: Oxford UP, 1983.

Smithson, Robert. *Robert Smithson: The Collected Writings*. Ed. Jack Flam. Berkeley: U of California P, 1996.

———. *Spiral Jetty*. Film. 1970. Museum of Modern Art, New York.

Sohn, Ho-Min. *The Korean Language*. Cambridge: Cambridge UP, 1999.

Solt, Mary Ellen, ed. *Concrete Poetry: A World View*. Bloomington: Indiana UP, 1970.

Spahr, Juliana. *Everybody's Autonomy: Connective Reading and Collective Identity*. Tuscaloosa and London: U of Alabama P, 2001.

Spivak, Gayatri Chakravorty. "Can the Subaltern Speak?" *Colonial Discourse and Post-colonial Theory*. Ed. Patrick Williams and Laura Chrisman. New York and London: Harvester Wheatsheaf, 1994. 66–111.

———. "An Interview with Gayatri Chakravorty Spivak." With Sara Danius and Stefan Jonsson. *Boundary 2* 20.2 (1993): 24–50.

Stewart, Garrett. *Reading Voices: Literature and the Phonotext*. Berkeley: U of California P, 1990.

Storr, Robert. *Robert Ryman*. London: Tate, 1993.

Susan Howe Papers, MSS. 201. Mandeville Special Collections. U of California, San Diego. Materials accessed May 27–June 1, 2007.

Takada, Mayumi. "Annihilating Possibilities: Witnessing and Testimony through Cinematic Love in Theresa Hak Kyung Cha's DICTEE." *Lit: Literature Interpretation Theory* 17.1 (2006): 23–48.

Terrell, Carroll F. *A Companion to the Cantos of Ezra Pound*. Vol. 2. Berkeley: U of California P, 1984.

Theresa Hak Kyung Cha Collection, Berkeley Art Museum / Pacific Film Archive. Materials accessed 22–25th May, 2007.

Theresa Hak Kyung Cha Collection, BAM/ PFA, Online Archive. Accessed on web

Apr. 2007 and Aug. 2008. <http://www.bampfa.berkeley.edu/collections/bam/texts/cha.ead.html>

Theresa Hak Kyung Cha Collection. California Online Archive. Accessed on web Jan. 2005 <http://www.oac.cdlib.org/findaid/ark:/13030/tf238n986k>

Thieme, John. *Derek Walcott*. Manchester: Manchester UP, 1999.

Thoreau, Henry David. *The Maine Woods*. Princeton: Princeton UP, 2004.

———. *Walden*. Oxford: Oxford UP, 1999.

Tiedemann, Rolf. "Dialectics at a Standstill." *The Arcades Project*. By Walter Benjamin. Trans. Howard Eiland and Kevin McLaughlin. Cambridge, MA and London, England: Belknap Press of Harvard UP, 1999. 929–945.

———. "Historical Materialism or Political Messianism? An interpretation of the theses 'On the Concept of History.'" Trans. Barton Byg, Jeremy Gains, and Doris L. Jones. *Walter Benjamin: Critical evaluations in cultural theory*. Ed Peter Osborne. London and New York: Routledge, 2005. 175–209.

Tisdall, Caroline, dir. *Arena: Joseph Beuys*. Television program. BBC. 1987.

———. *Joseph Beuys: We Go This Way*. London: Violette Editions, 1998.

Turner, J. M.W. *The Slave Ship (Slavers Throwing overboard the Dead and Dying—Typhoon coming on)*. Painting. 1840. Museum of Fine Arts, Boston.

Walcott, Derek. *Collected Poems 1948–1984*. London: Faber and Faber, 1992.

Walmsley, Anne. "A Sense of Community." *The Art of Kamau Brathwaite*. Ed. Stewart Brown. Bridgend, Wales: Poetry Wales, 1995. 101–116.

———. "Her Stem Singing: Kamau Brathwaite's 'Zea Mexican Diary.'" *World Literature Today* 68.4 (1994): 747–749.

Walvin, James. *Black Ivory: Slavery in the British Empire*. 2nd ed. London: Blackwell, 2001.

Webster, Jane. "The Zong in the Context of the Eighteenth-Century Slave Trade." *The Journal of Legal History* 28.3 (2007): 285–298.

Williams, Bernard. *Truth and Truthfulness: An essay in Genealogy*. Princeton: Princeton UP, 2004.

Williams, Emmett, ed. *An Anthology of Concrete Poetry*. New York: Something Else, 1967.

Williams, William Carlos. "The Poem as a Field of Action (1948)." *Selected Essays of William Carlos Williams*. New York: New Directions, 1969. 280–291.

Wong, Shelley Sunn. "Unnaming the Same: Theresa Hak Kyung Cha's *Dictée*." *Writing Self, Writing Nation*. Ed. Elaine Kim and Norma Alarcón. Berkeley: Third Woman, 1994. 103–140.

Yuval-Davis, Nira. *Gender and Nation*. London: Sage, 1997.

Index